# Ann Arbor Observed

# Ann Arbor Observed

*Selections from*
THEN & NOW

*Grace Shackman*

*Grace*

*Dec. 1, 2008*

*Mary,*
*you'll see your influence*
*all through this book.*
*Love,*
*Grace*

THE UNIVERSITY OF MICHIGAN PRESS | ANN ARBOR

2009   2008   2007   2006      4   3   2   1

*A CIP catalog record for this book is available from the British Library.*

Library of Congress Cataloging-in-Publication Data

Shackman, Grace.
    Ann Arbor observed : selections from Then and now / Grace
Shackman.
        p.   cm.
    Articles from the author's column Then and now originally appeared
in the Ann Arbor observer.
    ISBN-13: 978-0-472-03175-7 (pbk. : alk. paper)
    ISBN-10: 0-472-03175-9 (pbk. : alk. paper)
    1. Ann Arbor (Mich.)—History.   2. Ann Arbor (Mich.)—Social life
and customs.   3. Ann Arbor (Mich.)—Pictorial works.   4. Historic
buildings—Michigan—Ann Arbor.   5. Historic buildings—Michigan—
Ann Arbor—Pictorial works.   6. Ann Arbor (Mich.)—Buildings,
structures, etc.   I. Title.

F574.A6S47   2006
97.4'35—dc22                                        2006006207

# Acknowledgments

I owe thanks to so many, those who helped during the more than twenty years that I was writing these articles for the *Ann Arbor Observer*, plus the people who assisted as this book was being prepared, that there is no way I can list them all here. But by making an attempt, I can at least show how much backup there was in the community for this project.

To begin, I have to thank Mary and Don Hunt, not just for publishing my early articles, but for starting the *Observer*, a publication that looks at the big picture implications of life in Ann Arbor, an approach that I felt a great affinity to from the first. I am also eternally grateful that they sold the magazine to John Hilton and Patricia Garcia, who are continuing that philosophy. Much of my writing style has been guided by John Hilton, who taught me to look at the larger meanings of what I was writing rather than get bogged down in endless recitals of facts. On the other end, I've been blessed with a core of appreciative readers, many of whom have suggested topics and helped me find relevant information.

The first person to thank for this book is Peter Heydon, who was not the first to suggest I compile my articles into a book but was the first to offer to help. I am accordingly grateful for the underwriting of THE MOSAIC FOUNDATION (of Rita and Peter Heydon) based in Ann Arbor.

Since the *Observer* only in recent years began keeping digital records, I had to come up with copies of the pictures I originally used. Some I needed to re-borrow. Others I had kept copies of or the *Observer* had, but in all cases I had to contact the owner of the photos to get permission to reprint them. This meant calling up people, many of whom I hadn't seen in years, but they were all very helpful and encouraging, rummaging around if necessary to find the pictures and promptly signing permission slips. These wonderful folks are listed in the picture credits.

Members of the *Observer* staff, including John Hilton, Penny Schreiber, Caron Valentine-Marsh, and Sally Wright Day, let me mine their photo archives and provided electronic copies of back issues that were available.

The staff at the Bentley Historical Library, particularly Karen Jania and Malgosia Myc, helped me track down some of the photos I'd once used or find reasonable substitutes. The people at the University of Michigan Press, led by my editor Mary Erwin, were all a joy to work with as they strove for the best possible product within the bounds of reality.

Of course no acknowledgment is complete without thanking family members. I have to salute my two children, Josh and Leah, for putting up with my writing all these years. Not only was I often spacey when I was in the middle of thinking about an article, but back when all the bedrooms were being slept in, they had to live with a messy dining room with my work spread out all over.

And saving the best for last, my husband, Stan Shackman, would almost qualify as a coauthor because he was so much help with the photographs, scanning borrowed pictures and taking "now" pictures when needed. He also served as in-house technical support on a 24/7 basis.

# Contents

# Introduction

This book is a selection of historical articles that I wrote over a twenty-five-year period for the *Ann Arbor Observer*, documenting the history of Ann Arbor. Most were short "Then and Now" pieces, although a few were feature-length articles. I was amazed as I started sorting through my files at how many I had written. The large number of articles meant that I had to make some tough choices. Obviously this is not as complete a history as it would be if I included everything I wrote, but I hope it will provide an idea of the richness and variety of our community's heritage.

I started out selecting articles intuitively, but as I look back I can see certain principles at work. First, there were the articles that were much commented on when they first came out, such as the Underground Railroad piece and the one about the Frank Lloyd Wright house. I knew from the beginning that these were to be part of the book. Then there were those articles that I felt contained unique information because of the people willing to share their memories with me, such as drivers for the Artificial Ice Company or doctors who worked in home hospitals.

There also were articles about the nineteenth century that were straight archive research that I felt were worth saving in a more permanent form, including the pieces on Orange Risdon's 1825 map and the *Argus* newspaper. Some articles were selected because they cover ongoing concerns such as Allen's Creek and the Carnegie Library. Some were appealing because they brought back such happy memories to the people being interviewed, like the Michigan Union Opera article and the article about the municipal beach. Finally, some made the cut because they described an aspect of history that I felt needed inclusion, including the two articles about railroads, a major key to Ann Arbor's nineteenth-century success.

The articles are arranged in eight sections, but many of them could have been put in several places. And there are themes that run throughout. The heavy German contribution can be seen in the large number of German names in the Industry and Downtown Ann Arbor sections, Otto's Band in Recreation and Culture, and the Schwaben Halle in Social

Fabric and Communities. The fact that Ann Arbor was a close-knit community shows through in numerous places, from the story about Red Howard, a community policeman before the term was invented, to the article on the Hoyer dance studio, where the whole town showed up to watch "Juniors on Parade."

I've left the articles basically as they were, limiting myself to correcting mistakes and making small changes in cases where new information has come to light. I've also taken out a few paragraphs here and there that were meant to anchor articles to the moment in time when they were published but are no longer pertinent. I did not, however, have the heart to add "late" to descriptions of the people who have died since I wrote about or interviewed them. If individuals were alive when the relevant articles were written, I've left references to them in the present tense.

Ann Arbor is such a rich subject because it has an incredibly varied background for a city of its size. It developed in the nineteenth century as both a university town and an industrial town. Early settlers plied their trades and opened factories, while the University of Michigan brought in people with the background and leisure to enjoy the arts and to pursue new ideas.

The twentieth century added to the mix with the growth of research-related industry, which was attracted by the presence of trained university graduates. During the twentieth century the population of Ann Arbor became much more diverse, with people from around the world coming to work in the new industries or to become affiliated with the university.

Ann Arbor's growth and development provide a microcosm of American history, from nineteenth-century immigration to the Underground Railroad, from the early twentieth-century auto barons to the creation of the research university. All of these have left visible traces, both physically and in the community's institutions.

Historical facts give structure to the articles, while a comparison with the national scene at the time gives them context. But for me, the most engaging part of the majority of these pieces is the remembrances of long-time residents. These interviews give the articles another level of truth, a sense of what it was like to live during a particular time period.

When I started writing local history in the late 1970s, I was surprised to find how many remnants of an earlier Ann Arbor remained. I found people who remembered riding trolley cars, who recalled wading in Allen's Creek, and who knew about the Washtenaw County Poorhouse. Descendants of early settlers still lived in the area and were able to tell me stories about their ancestors' early struggles. Owners of downtown establishments that had been in families for generations related to me how their businesses began and how they evolved as needs changed.

People from a wide variety of backgrounds have generously let me interview them, giving me a wider view of Ann Arbor's mix of populations. The interviewees range from people who grew up in Ann Arbor's most elegant homes; to numerous people of German ancestry who have told me about their social groups, churches, and businesses; to second-generation participants in the Farmers' Market.

I also found that much of the material culture remained, and it, too, gave clues to how life was lived in the past. For instance, the diversity in population directly affected the housing stock, which ranged from small vernacular Greek Revival homes to elegant Italianate and Queen Anne residences. In the twentieth century, while working-class people were buying modest tract bungalows and ranch houses, a faculty couple was convincing the premier architect of their generation, Frank Lloyd Wright, to design a house for them.

University buildings also have many stories to tell, from the Detroit Observatory, which is a visible reminder of President Henry Tappan's commitment to science, to the Kelsey Museum and Lane Hall, buildings that speak to the large role religion once played in campus life.

People are always calling me up asking me if I ever wrote about subject X or if I can send them a copy of story Y. I hope that this book will make it easier for people to reread articles they remember, as well as introduce newcomers to the wide history available out our windows and down our streets.

# Public Buildings and Institutions

# The 1838 Jail

*Jailbreaks were a constant danger.*

Even in the good old days there were criminals. Ann Arbor was smaller and more neighborly in the nineteenth century, but there were still very serious crimes, including robbery and murder. Thus, there was a need for jails. For half the century, from 1838 to 1887, local wrongdoers were imprisoned in a Greek Revival building on North Main, where the Ann Arbor Community Center now stands.

When John Allen and Elisha Rumsey founded Ann Arbor in 1824, Rumsey gave the land bounded by Fourth and Fifth Avenues and Liberty and William Streets (now containing the downtown post office, the Blake Transit Center, and the former YMCA) to the community as a site for a jail. Allen contributed the block at Main and Huron still used for the county courthouse.

The county's first jail was built on Rumsey's square in 1829. The project was organized in a socialist fashion. "The citizens of Ann Arbor and vicinity contributed, each according to his ability, some timber, lumber, work or other materials necessary for the construction of a building that would answer for a county prison," wrote a local historian in the Charles C. Chapman 1881 *History of Washtenaw County, Michigan*. The wooden building included quarters for the jailer's family as well as one room for prisoners.

The first jail was notoriously insecure. According to O. W. Stevenson's *Ann Arbor: The First Hundred Years*, "No one could be sure that a prisoner who had been placed within its confines on any particular night would be found there the next morning." Less than seven years after it was built, a grand jury concluded that a new jail was needed. The county bought the land on North Main, four blocks from the courthouse, and the next year the Davison brothers began construction of a two-and-a-half-story red brick building.

The work evidently took several years to finish; local newspapers published numerous letters asking why it wasn't done yet and explanations

4

After the jail moved to downtown Ann Arbor, the old jail building on North Main was converted first to a private home and then to a gas station. *(Courtesy of Bentley Historical Library.)*

for the slowness of getting the necessary funds. Meanwhile, large numbers of prisoners continued to escape from the old jail—five when the door was opened for delivery of some dishes and seven others who managed to cut a hole through the floor.

"When erected [the Main Street jail] was considered a handsome building, in which the citizens felt a just pride," Chapman's historian wrote. William Spaulding, son of sheriff Ephraim Spaulding (who served from 1847 to 1852), had a less cheerful description in his memoirs, written in the 1920s. Spaulding remembered how "the family lived in a wing of the big gloomy jail, with its barred windows, in the lower part of town. 'When we lived in the jail' was a very common reference in our family, and there was no stigma attached."

Spaulding's entire family was involved in keeping the jail. "My brother James was old enough to act as 'turnkey,' which involved locking and unlocking cells at stated times," Spaulding recalled. "Imagine a boy serving in such capacity in one of our modern prisons."

The sheriff's wife, Jane McCormick Spaulding, cooked for the prisoners in her own kitchen. "Father and mother made due allowance for the fact that the jail was a place of enforced restraint. But, when these stern requirements were satisfied, every effort was made to treat the prisoners with consideration and kindness. . . . This policy not only contributed to the discipline and good order of the institution, but it actually gained the confidence and good will of many of the prisoners," Spaulding wrote. He went on to say that his parents often helped the families of prisoners and that after they were released, they often came by to "give good account of themselves and testify their appreciation. In testimony of this Mother treasured various keep-sakes of hand-craft which had been presented to her on such occasions."

ANN ARBOR'S CITIZENS had reason to worry about their safety even after the new jail opened. Criminals held there included horse thieves and bank robbers. Murderers were sent to the state penitentiary (as they still are today), but even they stayed in the county jail while they awaited trial. And despite the new jail's brick construction, jailbreaks in Ann Arbor were still rife. On June 1, 1842, the *State Journal* recorded that "Henry Andrews, indicted for larceny, made his escape from our jail on Sunday last by digging through the outer wall. He was not confined in a cell. He has acquitted himself without the assistance of judge or jury, and avoided his trial which was to have taken place today."

Chapman's history tells of two men convicted in 1857 for the murder of Simon Holden and sentenced to the state penitentiary for life. About a year after the sentence, the court ordered a new trial. "They were returned to Ann Arbor jail, but before court next convened they escaped from jail and were never re-captured."

Allen K. Donahue, who lived across the street from the jail, reminisced about it toward the end of his life in a 1943 *Ann Arbor News* interview. Many of his stories concerned escapees such as Charles Chorr, who was sentenced to hang for murder in 1843 but escaped and was never caught. Donahue recalled a pair of prisoners who got out through the jail's chimney in the middle of winter but were glad to be caught again because they were so cold. Two other prisoners tried to escape through the underground drainage pipe but couldn't get beyond a heavy grate and were dead by the time they were found. Another escapee, a horse thief, was shot and killed while trying to get to the stables.

There were escape attempts even during Spaulding's benign reign. "One story which my father told was of pursuing and capturing a number of prisoners who had escaped. There was a rough-and-tumble bout between the officers and the fugitives. Revolvers hadn't been invented, and shooting was not such a ready resort. Father grabbed one of the escapees, wrestled him down, and was sitting astride him, when he chanced to glimpse something out of one corner of his eye which caused him to dodge with the free part of his body. It was just in time to avoid a large rock which the fellow hurled at him: the missile whizzed by and split open the head of the prisoner beneath."

If Spaulding couldn't stop all escapes, his methods allowed him to stop one. "Once, when a gang of tough customers had just been incarcerated, they managed to secure from outside confederates, tools to saw their way out, and arms. They had nearly brought matters to a climax, and were prepared to murder the guard or anyone who opposed them, when a warning word was passed by one of the inmates to the sheriff. At least that was a substantial return for the humanitarian policy toward prisoners."

There were also quiet times in the jail. Donahue recalled that he had seen the jail "swamped with inmates and devoid of any life at all." An 1843 newspaper article noted little activity. "There is but one person in our jail and he is committed for want of bail to keep the peace. It is supposed that the man is partially deranged or he never should have been there." Unfortunately, the incarceration of mentally ill people is still an issue.

As THE COUNTY GREW, especially in the years after the Civil War, the Main Street jail became too small. After a new courthouse was finished in 1878, civic leaders began discussing building a new jail. They lost a ballot issue in 1884, but by selling the old jail they managed to raise enough money to buy land at Ashley and Ann. The jail stayed on that site, in two different buildings, until 1970, when it moved to its present location at Hogback and Washtenaw in Pittsfield Township.

John J. Robison, who had served as state senator, county clerk, and mayor of Ann Arbor, bought the Main Street jail in 1887 and made it into his family home. He took off the cellblock in back and used the bricks to build two houses to the south, one of which was turned into a store.

In 1917 Morris Kraizman bought the old jail and used it for a tire company, gas station, and scrap metal and junk store. Later it became the Pentecostal Church of God and then apartments. In 1951 it was severely damaged by fire. In 1958 what was left of the building was torn down. The Ann Arbor Community Center was built on the site two years later.

# The County Poorhouse

*It doubled as an insane asylum.*

People choose to go to the Meri Lou Murray Recreation Center and the County Farm Park, on the south side of Washtenaw between Platt and Medford, but in the nineteenth and early twentieth centuries it was the site of the county poorhouse, a place for homeless people of both sexes and all ages who had no other place of refuge.

The poorhouse sheltered a diverse group of unfortunates: the insane, alcoholic, feeble, indolent, senile, developmentally disabled, handicapped, injured, sick, transient, or just down on their luck. Their common denominator was their poverty. Some stayed only for a short time, but others remained until they died. If no relative claimed the body, it was buried on the premises or given to the U-M medical school. Some human bones found in the 1960s when Washtenaw Avenue was being widened were at first believed to be Indian relics until someone figured out that the road extended over the area used for the poorhouse cemetery.

Poor farms were the nineteenth-century solution to poverty. Reformers such as Dorothea Dix, a pioneer in the movement for specialized treatment of the insane, believed that placing people on working farms could make them into contributing members of society and also relieve the public of paying for their care. Most of the people who lived in poorhouses were not able to work, however, or if they could, were not very productive. Income from crops raised at the Washtenaw County Poorhouse helped defray costs, but except for a few years during the Civil War, it was never enough to cover all expenses.

The land for the Washtenaw County Poorhouse was purchased by the county in 1836 from Revolutionary War veteran Claudius Britton, to comply with an 1830 Michigan law directing each county to build a poorhouse. The county hired a keeper, always a local person with a farming background, who lived on the premises with a wife who cooked for the residents (or "inmates," as they were called in the official reports).

The farm included orchards of apples, peaches, and pears; livestock (pigs, cattle, sheep, and chickens); and gardens with vegetables and grains.

The Washtenaw County Poorhouse on Washtenaw near Platt housed a variety of unfortunates, from the mentally ill, handicapped, developmentally disabled, and injured to those just plain down on their luck. *(Courtesy of Bentley Historical Library.)*

"I would often see poor farm residents out in the fields pitching hay, always under supervision," recalled George Campbell, who grew up on nearby Cobblestone Farm. "The men worked the farm as long as it was done with horsepower, but they couldn't manage farm machinery. The women residents helped in the kitchen, setting the tables or peeling potatoes. During the day they would sew." Campbell also remembered that Platt Road used to be known as "Pauper's Alley" and that "poorhouse residents used to sneak away and, using a little money they might have gotten from relatives, buy some tobacco at McMillan's store on Packard, where the gas station is now."

Poorhouses are usually depicted as bleak, terrible places, but Ann Arborites old enough to remember believe this one was not such a bad place. "It was a lot nicer than old age homes are today. Those who could work, did, and there was a nice visiting room. No one minded going there to live," recalls lifelong Ann Arbor resident Arthur Rieff. Edith Staebler Kempf agrees it was a pleasant enough place, especially with all the homegrown food, but says there was enough of a social stigma in being there that she was taught in her childhood to refer to it not as the "poor farm" but as the "county home." She adds, "People of means were ostracized if they let their relatives live there."

After the welfare system was created in the 1930s, the farm changed from a home for poor people to a place for people who needed continual medical care but could not afford it. The farmland was rented to Ralph

An 1830 Michigan law required each county to have a poorhouse. The county infirmary, the successor to the poorhouse, was for poor people who needed continual medical care. Built in 1917, it closed in 1971 and was torn down in 1979. *(Courtesy of Washtenaw County.)*

McCalla, who continued raising cattle and growing crops until 1960. According to McCalla, "Some of the poorhouse residents still helped. They would come down to the barn and feed the livestock just to have something to do."

The county infirmary, as it was known after 1917, was closed in 1971 after county officials decided it would cost too much to modernize. It was torn down in 1979. For a time, St. Joseph's Mercy Hospital seriously considered building on the site, and doctors' offices were built on the eastern side of Platt in anticipation of this move. After St. Joe's decided to locate elsewhere, debate centered on whether the land should be used for new county buildings or for a park.

After the county commissioners decided to keep the county courthouse in downtown Ann Arbor, the County Parks and Recreation Department went to work creating the County Farm Park. Today the 127-acre park includes a parcours (a jogging-exercise trail patterned after European fitness courses), a woodland trail, and Project Grow gardens. The Meri Lou Murray Center, named after a former county commissioner who was responsible for starting the county parks system, was opened in 1991.

# The Private Hospital Era

*Between 1875 and 1945, the city was home to seventeen proprietary hospitals. Ann Arborites could go to Dr. Cowie for a difficult diagnosis, study nursing with Dr. Peterson, get cuts stitched by Dr. Gates, and have their babies in Nurse Grove's home.*

When Dr. Carl Malcolm Jr. started practicing in Ann Arbor in the 1930s, many patients still expected him to treat them at home. When he urged them to go to the hospital, Malcolm recalls, "they thought it was the end of things."

Malcolm's older patients had been born in a time when anything a doctor could do to help he could do in their homes. As recently as the mid-1800s, hospitals were charity institutions for those who had no home to be sick in—"refuges mainly for the homeless poor and insane," according to Paul Starr's *The Social Transformation of American Medicine*.

Starr's fascinating medical history explains how, "in a matter of decades, roughly between 1870 and 1910, hospitals moved from the periphery to the center of medical education and medical practice." A string of breakthroughs, including antisepsis, anesthesia, and X-rays, transformed surgery from a desperate last resort into a routine medical tool. At first, doctors performed surgery in people's homes—Elsa Goetz Ordway remembers the family physician operating on her mother on the dining room table in 1914. But as medical standards rose, more and more doctors preferred to work in hospitals, which gradually evolved from shelters for the poor and the dying into, in Starr's words, "doctors' workshops for all types and classes of patients."

Today, Ann Arbor's three huge hospitals—the U-M, St. Joe's, and the VA—together handle more than a million patient visits every year. But it took a long time to get there. Both the University of Michigan Hospital (1869) and St. Joseph Mercy Hospital (1911) started out serving mere handfuls of patients in converted homes. For two generations, they shared the town with numerous small hospitals owned by individual practitioners.

Between 1875 and 1945, Ann Arbor had at least seventeen "proprietary" hospitals. All were located in converted houses. Otherwise, they were as different as the personalities and medical specialties of their owners.

The hospitals' owners included some of the most distinguished physicians in the city. Dr. David Murray Cowie founded the U-M pediatrics department, cared for patients at the U-M Hospital, and engaged in extensive research while also running his own hospital in a former mansion on South Division Street. His colleague Dr. Reuben Peterson, U-M professor of "women's and children's diseases," established a private medical complex that eventually filled ten buildings on Forest, Church, and South University. At the other end of the spectrum, nurse Josephine Grove took patients into her own home on Huron near Revena, caring for them around the clock. And Neil Gates, a down-to-earth general practitioner, attempted to treat almost every kind of medical ailment, whether in a patient's home, in his downtown office, or in his hospital on South Fifth Avenue.

## Dr. Cowie's Exclusive Clientele

Dr. David Cowie's sprawling brick mansion at 320 South Division is by far the most impressive surviving former hospital. In its day, it was also the most prestigious.

Cowie was born in Canada in 1872 to Scottish parents (his obituary called him "as Scotch as MacGregor"). He came to Michigan in 1892 to attend Battle Creek College but soon transferred to the U-M, where he graduated from the medical school and was hired as an assistant in internal medicine in 1896. He earned a second medical degree at the University of Heidelberg in 1908, the year he married Anna Marion Cook, who was also a doctor, although there is no evidence that she ever practiced medicine.

When Cowie returned from Germany, he was asked by medical dean George Dock to start a pediatrics department at the U-M Hospital. He opened his private diagnostic hospital a few years later, starting out with four rooms on the second floor at 122 North Fourth Avenue.

In 1918, Cowie tripled the number of patients he could serve by buying the home at 320 South Division built in the mid-1880s for Adelbert Noble, proprietor of the Star Clothing House. Cowie added on an institutional dining room and kitchen to the back of the house and built a third floor for additional patient rooms. Set up to provide complete medical and surgical services, the hospital boasted an automatic elevator, and every room had running water. The nurses wore pink uniforms.

Edith Staebler Kempf, whose in-laws lived next door in what is now

Dr. David Cowie took care of patients in his private hospital at 320 South Division, now an apartment building. He is best remembered today as the instigator of adding iodine to salt to prevent goiters. *(Photograph of Dr. Cowie courtesy of Bentley Historical Library; photograph of 320 South Division courtesy of Stan Shackman.)*

the Kempf House Center for Local History, remembered Cowie Private Hospital as "a hospital for rich women." But according to the *Medical History of Michigan*, published in 1930 by the Michigan State Medical Society, some exceptions were made. The authors wrote of Cowie's "ministration to semi-indigent gentlefolk" as "a pleasant feature" of the hospital.

Retired surgeon Thurston Thieme sometimes assisted with operations at Cowie's as a U-M intern. He agrees with Kempf about the high-toned clientele. He remembers setting out the sterilized instruments for Dr. Frederick Coller, the distinguished chairman of surgery at the U-M, while Coller complained that the patient should have come to the U-M Hospital for the operation. But according to Thieme, "Cowie had the best families as patients. He got the necessary doctors to come in."

Cowie attracted patients from all around the state. Dr. Allen Saunders, a local pediatrician who grew up in Coldwater, remembers that a number of relatives and family friends chose to come to Cowie's in Ann Arbor rather than be treated locally.

Cowie's prominent patients included Francis Kelsey, U-M professor of Latin and director of Near East research. Kelsey, for whom the Kelsey Museum was named, was a friend and admirer of Cowie's. In a 1924 letter to philanthropist Horace Rackham, who underwrote his archaeological work, Kelsey wrote that his wife, Isabelle, was sick but was receiving expert care from Cowie: "I have a friend who is a scientific physician in charge of a private hospital where obscure cases of her sort are investigated. She is there now and her case is being studied with the help of the x-ray and other means of diagnosis." It is not known what Cowie found, but Isabelle Kelsey lived another twenty years, to the age of eighty-two.

Francis Kelsey was not so lucky. In 1927, he returned from a dig in Egypt in failing health and immediately checked into Cowie's hospital. Too weak to give the paper on his findings that he had come home expressly to deliver, he got out of his sickbed to go to the meeting and hear someone else read it for him. He came back to the hospital and died a few weeks later.

Though his hospital was exclusive, Cowie's research ended up benefiting children throughout the state and the nation. At the time, many children in the Great Lakes region suffered from goiters—swollen thyroid glands in the neck—due to a lack of iodine in the soil. At Cowie's suggestion, a state commission was appointed in 1922 to study the problem. Cowie chaired the group, which first considered adding the iodine to drinking water. When that proved too expensive, they switched to the idea of adding it to table salt. At their urging, iodized salt was marketed in Michigan starting in 1924. Before Cowie began his crusade, 35 percent of Detroit schoolchildren suffered from goiters. With the introduction of iodized salt, the incidence was reduced to 1.4 percent. The use of iodized salt spread throughout the country and is commonplace today.

Cowie died on January 27, 1940. He became sick while on the way to his cottage in the Irish Hills; returned to Ann Arbor; and entered his own hospital, where he died of a coronary thrombosis. "Dr. Cowie's interests extended far beyond the limits of his profession," the *Ann Arbor News* wrote. "He was widely read, of broad human sympathies, quiet in demeanor, yet forceful. Literally hundreds of children owed their lives to his professional knowledge and unusual sympathetic insight." After Cowie's death, his hospital was divided into apartments, a use it still retains.

## DR. PETERSON'S MEDICAL EMPIRE

Like Cowie, Reuben Peterson served people who were willing to pay for better service than was available in the public hospitals of the time. Thurston Thieme remembers Dr. Peterson's Private Hospital as "a fine hospital, greatly respected and well known." His patients were all women and children, some of whom came from other towns and even other states.

For most of its early years, Peterson's hospital was located in a former fraternity house at 620 South Forest. He was so successful that he expanded into surrounding buildings, until he had the capacity to treat forty patients and train sixteen nurses. His private medical empire eventually included an annex at 614 Forest; a maternity hospital at 610 Forest; five residences for employees and nursing students on Forest, Church, and South University; and two hospitals, run for him by other doctors, at 1216 and 1218 South University.

Peterson was born in Boston in 1862; he received both undergraduate and medical degrees from Harvard, graduating in 1889. He set up the nurse's training program at St. Mark's Hospital in Grand Rapids and taught gynecology at Rush Medical School in Chicago before accepting an appointment to the U-M medical school in 1901. He started his hospital the next year. "The University of Michigan Hospital contains 225 beds," he wrote to explain the move. "It is full to overflowing the year around and many patients are compelled to board outside and wait for beds."

Peterson's hospital opened in June 1902 in an old house at 1215 South University. Peterson's partners, Fantine Pemberton, an early graduate of the new U-M nursing school, and her widowed mother, Laura Pemberton, rented and furnished the hospital building. Besides serving for many years as Peterson's superintendent of nursing and matron, respectively, the two women also provided household goods, equipment, and tableware of their own for use in the hospital. A few months later, the hospital moved to the larger house at 620 Forest.

*Left:* Reuben Peterson by his wife's roses. *(Courtesy of Linda Strodtman.)*
*Below:* Peterson's student nurses pose in front of one of the houses in his hospital complex. *(Courtesy of Linda Strodtman.)*

Nurses' graduation dinner decorated with Mrs. Peterson's roses. *(Courtesy of Linda Strodtman.)*

PETERSON RAN HIS OWN nurse's training program at his hospital. He awarded the first degrees in 1907, the same year he incorporated the school and bought out the Pembertons' interest. (Both women continued to work for him.) By 1909, he had six nurses in training. In 1912 Peterson set up the hospital annex and the next year the maternity hospital.

Peterson did not strictly separate his private life from the hospital. In 1910, he installed a "laundry appliance and mangle" in the basement of the hospital and hired Mary Simons and her husband for laundry work, with the understanding that they also would do his wife's laundry. (He had married the former Josephine Davis of Elk Rapids in 1890.) When he used 614 Forest as a home for nurses, he and Mrs. Peterson furnished it with a piano from their home.

In 1920 Peterson decided to discontinue the nurse's training school, "because of the difficulties in maintaining a high standard of training under present conditions." Nursing historian Linda Strodtman explains that "as nursing standards developed, it was not sufficient to just offer women's care." After 1920, Peterson confined his work to one building, keeping 620 Forest as the hospital and the house next door at 614 for a nurses' home and selling or renting the rest of his property. Shortly after, in 1922, he was promoted to head the ob-gyn department at the U-M medical school.

Clara Schnierle worked at Peterson's hospital from 1928 to 1932 as a cook's helper. She remembers Peterson as a good man and a good doctor—reserved, but still someone you felt comfortable around. "He was strict, like everyone in those days," Schnierle recalls. "You did your duties as he wanted; if you didn't like it, you moved on." Schnierle lived on the third floor of the hospital, which also contained the operating room. On the second floor there were eight private rooms and a nursery where the newborns slept in little baskets.

As a boy, book manufacturer Joe Edwards had his tonsils out at Peterson's. Many women were there for childbirth, but some came with illnesses. According to Schnierle, the patients generally chose Peterson's so they could have a private room and avoid the medical students at University Hospital. Maternity patients stayed two weeks, sitting up only after ten days. If they had twins, they stayed three weeks. Some of the patients hired their own personal nurses. Schnierle remembers a preemie, born three months early, who was tended by two nurses in twelve-hour shifts. The mother was cared for by two other private nurses. After three months in the hospital, the baby and mother went home, accompanied by all four nurses.

Schnierle recalls that Dr. Peterson came by every day, usually in the afternoon, after attending to his work at the university. He spent every summer, when the university was in recess, at his summer home in Duxbury, Massachusetts, arranging with other doctors to take care of emergencies and putting off elective surgery until he returned in the fall.

In 1931, Peterson retired from the university. When Schnierle left to get married in 1932, she was not replaced because Peterson's hospital was shrinking again. It closed for good the next year, and Peterson moved permanently to Duxbury, where he died on November 25, 1942, at age eighty. His hospital became a rooming house and later was torn down to make room for the Forest Avenue parking structure.

NURSE GROVE'S HOME HOSPITAL

Most proprietary hospitals were owned by doctors. But the Grove Cottage Hospital, 1422 West Huron at Revena, was owned and operated by nurse Josephine Grove and her husband, Otto, who was listed in the city directory as a traveling salesman.

The Groves turned their home into a hospital in the mid-1920s and ran it until Otto's death in 1934. Upstairs were two bedrooms for patients (they kept the third bedroom for themselves). Downstairs another bedroom was available for overflow patients. The upstairs bathroom served visiting doctors as an operating room. Mrs. Grove herself cared for her patients around the clock.

Most of Grove's patients were referred by a neighbor, Dr. John Gates, who lived at 201 South Revena. Many were women giving birth. Helen Wolf Curtis remembers that her brother was born at the Grove Cottage Hospital in 1927. Her family lived at 110 South Revena, so when her mother, Lucy Wolf, went into labor, she just walked down the street. After Dr. Peterson's hospital closed, his former employee, Clara Schnierle, chose to have her first child at Grove's. She explains that in those days people differed on whether to have their babies at home or in the hospital. Schnierle and her husband decided they would rather have the first one in a hospital, so their physician, John Gates, recommended the Grove Cottage Hospital. Schnierle remembers Mrs. Grove as "very pleasant, very serious-minded."

Sophie Walker, who lived nearby at 330 South Seventh, had her baby at Grove's hospital in 1928, not with Dr. Gates, but with another doctor, whom she chose because he spoke German. She had come from Germany just two years before. She liked Grove's hospital because it was like a private home, but she has a sad memory of the patient in the other room crying after giving birth: she wasn't married and was giving up her baby for adoption.

Maternity was not the only service offered. When Helen Wolf Curtis was a girl, she fell off the front stoop and broke her arm, and Dr. John Gates set it. Eleven years later, in 1929, she had the plate taken out at Grove's hospital, and while she was there she also had her tonsils and adenoids out. She remembers the hospital as "a wonderful place, not very plush but neat and clean."

## Dr. Gates's General Hospital

Dr. John Gates's elder brother, Neil, was also a doctor, a well-loved general practitioner. But according to his grandson Jeff Rentschler, he struggled financially until he bought his own hospital.

Gates's hospital at 314 South Fifth Avenue (now the parking lot of the Federal Building) exemplified a general practitioner's proprietary hospital. Neil Gates was the classic GP—he made house calls even in the worst weather, never took vacations (another grandson, David Gates, remembers him saying, "I'll take a vacation on the day nobody gets sick"), and was rarely allowed to sleep through the night. He smoked cigars constantly; people said they didn't recognize him without one. His niece Janet Ivory remembers him coming to her house when she was sick as a little girl. "When I smelled the cigar smoke, I felt better because I knew he was there. I knew I would get better."

Gates was born in Ann Arbor in 1873, the son of contractor John Gates and Dora McCormick Gates. He graduated from the U-M medical school in 1897 and started his career in Dexter. In about 1900 he built the Gates Block there as an office and infirmary (it is now occupied by insurance and real estate offices). Ten years later he moved to Ann Arbor and opened an office at 117 East Liberty, but he still kept up his large rural practice.

In the early days, Gates made house calls in a horse and buggy. In later years, his daughter, Lois Gates Rentschler, would drive him, often taking her son, Jeff, along. Jeff and his mother would usually stay in the car or walk around outside, but he has one memory of going inside the house of an elderly woman in Dexter and eating homemade graham crackers with butter in front of her wood-burning stove.

During the flu epidemic of 1918, Gates ministered heroically to his rural patients. The epidemic hit Ann Arbor in the fall but didn't get out into the country until the winter. Gates usually made winter visits in a one-horse sleigh that he drove himself, but during the epidemic he hired

Dr. Neil Gates ran the city's last private hospital at 314 South Fifth. Unable to keep up with advances at public hospitals, it closed after his death in 1945 and was torn down in 1973. *(Photograph of Dr. Gates courtesy of Jeff Rentschler; photograph of 314 South Fifth courtesy of Jeff Rentschler.)*

a two-horse wagon and a driver so that he could sleep between visits. During the terrible epidemic, which claimed 548,000 lives nationwide, it was the only rest he got.

Gates made a lot of his own medicine using natural materials—plants, weeds, bark, fungus—that he mashed with a pestle. For refined ingredients, he dealt exclusively with Fischer's Pharmacy. David Gates remembers that his grandfather carried three or four bags filled with all sorts of medicines, including some sugar pills he gave to people with imagined illnesses.

The Ann Arbor Railroad tracks ran right behind Gates's house at 440 South Main. When he was at home, his wife would put a scarf on the pole of the birdhouse in the backyard, so the train crews could stop if they had a medical problem. They would toot their whistle, and Gates would come out to take a cinder out of an eye, treat a burn, set a broken arm, or help a passenger with motion sickness.

Despite all his business, Gates for many years didn't make much money. David Gates remembers that his grandparents had a monster icebox and a big pantry, usually filled with eggs, chickens, and whatever produce was in season, contributed by patients who couldn't afford to pay in cash. But Jeff Rentschler says their grandfather did much better after he started his own hospital in 1924.

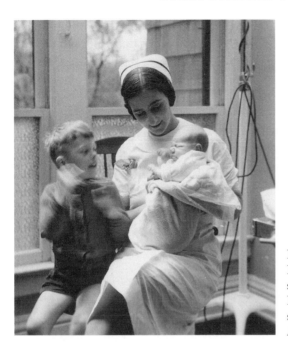

Dorothy Jolly, nurse at Dr. Gates's hopsital, shows a new baby to Jeff Rentschler, Gates's grandson. *(Courtesy of Jeff Rentschler.)*

The hospital Gates bought was an old Queen Anne house on South Fifth Avenue, built about 1895, complete with tower and wraparound front porch. In 1906, U-M medical professor Cyrenus Darling had converted it into a hospital with its own operating room and eight private patient rooms. In 1911, Darling became one of eight founding staff doctors at St. Joe's, which started out in a former rooming house on the corner of State and Kingsley. For a few years Darling worked at both hospitals, but in 1916 he decided to concentrate on St. Joe's. The hospital was run by James and Muriel McLaren as "Maplehurst" until Dr. Gates bought it in 1924.

Gates modernized the hospital by adding an X-ray facility, a second operating room (used mainly for delivering babies), and two wards, raising its capacity to twenty-eight patients. In his book *Historic Michigan*, George Fuller called Gates's hospital "one of the most complete and up-to-date of the many privately owned institutions of its kind in the United States."

As in his office and rural practice, Gates continued to treat whatever needs his patients had, although he had a reputation for being particularly good at stitching. W. H. Priestkorn went there as a boy to have his appendix out. Nate Weinberg's mother was operated on for pleurisy. Sam Schlect remembers someone he knew being stitched up by Dr. Gates after a Fourth of July explosion slashed his cheek.

Gates had a lot of maternity business. Mary Schlect, Sam's wife, gave birth to their daughter there in 1943. Sam was in the army, so she came with her neighbor, Gladys Water, who also was pregnant, and stayed in a three-bed ward. She remembers that the fee was $110, reduced to $100 if paid in cash. Election worker Bev Kirsht, who was born in Gates's hospital, reports that her father, George Lirette, was in the delivery room both for her birth and that of her sister. Years later, the Lamaze Association would have to fight local hospitals for this privilege, but Gates was ahead of his time on the issue. He routinely told the men, "Go out and take off your tie and jacket and come back in. It's your baby, too." David Gates believes there was a large influx of babies named Neil from the Gates's hospital—he says that when his grandfather delivered a boy he would hold him up and say, "If you don't know what to name him, name him 'Neil.'"

Gates never retired. During World War II he was able to continue his usual rural calls, thanks to a special permit that enabled him to buy gasoline and hard-to-obtain tires, both rationed. He was also issued extra ration coupons to buy food for the patients in his hospital.

Dr. Gates died on July 16, 1945. By then, his was the last surviving private hospital in the city. The rest had slowly died out, unable to compete with St. Joe's, which had built a big hospital on Ingalls in 1913, and the U-M, which had built a large modern hospital in 1925.

Of all hospitals, Paul Starr writes, the proprietary hospitals' "rate of institutional survival was the lowest. In this regard they were typical of small businesses; they opened and closed with the vicissitudes of personal fortune." Ann Arbor's experience bears this out. None of the hospitals survived their owners. After Gates's death, his hospital was converted to a rooming house. The turreted building was torn down in 1973 to make room for the Federal Building.

## Proprietary Hospitals

The following list of proprietary hospitals and the doctors who owned them was compiled from the city directory and from people's memories.

Ann Arbor Private Hospital, Mrs. Margaret Kelly, proprietor, Huron near First and then 1129 Washtenaw Avenue
Ann Arbor Sanitarium and Private Hospital, Dr. James Lynds, 403 South Fourth Avenue (now Muehlig's Funeral Chapel)
Bethel Faith Home, Mrs. Augusta Whitlark, matron, 126 Observatory
Dr. William Blair, 311 South Division Street

Burrett-Smith, Dr. Cyrus Burrett and Dr. Dean T. Smith, first at 721 East Washington and then at 416 South Fifth Avenue

Classen Private Hospital, Dr. Carrie Classen, osteopath, 429 Hamilton Place

Cowie Private Hospital, Dr. David M. Cowie, 320 South Division Street

Curtrest Maternity Home and Hospital, Mrs. Severine C. Curtiss, 1100 East Huron Street

Dr. Neil Gates, 314 South Fifth Avenue

Grove Cottage Hospital, Josephine and Otto Grove, 1422 West Huron Street

Herdman's Private Hospital, Dr. William James Herdman, 709 West Huron Street

Institute of Ozonotherapy, R. M. Leggett, manager, 120 North Fourth Avenue

Maplehurst, James and Muriel McLaren, first at 314 South Fifth Avenue and then at 822 Arch

Dr. Katherine Martin, 120 North Fourth Avenue

Dr. Peterson's Private Hospital, Dr. Reuben Peterson, 620 South Forest Avenue

Vreeland Maternity Home, Mrs. Velva C. Vreeland, 315 West Mosley

Washtenaw Private Hospital, also known as Dr. Cummings's Private Hospital, Dr. Howard Cummings, 216 North State Street

# Ann Arbor's Carnegie Library

*The steel magnate's gift was grafted onto the public high school.*

People who looked at the old Frieze Building on Huron opposite North Thayer couldn't tell that part of it was actually a distinct structure, set closer to Huron Street and built of stone blocks rather than brick. The main brick building was built in 1907 as Ann Arbor High School. The smaller stone one was built the same year, as one of America's 1,679 Carnegie libraries.

Andrew Carnegie (1835–1919) was a Scottish immigrant who made his fortune in steel (he replaced many wooden bridges with steel ones) and railroads (he introduced the first sleeping cars). After he sold Carnegie Steel to financier J. P. Morgan in 1901, he devoted his energies to giving away his vast fortune for social and educational advancement.

Carnegie believed that great wealth was a public trust that should be shared. But he did not believe in straight almsgiving. (This was, after all, the Carnegie who broke the 1886 strike at his steel plant in Homestead, Pennsylvania, with two hundred Pinkerton detectives. It took the state militia to put down the riots that resulted.) Building libraries to encourage self-improvement was consistent with Carnegie's philosophy of helping people help themselves. He paid for the buildings but required the community to provide the site and to pay for books and maintenance in perpetuity.

At the time it was built, Ann Arbor's Carnegie library was believed to be the only one in the country attached to another building. But it was a natural pairing in a town where the library and the high school had already been associated for nearly fifty years. The contents of the high school's library, which started operating in 1858, were the city's first publicly owned books. In 1883, the collection was given its own quarters on the second floor of the school, and Nellie Loving was hired to be the first librarian. At this time, or soon after, the general public also was allowed to use the library, thus setting the precedent, continued until 1995, of the school board taking responsibility for the public library. Today it is a district library with its own elected board.

The Carnegie Library—Ann Arbor. Mich

Postcard view of Ann Arbor's Carnegie Library. It was said to be the only one in the country attached to another building. *(Courtesy of Bentley Historical Library.)*

ANOTHER SOURCE OF BOOKS for nineteenth-century readers was the Ladies Library Association. It was organized in 1866 by thirty-five women as a subscription library, based on a model started by Benjamin Franklin. By 1885, members had raised enough money—through Easter and Christmas fairs, lectures, cantatas, and strawberry festivals—to build their own library on Huron Street between Division and Fifth, in a building since torn down to make room for Michigan Bell.

In 1902, Anna Botsford Bach, then president of the Ladies Library Association, suggested applying for a Carnegie grant to build a city library. The city's application was supported by the school board, the city council, and the Ladies Library Association. But after Carnegie granted $20,000 for the project in 1903, the applicants could not agree among themselves on a site. (The school board wanted the new library to be near the high school so the students could continue using it. The Ladies Library Association thought an entirely separate location would better serve the general public.) The deadlock was resolved only after the application was resubmitted in 1904 without the participation of the Ladies Library Association. This time, the city and school board were awarded $30,000.

The Carnegie grant came just in time: on the night of December 31, 1904, the high school burned down. Luckily, school officials and students who rushed to the scene were able to save most of the library's eight thousand books before the building was destroyed.

A few months later, voters approved a bond issue to build a new school. The school and the library went up simultaneously; both were designed by architects Malcomson and Higginbottom of Detroit, who specialized in school architecture, and built by M. Campbell of Findlay, Ohio. (The interior finishing work was done by the Lewis Company of Bay City, which later began building kit homes.) Despite its unusual connection to the high school, the library looked much like other Carnegie libraries: large pillars on the front, big windows, high ceilings, and a massive center staircase. The board of education, pleased with the result, called the new building "beautiful and commodious."

In 1932, the high school library moved into separate quarters on the library's third floor, but students continued to use the lower floors after school. Gene Wilson, retired director of the public library, remembers that when he began working there in 1951, the busiest time of day was right after school, when the students would flock over to do their homework. By the time Wilson came to the library, the once spacious building was, in his words, "obscured by shelving on top of shelving. It was a rabbit warren of a building, typical of libraries at the end of their life, with six times as many books as planned for with stacks all over."

Since the late 1940s, citizens' groups had been talking about the need for a new library. The school board took action in 1953, selling the high school and library building to the U-M for $1.4 million. (By then the new Ann Arbor High—now Pioneer—was under construction at the corner of West Stadium and South Main.) The board used the proceeds of the sale to buy the Beal property at the corner of Fifth and William as the site for a new library, ending nearly a century of close association between the high school and the public library.

The library remained in the old Carnegie building for a few years after the high school moved out. It left in 1957, when the new public library on Fifth Avenue was ready for occupancy.

The university remodeled and enlarged the old library and high school building and renamed it the Henry S. Frieze Building, after a professor of classics who also had served as acting president. In 2004 the university announced plans to build a dormitory on the site.

# Red Howard, Small-Town Cop

*Tough and outgoing, he embodied the AAPD for forty years.*

Sam Schlecht still remembers a run-in he had with Ann Arbor police-man Red Howard in the 1920s. On a Halloween night, when Schlecht was about ten, he and a buddy played a prank on a neighbor. "We took a couple of big garbage cans and dumped them on the porch," Schlecht recalls. This act was evidently witnessed, because they had run only a couple of blocks before they were overtaken by Howard, driving the police department's red Buick touring car.

The boys confessed to the crime. "I wasn't going to lie, because if it got back to my grandmother I would really be up a creek," Schlecht recalls. Howard told them he was taking them in. After driving toward the police station long enough to make them thoroughly frightened, Howard turned back to the scene of the crime, where he set them to work cleaning up the porch. Schlecht, of course, never performed that act of vandalism again.

When Red Howard joined the police in 1907, Ann Arbor was a town of about fourteen thousand people. Though the city grew severalfold during his forty years on the force, he always remained a small-town cop. He handled wrongdoers more like a strict parent than a legal functionary. "The word was that Red never arrested anyone, but he did more good than anyone else," recalls Warren Staebler. "A good licking down did more good than fining."

A big man, six feet two inches and of impressive girth, Howard kept order more by his commanding presence than by his billy club or gun. Although he never advanced beyond the rank of sergeant, he embodied the department to Ann Arborites of his era. People still remember him vividly more than fifty years after his death.

To Howard, what we now call "community policing" was second na-ture. He "would walk up and talk to anyone," recalls Bob Kuhn, who lived on Catherine Street. "He was super to kids," remembers Mary Schlecht. "Everyone liked him," agrees Jim Crawford, former head of the Black Elks. On good terms with the Main Street merchants, he was

Red Howard on the job. *(Courtesy of Roseann Ingram.)*

Celebrating retirement with Mayor Robert Campbell and future police chief Walt Krasny. *(Courtesy of Roseann Ingram.)*

Fishing at Crooked Lake. *(Courtesy of Roseann Ingram.)*

equally comfortable in the rougher bar areas. "No one scared him," says his daughter, Roseann Ingram.

As Sam Schlecht found, Howard often acted as judge and jury as well as policeman. When Dick Tasch was a U-M freshman, he and some classmates printed up broadsides taunting the sophomore class and pasted them surreptitiously on State Street buildings. "One night, about one AM, we put a whole bunch at Goldman Cleaners and Quarry Drugs," Tasch remembers, "and were going around the corner when there was Red Howard standing. We took off running."

A local boy, Tasch was able to duck out of sight and escape, but the others were caught. Tasch drove by later and found his classmates carrying pails and scrub brushes, cleaning up. "You didn't go to court," Tasch recalls. "He'd punish you on the job."

Though overweight and a heavy smoker, Howard could outrun most criminals. He kept his strength up his whole career. Duane Bauer, who joined the force the year before Howard retired, remembers an incident at Michigan Stadium when two drunks were creating a disturbance down by the field. "Red took both by the neck and took them up seventy-two steps. He was a powerful man."

Before and after football games, Howard also directed traffic at the corner of State and Packard. When people asked if he wasn't scared of being run over, he'd reply, "If they hit me, they'll get a big grease spot." Not surprisingly, he made a big impression on out-of-towners. Bauer, who took over that intersection after Howard retired, recalls, "More people wanted to know what happened to big old Red."

HOWARD'S REAL FIRST NAME was Marland; he got the nickname Red as a schoolboy because of the color of his hair. He was born in 1878 in Saline, the son of an Irish produce merchant, and grew up on Hiscock Street in Ann Arbor.

At the time, half the town was of German descent. Howard learned to speak the language from other kids in the neighborhood. ("He could rattle off German like anything," his daughter remembers.) He was often called the German Irish cop, because he always lived in German neighborhoods and enjoyed German beer and German food.

Howard quit school when he was eleven and worked at a grocery store and then at Godfrey Moving (he was a relative of owner Dana Creal) before joining the police. He married Rose Galligan of Northfield Township in 1903, and they lived at 410 West Washington, where the Y now stands. Along with their own four children, the Howards usually had other relatives living with them.

Howard's personal life mirrored his police style. He was warm and loving but also strict. He told his sons, "If you get arrested and go to jail, don't call me." He kept a careful eye on his girls. "I couldn't do anything that wouldn't get back to him," recalls Ingram. His granddaughter Joan Dwyer Hume, who also lived in the house, recalls that Howard checked out all her boyfriends to make sure they didn't have police records. But Hume also has wonderful memories of walking home from St. Thomas School when Howard was walking his beat on Huron Street. He'd watch for her so that he could take Hume and her friends to Candyland for ice cream.

In 1937, after thirty years of service and completion of a training course on new police methods, Howard was promoted to sergeant. "Even after he was a sergeant, he'd still go out on the beat because he loved it," recalls Ingram. "He went down to Main Street, where everyone knew him and thought he was the greatest. He didn't give two hoots for an office."

Howard's personality and seniority won the respect of his fellow officers (there were eight when he started, more than forty by the time he retired). "He was the only policeman who could bring a bottle of beer with his lunch," Bauer remembers. John Walter, who joined the police the same year as Bauer, recalls that they called Howard "Pappy" because he was the oldest man on the force. "He was a joyful guy," says Walter. "We kidded him an awful lot. He took it and gave it back."

Howard didn't retire until he was sixty-nine. "All I ever wanted to do was police work," he told Ingram. "I loved every minute." His family held a huge retirement party in his honor. Afterward, Howard spent more time at his cottage on Crooked Lake. He loved to fish and had a boat that was specially built to hold his weight.

In declining health, he also spent time in the hospital. Ingram and Hume remember coming to visit him and finding three clergymen sitting at his bedside: the ministers from Zion and Bethlehem and Father Carey from St. Thomas. They were discussing fishing.

Howard died of lung cancer in 1948, just a year after he retired. His funeral was held at St. Thomas with Police Chief Casper Enkemann and Judge Jay Paine among the pallbearers. "When he passed, we learned a lot," his daughter recalls. "It was such a big funeral. Police came from out of town, firemen, and people he helped. He made an impression. He had more friends than he ever knew."

# The Farmers' Market

*The future of the city-owned market looked bleak a decade ago, but today the biggest problem is competition for space.*

"I have been to markets all over the world," says Al Kierczak, a farmer who's been coming to the Farmers' Market since 1927, "and Ann Arbor is the nicest. It has the most variety." His wife, Florence, confirms that wherever they travel, Kierczak spends part of their vacation taking a busman's holiday, checking out the local markets in Europe, South America, and Japan.

Kierczak started coming to the Ann Arbor market with his parents when he was eight years old, riding in from their farm near Milan in an open Model T pickup. In those days the market was held around the old courthouse at Main and Huron, which had sweeping lawns on all four sides. Kierczak's dad and the other farmers would back their trucks up to the sidewalk and set up tables to display their produce. If it was a hot day, they'd put up umbrellas.

The curb market, as it was originally called, was started in May 1919 by the Community Federation, composed of representatives from several women's organizations. The group believed it could cut food costs by eliminating the middleman. In fact, several grocers, fearing the competition, went to the common council to object to the plan. They were overruled, and the council and the board of public works approved the federation's request to let the farmers sell from the streets adjacent to the courthouse.

The original market began with ten farmers on the Main Street side of the courthouse. According to Rudy Weiner, each farmer sold something different: Adolph Weiner, Rudy's father, sold flowers (he had emigrated from Austria, where he was head gardener for Emperor Franz Joseph); Flora Osborne sold celery, Chinese cabbage, and onions; and the Riecherts of Chelsea sold fruit. Many of the farmers came in horse-drawn wagons. They'd leave their wagons at the curb and stable the horses in the dairy barn on the corner of Miller Avenue and First Street. If they had any produce left at the end of the day, they'd hitch up the horses and peddle it around town.

The curb market.
*(Courtesy of Bentley Historical Library.)*

The city's growth has long since overrun some of the early growers' farms. The Weiners' farm was on Packard, near where the Darlington Lutheran Church is now. The Osborne place was near today's city airport, and the Dickinsons, another early market family, had a farm on Broadway. The market organizers talked of limiting the market to only Washtenaw County farmers, but since one of the early participants was from outside the county, they decided against it. But another rule they made at the time is still rigorously enforced: everything sold at the market must be produced by the vendors themselves.

THE EARLY VENDORS sold everything their farms produced: not just vegetables, fruit, and flowers but also honey, eggs, dairy products, baked goods, and poultry—chickens were the most common, but turkeys, ducks, and geese also could be found at the market. Esther Kapp remembers that her family sold beef and pork that her father butchered. Several people even remember seeing dressed muskrat for sale.

With so many things for sale, it's obvious why some of the local merchants were worried about the competition. But, bowing to the inevitable, some began buying market produce—such as seasonal strawberries or Flora Osborne's onions—by the crate or bushel to resell in their stores. Not wanting to sell out and disappoint their regular clientele, some of the farmers set aside a certain amount for wholesale or brought in an extra buggy load for the stores.

As the number of farmers increased, people objected to clogging up Main Street, so the market moved to the Fourth Avenue side of the courthouse and then eventually wrapped around onto Ann Street. The market never used the Huron Street side, since it was too busy a street to block off. (Before expressways, Huron/Washtenaw was the main highway through town.) During the peak of the growing season, there were so many farmers that the market expanded to the other side of Fourth Avenue, in front of what was then the YMCA and is now the county annex. To limit traffic congestion, the farmers who used that space had to move their trucks out of the way after they unloaded. The market was such a success that in 1921 the common council decided to take it over. It has been a city market managed by a council-appointed commission ever since.

Anna Biederman was the city's first market master. Born in Germany, she moved to Ann Arbor with her husband, John, and raised nine children. "She knew all about growing," says Warren Staebler, who remembers her as the director of the victory garden he was involved in as a child during World War I, on land between Seventh and Eighth Streets. Biederman did the same in World War II and between the wars directed the children at Bach Elementary School in gardening on their own plots on what is today the school's playground.

Biederman traveled to other markets around the state and became an authority on how to organize a community market. "Throughout the trying early years and the development into the present large market Mrs. Biederman has been the ruling spirit," claimed a 1934 *Ann Arbor News* article. Her grandson, John Biederman, remembers her as "a little, short, chubby woman, very outspoken. When she ran the market, she ran the market."

John remembers that his family benefited from one of the perks of Biederman's position. "On market days we would get a call from Grandma saying, 'I've got a whole bunch of cabbages, or carrots, or beets. Come get them.' The farmers would give them to her, and there would be too much for two people to eat."

As the amount of traffic and the number of sellers increased in the 1920s, the courthouse square became a less satisfactory location for the market. In 1931, Gottlob Luick, a former mayor (1899–1901), solved the problem by donating land for a permanent site between Fourth Avenue and Detroit Street, which had been used by his lumber company. Adolph Weiner worked with Luick to design the market.

It was the midst of the Depression, so the city didn't have money to develop the site, but the farmers made do, selling their produce from the sidewalk that fronted Detroit Street. They used wooden sheds from the old lumberyard for protection in rain and to keep warm in the winter. They created more space by adding a boardwalk along the northern edge of the property, creating an L-shaped layout. The wooden walkway protected people from the mud and also helped level a sloping piece of land. "It was three feet at the highest and then tapered down," recalls fruit grower Alex Nemeth, who, like Al Kierczak, starting coming to the market with his parents when he was a child. "I'd crawl under it with the other kids, looking for coins that dropped through."

From 1938 to 1940, the present 124-stall market was built by the federal Works Progress Administration (WPA), a Depression-era jobs program. WPA workers roofed and paved the market and added another short wing extending west from Detroit Street. A market headquarters, a small tan brick building, was built in the middle, where the parking coin meter is today. Market managers used the back room for an office, while farmers used the lounge in front to get warm and to eat sack lunches.

Shortly after the market was finished, Charles McCalla built a cinderblock building just north of the market for his Washtenaw Farm Bureau store. He used the new building as a store and feed mill and the old lumber warehouse on the corner of Fifth and Kingsley for storage and parts. (Both buildings are now part of Kerrytown.)

McCalla ground grain into livestock feed and sold prepared feeds, seeds, pet supplies, and penny candy. With such a convenient location, many market farmers bought supplies there. In 1962, McCalla's son and daughter-in-law, Ray and Shirley McCalla, took over the business and renamed it Washtenaw Farm and Garden Center. In 1969, they sold the buildings to Kerrytown's developers and moved their operation to Dexter.

Another nearby business that catered to the farmers was a small eatery run by Bill Biederman, Anna's son. At the time the WPA market was built, there were still four houses along Fourth Avenue west of the market. Bill Biederman lived in one of the houses and ran a modest restau-

WPA construction. Note the old lumber sheds on the right. *(Courtesy of Bentley Historical Library.)*

rant in his kitchen, serving breakfasts and light lunches—hamburgers, chili, soup. John Biederman worked as a dishwasher and cook for his uncle when he was a teenager. He remembers there were about nine stools and some little armchairs. When Anna Biederman retired, Bill took over as market manager.

During the food shortages of World War II, the market was busier than ever. Mildred Parker remembers customers lining up five or six stalls back to buy her chickens. "Finally," she remembers, "I counted how many were left and then came out and said I'd sell one to each and the rest should go home."

FROM ITS INCEPTION through the 1960s, market stalls were in great demand. "Quite a few [growers] would stay all night the night before to get a preferred spot," Alex Nemeth remembers. Bob Dieterle, who still works the family farm near Saline, remembers that his mother used to go at 2 AM and park across from the armory to make sure she'd get a stall.

Once they had secured a spot, many stayed up all night, or close to it, getting ready for the market. Dieterle's wife, Luella, used to spend the night picking flowers, a flashlight under her arm. Esther Kapp remembers harvesting until 1:30 AM and then rising again at 4 AM for the trip to town. Her three brothers stayed behind on the farm on Northfield Church Road to continue picking; while Kapp and her mother sold, her dad would drive back and forth all day to pick up fresh produce.

Winter was an even more trying time. Bob Dieterle didn't miss a Saturday for fifty-seven years. "People depended on us to bring eggs," he says. "Once when there was a big snowstorm, when we still had horses, I knew my dad's '34 Ford couldn't reach the corner [to the main road], so I had the horses pull it there. I met him there with the horses when he returned at three." Mildred Parker remembers selling eggs on a day when it was nineteen degrees below zero. "I had just the empty containers on the table. When I made a sale, I'd go to the truck, but every carton had at least one cracked egg. I could see they were frozen, so I just went home." The farmers dressed warmly and rigged up homemade stoves, called "salamanders," to keep warm.

Over the years, fewer and fewer people were willing to endure such hardships. For one thing, health regulations kept limiting what the farmers could bring to the market. In the 1950s, stricter standards stopped the sale of unrefrigerated dairy products: butter, milk, cottage cheese, buttermilk. Next, the state barred the farmers from selling meat. Kapp recalls, "We always had the meat in ice. It was a Lansing problem, not the meat inspector's. We went up to Lansing to complain, but they had made up their mind." In 1977 baked goods were banned unless they were prepared in a separate, licensed commercial kitchen.

The market went through a low point in the 1970s and 1980s. With farmers finding it harder to stay in business and local retailers luring shoppers away with more and better produce, the number of vendors plunged 40 percent between 1976 and 1988. That year, the *Observer* published an article asking, "Will the market survive to the year 2000?"

To keep the market going, the commission implemented two important changes. Some veteran growers were allowed to spread out, renting three or even four stalls. And for the first time, a dozen booths were permanently rented to craftspeople—woodworker Coleman Jewett's Adirondack chairs, for instance, are now a fixture at the market's north end.

Today the market is again full. According to Maxine Rosasco, market manager since 1987, there is even a waiting list: the 54 produce vendors and 144 craftspeople who currently rent daily as space permits want to be assigned permanent stalls.

While the turnaround is good news for the market, it also means that the two stopgap changes in the 1980s have become a problem. Pointing to their numbers, the craftspeople are lobbying for more space. "We set up Sunday for an artisans' market, but they'd rather come on Saturday," says Rosasco. And there is also friction among the growers themselves.

The waiting list for produce vendors is surprising—after all, farming has only gotten tougher in the last decade, and farms around the city

The Farmers' Market in the 1950s. *(Courtesy of Olive Conant.)*

have continued to be gobbled up by new subdivisions. But those losses have been more than made up for by growers coming from farther afield, as far away as Allen and Coldwater. And despite increased competition from supermarkets and produce markets, shoppers have continued to flock to the market for specialties, like Ken King's organic produce and George Merkle's Chinese vegetables.

"Buyers are more sophisticated," says Florence Kierczak. "Years ago we didn't sell kohlrabi; people didn't know what it was. Now they do." The Nemeth family has expanded its variety of fruit, offering customers different tastes and also gaining a longer harvest. And many growers have responded to shoppers' demands for bedding plants, especially perennials, as well as for cut flowers and herbs.

The downside of the market's resurgence is growing tension between longtime vendors and newcomers who'd like to get into the market. Some of the growers on the waiting list think that the vendors with four stalls should be made to give one up.

That, of course, isn't going over well with the veteran growers. Says Mildred Parker, "They think they should get a stall right away. Some of us waited four or five years, or even ten, to get where we wanted." The growers with multiple stalls say they need the space because they have to sell more now to make up for rising costs—for instance, new state health rules require farmers making apple cider to have a separate press building with a cement floor. "One stall was adequate for each farm in the early days," says Alex Nemeth. "Now you need two or three to make a living."

PHYSICALLY THE MARKET'S LAYOUT hasn't changed much since the WPA finished its work, except for gradual expansions as houses on Fourth Avenue were acquired and demolished or moved. In 1980, city voters turned down a bond proposal to rebuild and winterize the market, apparently feeling the changes would make it too glitzy (although most of the farmers would have appreciated the warmth!). But by saving up vendors' fees, the market commission was able to replace the roofs and gutters and build a new office at the market's south end.

Crowds at the market remain strong, especially in midsummer when foot traffic gets so thick shoppers sometimes find it hard to move. The farmers for their part have warm feelings for the market beyond just making a living. Many have been involved for several generations and have become close friends, almost family, with their fellow farmers. Parker first brought her daughter in a playpen. In later years, her daughter became such good friends with the Kapps' daughter that people didn't know which kid belonged with which stall. The farmers have also made friends with their customers over the years. Says Olive Conant, "They'd talk to you, tell you things they wouldn't tell others—they think farmers have a more down-to-earth life."

# The University of Michigan

## The Detroit Observatory

*It launched the U-M on the path to greatness.*

"How can we truly be called a nation, if we cannot possess within our-selves the sources of a literary, scientific, and artistic life?" asked Henry Philip Tappan, the first president of the University of Michigan, at his inaugural address in 1852. Henry N. Walker, a prominent Detroit lawyer in the audience, was inspired by Tappan's vision and asked what he could do to help. Tappan suggested he raise money to build an astro-nomical observatory.

Born into a prominent New York family, Tappan had astonished his friends by agreeing, at age forty-seven, to head what was then an obscure frontier college. The attraction for Tappan, who previously had been a minister, professor, and writer, was the chance Michigan offered to put his educational philosophy into practice—"to change the wilderness into fruitful fields," as he put it in his inaugural address.

An adherent of the Prussian model of education, Tappan believed that universities should expand their curriculum beyond the classics to teach science and encourage research. An observatory would embody the new approach perfectly—and Walker was ideally positioned to make it a reality.

Walker was a former state attorney general who often handled rail-road cases. Well connected to both intellectuals and businesspeople in Detroit, he attracted contributors who desired to advance scientific knowledge, as well as those who were interested in astronomy's prac-tical uses, particularly in establishing accurate time.

Because Walker raised most of its $22,000 cost from Detroiters, the building was named the Detroit Observatory. Tappan originally planned to have just one telescope, a refractor, suitable for research and instruc-tion. But Walker offered to pay for a meridian-circle telescope as well. It would be better suited for measuring the transit of the stars and thus for establishing more accurate time—a matter of vital importance to railroads, which needed to run on schedule.

The regents sited the observatory on a four-acre lot, high on a hill outside the city limits. Although only half a mile east of central campus, it was then considered way out in the country. In the early days it could be reached only by a footpath, and astronomers complained of the long walk.

Tappan said later that he took credit for everything about the observatory except its location, which he would have preferred to be on the main campus. "It has proved an inconvenient location, and has caused much fatigue to the astronomer," he wrote. However, the remote site probably saved it: nearly every building of its age on central campus has long since been torn down.

In 1853, Tappan and Walker traveled to New York to order the refracting telescope from Henry Fitz, the country's leading telescope maker. With an objective lens twelve and five-eighths inches across, it would be the largest refractor yet built in the United States and the third largest telescope in the world, after instruments in Pulkovo, Russia, and at Harvard.

Meridian-circle telescopes were not manufactured in the United States, so Tappan went to Europe. On the advice of Johann Encke, director of the Prussian Royal Observatory in Berlin, he ordered a brass meridian-circle telescope from Pistor and Martins, a Berlin firm.

Tappan asked several American astronomers to head the new observatory, but they all turned him down. At that point he thought of Franz Brunnow, Encke's assistant, who had been very enthusiastic about the project. Some objected to hiring a foreigner as astronomer, but Tappan prevailed. And certainly Brunnow was eminently qualified—he was the first Ph.D. on the U-M faculty. Under his direction, Ann Arbor soon became "the place to study astronomy," according to Patricia Whitesell, the observatory director and curator and author of *A Creation of His Own: Tappan's Detroit Observatory*. Brunnow socialized with the Tappans and in 1857 married Tappan's daughter Rebecca.

Tappan launched many other initiatives to turn the U-M into a first-rate university. He moved the students out of the two classroom buildings, letting them board in town, to make more space for academic uses—classrooms, natural history and art museums, and library. He encouraged the growth of the medical school, started the law school, and built the first chemistry laboratory in the country to be used exclusively for research and teaching. Under his leadership, the U-M granted its first bachelor of science degrees in 1855, its first graduate degrees in 1859, and its first civil engineering degrees in 1860.

But Tappan also made enemies—people who found his changes too precipitous or his manner too haughty. In 1863, Tappan was fired in a

The earliest known picture of the observatory, circa 1858. The man is probably first director Franz Brunnow with his father-in-law's dog, Leo. *(Courtesy of Bentley Historical Library.)*

surprise vote by a lame-duck board of regents. Tappan moved his family to Europe, never to return; he died in Switzerland in 1881. Fortunately, his successors continued on the course he'd set, securing the U-M's reputation as one of the nation's leading universities.

BRUNNOW RESIGNED AFTER Tappan was fired; his star student, James Craig Watson, succeeded him. During Watson's tenure, a director's house was added to the west side of the observatory.

In 1908 an addition was built to the east to hold a thirty-seven-inch reflector telescope. But as the campus grew out to the observatory, lights from the power plant (1914) and from the Ann Street hospital and Couzens Hall (both 1925) interfered with viewing. Over the decades that followed, the astronomy department transferred its serious research to a series of increasingly remote locations (currently Arizona and Chile). But the old observatory continued to be used for educational purposes until 1963, when the Dennison physics and astronomy building was completed.

In the tight-budget 1970s, there was talk of bulldozing the observatory. After World War II, the director's house had been torn down to

The observatory with the director's house on the west side. While Brunnow was able to live in the president's house, Watson, the next director, needed a home, so one was built that connected to his office in the observatory. *(Courtesy of Bentley Historical Library.)*

make room for an expansion of Couzens Hall, and the 1908 addition was razed in 1976 when the university decided it was too run down to maintain. But the original observatory was saved—though the rescue took a three-part campaign lasting close to thirty years.

Step one took place in the early 1970s, when a group of local preservationists led by John Hathaway, then chair of the Historic District Commission, and Dr. Hazel Losh, legendary U-M astronomy professor, convinced the university to give it a stay of execution.

Next, enter history professors Nick and Peg Steneck, who were called in by Al Hiltner, then chair of the astronomy department, and Orren Mohler, the former chair. Peg Steneck remembers that on her first tour of the building "squatters were gaining access by climbing the chestnut tree out front and entering through the trapdoor in the roof. Evidence of occupancy, such as mattresses and Kentucky Fried Chicken boxes, littered the dome room, and a mural was painted around the wall of the dome."

Nick Steneck tried to keep the building in use, setting up his office there, teaching classes, and using the upper level for the Collegiate Institute for Values in Science. Peg Steneck started research on the observatory's history, which grew into a course she still teaches on the history of the university. Under the Stenecks' prodding, the university took steps to stop the deterioration, fixing the roof, masonry foundation, and stucco.

Step three took place in 1994, when the university history and traditions committee asked vice president for research Homer Neal to restore the observatory. Neal assigned Whitesell, who was working in his office, to write a proposal, which she happily did, starting with Peg Steneck's research.

Whitesell had a Ph.D. in higher education, was interested in both historic preservation and the history of science, and had long admired the observatory. Her new assignment, she says, "was a dream come true." Neal agreed to the restoration and appointed Whitesell project manager.

Like the original construction, the million-dollar project, spearheaded enthusiastically by Anne and Jim Duderstadt, was paid for by gifts from private donors. The work began in June 1997 and was completed a year and a half later.

The university's first total restoration project, the observatory has a lot of "first" and "only" distinctions. It is the oldest unaltered observatory in America that has its original instruments intact, in their original mounts, and operational. The meridian-circle telescope is the oldest in its original mount in the entire world. The building is the second oldest on campus (next to the president's house) and the oldest unaltered one.

Restored, the observatory serves both as a museum of astronomical history and as a location for many academic events.

# The Remarkable Legacy of
# Francis Kelsey

*At the turn of the century, a U-M Latin professor single-handedly amassed the university's amazing collection of antiquities.*

Who can imagine Barbie dolls as educational tools? The Kelsey Museum of Archaeology can, and did. On family days, held regularly to teach area children about ancient Egypt, kids get to mummify Barbie.

The young students "disembowel" the previously prepared dolls, extracting walnut lungs, gummy worm intestines, raisin livers, and jelly bean stomachs. These "entrails" go into "canopic jars" made from empty film canisters. The children then wrap their dolls in a white, linenlike packing material and place each one in a sarcophagus—a shoe box spray painted gold.

Lauren Talalay, the Kelsey's associate director, says the idea of using Barbies came to her in a dream one night after she'd been approached by the Ann Arbor Hands-On Museum to develop a program for children. She laughingly says, "Barbies deserve this." Besides making mummies, the children participate in a sandbox dig, make bead necklaces, and learn to write hieroglyphs.

The Kelsey is unique among U-M museums because it serves both teaching and display purposes. Organized in 1929 to house a collection started in 1893, it now has more than one hundred thousand artifacts from all over the Mediterranean world, spanning a period from 2700 BC to 1100 AD. Long a great resource for U-M faculty and students, as well as the international academic world, the Kelsey in the last ten years has extended its mission to reach the community at large with lectures, minicourses, and tours to archaeological sites. To reach more school-age children, the museum created "Civilization in a Crate," sets of teaching aids on thirteen subjects ranging from the Argonauts to ancient social problems. The idea has been picked up by institutions as far away as Japan.

THE DAY I VISIT, docent Susan Darrow, a social worker by profession, elegantly dressed in a brown dress with a coordinating scarf, is teaching a group of seventh graders from Southfield about daily life in ancient Egypt. She's using artifacts from Karanis, the Kelsey's first dig (1924–35) and the source of almost half the museum's holdings. As the children sit around a large table in a windowless basement room of the museum, Darrow, wearing protective gloves, holds up various objects sealed in plastic bags and asks the kids to guess what they are. She begins with items that would be used at the start of a day two thousand years ago: comb, perfume bottle, kohl mascara container (one of the kids says in disbelief, "They used makeup back then?"), a pull toy, and even breakfast food— a piece of bread, which leads the kids to joke, "It must be kinda stale." This group is part of the Chavez-King project, intended to interest students considered non–college bound to set their sights higher and consider a wider variety of professions, such as archaeology.

When Darrow finishes, she leads the group upstairs, turning them over to docent Tammy Vaughn, a blond, blue-jeaned Eastern Michigan University student. Vaughn takes them on a tour of the first floor, the only public part of the museum; the rest of the building is used for offices, classrooms, and storage. Built in 1891 as the headquarters for the U-M Student Christian Association, the building still has many elegant accoutrements—tiled fireplaces, inlaid wooden floors, even a genuine Tiffany stained-glass window. There is display room to exhibit only about .5 percent of the museum's holdings at any one time, but exhibits change regularly. Usually Greek and Roman artifacts are displayed on the south side and Egyptian and Near Eastern pieces on the north.

Vaughn leads the group into an exhibit on the north side called "Death in Ancient Egypt: Preserving Eternity." They watch intently as she shows them the mummy of Djheutymose, ask "Where's his tail?" about a cat mummy, and then gasp almost in unison when she shows them the mummy of a little boy about five. Vaughn explains that mummifying people was the Egyptians' attempt to defeat death.

THE MUSEUM'S FANTASTIC COLLECTION was started by Francis Kelsey, a U-M Latin professor from 1889 to 1927. He began the collection as a teaching aid on his first sabbatical, and he continued adding to it on every sabbatical and leave of absence thereafter. He moved from buying artifacts with his own funds to raising money for acquisitions and then, after World War I, to conducting his own digs. Kelsey had the advantage of starting his collecting before laws were passed prohibiting the removal of historic artifacts from the countries of origin. But he was far more than a treasure hunter. The Kelsey's collection testifies to his wide-ranging interests in all aspects of ancient history.

Kelsey was born in 1858 in Ogden, New York, and educated at the University of Rochester. Early pictures show a dark-haired, serious young man, but most surviving photos show a graying, bearded gentleman, dressed formally even on archaeological sites. "He had a heavy beard and rode a bicycle," recalled the late Charles A. Sink in the book *Our Michigan.* Sink and Kelsey worked closely over the decades when Kelsey was president and Sink the administrator of the University Musical Society. "He was a bit pompous in manner and exceedingly polite," wrote Sink.

Reading Kelsey's papers at the Bentley Historical Library, one senses a continual conflict between his old-world politeness and his drive to secure artifacts for the university. He was relentless in asking for help, yet apologized as he did so. "I cannot tell you how sorry I am to bother you with this matter," he wrote while seeking more money from W. W. Bishop, the U-M librarian who handled acquisition funds. "My only excuse is that we have here a unique opportunity and it seems to me that duty both to our subject and to the university requires us to put forth every effort."

Kelsey followed up on any suggestion that might lead to a find or a potential donor, and he went to great lengths to please contributors. For instance, he persuaded Horace Rackham, Henry Ford's lawyer and U-M contributor (the Rackham Building is named after him), to finance the first two excavation seasons at Karanis. Kelsey bought two rugs for Rackham during the dig and begged to be allowed to buy him something more, writing, "I had so much pleasure in hunting out those two rugs, and became so much interested in them that I do wish you would think of anything else that you would like from the Near East." Kelsey may have gone overboard in his efforts to keep Rackham interested. In January 1923, Rackham wrote from Pinehurst, North Carolina, "Please do not send any more [photos of the excavations]. I am here to play golf and escape business of every kind."

Kelsey wooed another rich Detroiter, Charles Freer, who had made his money manufacturing railroad cars, as well as local people such as G. Frank Allmendinger, owner of several Ann Arbor mills. (Allmendinger procured funds from the Michigan Millers Association to purchase a Roman mill.) But Kelsey did not use people. Many of the donors he worked with became lifelong friends, and he was always willing to return their favors. For instance, he looked after the sons of David Askren—a medical missionary who had helped him secure Egyptian papyri—when they came to the United States, getting them medical help and scholarships.

Kelsey (*in dark suit*) personally chose Karanis in Egypt as the site for the U-M's first archaeological dig and then persuaded Horace Rackham to finance the expedition. (*Courtesy of Bentley Historical Library.*)

Kelsey made his first purchase for the university in 1893, while on leave to study archaeological sites. In Carthage he met a Jesuit priest, Father R. P. Delattre, who took a liking to him and sold him 109 items collected over forty years of excavations there, including lamps, vases, and building materials. According to *The University of Michigan: An Encyclopedic Survey*, "a warm and lasting friendship sprang up between the American scholar and the priest of the Hill of Byrsa. As a lasting reminder of the kindness shown him, Professor Kelsey assigned accession number one in the museum records to a fragment of an ancient Roman lamp. It was the discovery of this lamp that had induced Father Delattre in the early years of his life in North Africa to undertake the careful excavation of the Roman sites at ancient Carthage." By the time Kelsey returned to Ann Arbor, he had amassed more than one thousand other specimens from Rome, Sicily, Capri, and Tunis.

Limited by budget and time constraints, Kelsey multiplied his achievements by enlisting others. For example, a colleague, Walter Dennison, while teaching in Italy, heard of a parish priest, Giuseppe de Criscio, who had a large collection of Roman and Greek inscriptions. De Criscio lived north of Naples in Pozzuoli (now famous as the hometown of Sophia Loren), a volcanic area rich with remains of earlier civilizations. When Dennison informed Kelsey that de Criscio was willing to sell his collection to a university, Kelsey went to work raising the necessary funds, buying the collection in three installments starting in 1899. The largest part of it is a collection of 267 inscriptions, mainly marble tombstones. Because these inscriptions include information such as the occupation and nationality of the deceased, they tell a lot about daily life in a Roman seaport more than two thousand years ago. Today, some of the items from the de Criscio collection are usually on display in the Kelsey's south gallery.

Kelsey met David Askren in 1915 while sailing to Italy to work on the estate of his late friend Thomas Spencer Jerome (whose bequest still pays for the Thomas Spencer Jerome Lectures in Classical Studies). Kelsey soon interested Askren in his endeavors, and before they parted, Askren agreed to become a U-M agent in Egypt. During World War I, nothing could be shipped out of Egypt, but Askren bought and saved material for Kelsey. He reported to Kelsey, "I have been gathering odds and ends that I can get cheaply and have now at least 300 fragments of papyri and parchment writing in Greek and Coptic."

After the war, Kelsey returned to the Near East. The papyri Askren had obtained, supplemented with other purchases Kelsey made on this trip, were the start of the university's current excellent collection, now housed in the Harlan Hatcher Graduate Library. Kelsey traveled around, making further purchases and looking for possible excavation sites. He returned to Ann Arbor with three suggestions: Antioch of Pisidia in Turkey, Carthage in Tunisia, and Karanis in Egypt. After exploratory digs at the first two sites in 1924 and 1925, he chose Karanis as the most promising site.

KARANIS, A GRECO-ROMAN farming community about fifty miles southwest of Cairo, interested Kelsey because the area was rich in papyri. In addition to a generous $10,000 grant from Rackham, Kelsey secured donations of a Dodge sedan and a Graham truck and brought along his son, Easton, as chauffeur. The dig found extensive and valuable collections of papyri, coins, and glass; Kelsey meticulously documented where every item was found to help assign each to its proper historic period. George Swain, a Latin instructor at the university who was also a professional photographer, photographed the excavation. His twelve thousand photos form an important part of the Kelsey Museum's photography collection and are still a valuable resource for researchers.

Kelsey was as interested in spreading knowledge of the ancient world as he was in acquiring its artifacts. He convinced Saginaw lumber baron Arthur Hill (the U-M regent for whom Hill Auditorium is named) to start a fund to publish humanistic studies series, and he persuaded Charles

Freer to leave a bequest to continue scholarly publications. Kelsey himself wrote textbooks and translated many works, including an edition of Caesar's *Commentaries on the Gaelic Wars*, for many years the standard text. (The edition was so well known that Kelsey was introduced at a talk in Denver as the author of Caesar's *Commentaries*.)

Kelsey's contributions were not confined to classical studies. He persuaded Catherine Pendleton, whose late husband, Edward, had been interested in ancient history, to endow a library in the Michigan Union and establish a number of scholarships. An ardent music lover, Kelsey persuaded the regents to locate Hill Auditorium on its present site, and he raised money for it and for its organ. He also secured the Stearns Collection of rare musical instruments for the university.

In May 1927, Kelsey returned early from the third season at Karanis to give a paper on his latest findings but became very ill. Though he left his bed at Cowie's Hospital on Division Street to attend the meeting, someone else had to read his paper for him. He died May 14, 1927, of a heart attack. On the very day he died, twenty-two large cases of archaeological specimens he had sent from Egypt arrived in Ann Arbor. Speaking at Kelsey's funeral, U-M president Clarence Little described him aptly as "combining a rare degree of tact with pertinacity."

Two years after Kelsey's death, his extensive collections—scattered around campus in his office, the basement of Alumni Memorial Hall (now the art museum), and the campus library—were brought together to their current home in what was then known as Newberry Hall. Kelsey had no doubt been familiar with the building, since early University Musical Society concerts were held in its auditorium. Orma Fitch Butler, who had served as Kelsey's assistant and was very familiar with the collection, became the museum's first curator, while John Winter, professor of Latin and Greek, served as the first director. They moved the collections in but otherwise left the building much as it had been when it was occupied by its builder, the Student Christian Association. The downstairs area was arranged for displays: a site room, a household room, a materials room, and a room devoted to sociological exhibits. The upstairs was converted into offices.

Meanwhile, the excavations at Karanis continued until 1935. Data from the dig form an amazingly complete picture of daily life in a Greco-Roman outpost and are still the basis of much scholarly research. The Karanis artifacts make the museum especially strong in glass, pottery, and textiles. In the early days of excavating, when most archaeologists were looking only for sensational finds like the King Tut tomb found by Howard Carter in 1922, Kelsey realized that information about daily

In 1929, two years after Kelsey's death, his collection was moved into what is now the Kelsey Museum, an 1891 building that originally was the home of the Student Christian Association. *(Courtesy of Bentley Historical Library.)*

life was equally important. He worked with his team to see that every item was treated carefully and recorded precisely.

Before the Great Depression ended excavations, the university participated in several other digs, including two more in Egypt, one at Sepphoris (Zippori) in Palestine, and—second in importance only to Karanis—one at Seleucia on the Tigris in Iraq. Under the leadership of Leroy Waterman, and later Clark Hopkins, the Seleucia dig yielded another ten thousand artifacts and provided valuable information about the town, founded by Seleucus Nicator, one of the generals of Alexander the Great.

After an almost twenty-year hiatus occasioned by the Depression and World War II, the Kelsey Museum began organizing expeditions again in the 1950s. The first of these, in 1956, was Saint Catherine's monastery in Israel, which is one of the oldest monasteries in existence, with a priceless collection of Byzantine religious art and manuscripts. Rather than removing artifacts for the museum, the emphasis this time was on learning from them, photographing and taking notes on the artifacts found.

Subsequent Kelsey Museum digs, done in conjunction with other universities or museums, have explored sites in Tunisia, Israel, Libya, Syria, and Egypt. Current Kelsey expeditions are at Paestum, Italy, investigating a Greek sanctuary; Leptiminus, Tunisia, where the researchers created a museum to display their findings; Pylos, Greece (a new kind of survey in which researchers are walking across the countryside, collecting signs of past human activity); and Abydos, Egypt, where the museum is doing an archaeological survey in an ancient cemetery. Smaller projects include Lauren Talalay's dig at Euboea, Greece, and John Cherry's investigation into digging in Albania, which had been closed to outsiders for almost forty years.

ALTHOUGH IT NO LONGER obtains artifacts from digs, the Kelsey still adds to its collection with gifts and carefully considered purchases. Karanis artifacts remain the star attraction; Francis Kelsey's findings are still considered the best collection in the world illustrating life in a Greco-Roman outpost. The ten thousand artifacts gathered by Waterman and Hopkins in Iraq are also considered important, especially because it is now much more difficult for Western scholars to enter the country. In many other areas, the Kelsey is considered to have the best collection in North America. Particular strengths are in glass (while the Corning and Toledo museums have more pieces, the Kelsey's are arguably more valuable because their sources can be documented); textiles, particularly late Roman and early Byzantine; and Latin inscriptions (with the de Criscio collection giving them the edge). Other treasures include eight thousand nineteenth-century photographs, largely of archaeological sites, and all twenty-three volumes of the reports of the scholars who accompanied Napoleon's expedition to Egypt at the beginning of the nineteenth century.

Yet despite the Kelsey's wonderful collections, the U-M's budget crunch in the 1970s threatened to close it or to merge its collections with those of the university Museum of Art. Ultimately, the Kelsey was saved, and classical studies professor John Pedley, a member of the four-person review committee, was appointed its director. One of the first things Pedley did was to hire a British Museum expert to assess the collection. The assessor reported that the textiles, bronzes, bones, and ivory were in grave condition; he recommended that a conservator be retained and that the collection be cataloged and records computerized. Conservator Amy Rosenberg was hired, and work began on cataloging the collection. But preserving the artifacts took longer because it required a large amount of money.

Elaine Gazda replaced Pedley in 1986 so he could concentrate on his research in Paestum, Italy. Gazda set the museum on its present course of outreach to the community. She also has been able to achieve the long-desired goal of building a climate-controlled storage area. Located on a newly created third floor in the upper half of the original building's auditorium, the storage area now holds 85 percent of the museum's collection. It was funded by a $250,000 gift from New York real estate developer Eugene Grant, a U-M alumnus, and additional contributions from private donors; the university; and the Kelsey Associates, a volunteer support and fund-raising group organized in 1979. In 2006 the Kelsey broke ground for an expansion of their building.

Although Francis Kelsey died in 1927, his influence is still strongly felt, not only through his collection but also in ongoing research. Terry Wilfong, the curator in charge of fieldwork, is making Karanis information available to both scholars and the general public on the Internet. Wilfong also serves as a clearinghouse for other Karanis information, collecting papers from scholars around the world and helping to get them published in scholarly journals. Eventually Wilfong would like to return to Karanis to reassess the original work and do new excavating.

# The Botanical Gardens

*Primoses, Chinese chestnuts, and pinochle in the boiler room*

Since 1960, the U-M botanical gardens have been on Dixboro Road straddling Superior and Ann Arbor Townships. But for forty-five years before that, they were in the heart of what is now Ann Arbor's south side. The fifty-two-acre gardens off Iroquois, now Woodbury Gardens apartments, played an important part in university life from 1916 to 1961.

"It was not landscaped for beauty but for [growing] specific plants," recalls Chuck Cares, who later landscaped the present gardens. "There were pretty plants, of course, but no aesthetic principle was involved."

"Plants were grown for research, university classes, and decorations for university functions," explains Dorothy Blanchard, whose mother, Frieda Blanchard, was assistant director from 1919 to 1956. Though "it was not a place for the general public," Blanchard says, "visitors did occasionally come out and were shown around by Mother."

The university's first botanical garden was planted on the Diag in 1897, near what is today the graduate library. In 1906 it moved to the newly acquired Arboretum. In 1913, finding the Arb's hilly terrain not conducive to growing plants in controlled conditions, the university bought the Iroquois site.

Harry Gleason, the new garden's first director, wrote that it was "located immediately beyond the city limits south of Ann Arbor, near the Packard street road, and comprises twenty acres of level fertile land." As surrounding parcels were purchased, the gardens grew to 51.72 acres.

Harley H. Bartlett replaced Gleason in 1919. "The chief thing that attracted me to the University of Michigan before I knew what a generally delightful place Ann Arbor was, was the new botanical gardens, which would provide perhaps the best facility in the country for work in genetics and plant breeding," Bartlett wrote in his 1923 Harvard alumni report.

Bartlett was born in Montana in 1886, graduated from Harvard with a chemistry degree, and then worked as a chemical biologist for the U.S. Department of Agriculture. While in Washington he became interested in the work of Dutch botanist Hugo DeVries on evolution and began to research the genetics of genus *Oenothera*, an evening primrose. He

The original botanical gardens were right on campus in front of the old library, about where the graduate library now sits. *(Courtesy of Bentley Historical Library.)*

accepted an assistant professorship at the U-M in 1915 and, as soon as he could, planted rows of *Oenothera* at the new botanical gardens to continue his research.

"The development of the garden has been my chief interest since coming to Michigan," Bartlett claimed in the alumni report—an impressive claim, considering his many competing interests. "A Renaissance man, he [Bartlett] knew a little about everything," recalls Ed Voss, emeritus professor of botany. "If you asked a question, he'd give you a reference off the top of his head." In addition to directing the gardens, Bartlett chaired the botany department, taught classes, frequently traveled to Asia and Latin America to collect rare plants, published prolifically, and was much in demand as a consultant to federal agencies.

Bartlett's secret was that he had accepted the gardens' directorship on the condition that graduate student Frieda Cobb be appointed the assistant director. While Bartlett dealt with the public and with the university administration, Cobb managed the gardens' day-to-day operations, taking over completely during Bartlett's frequent absences. "She kept things at an even keel," recalls Voss.

Frieda Cobb had come to the U-M at Bartlett's suggestion and was working on her Ph.D., continuing his *Oenothera* research. They had met through her brother, Victor Cobb, a classmate of Bartlett's at Harvard. She arrived in Ann Arbor in 1916 and in 1920 was the first of Bartlett's students to earn her doctorate. Two years later she married Frank Blanchard, a herpetologist whom she had met in graduate school.

The actual work of growing the plants was done by a series of excel-

Dorothy Blanchard's kindergarten class looking at the giant chrysanthemums in one of the Iroquois site greenhouses, 1930s. Although the botanical gardens were not generally open to the public, Blanchard obviously had pull since her mother was the assistant director. *(Courtesy of Dorothy Blanchard.)*

lent gardeners, the last of whom, from 1935 on, was Walter Kleinschmidt, who was promoted to superintendent. Part of his job was tending the rare plants brought back from various expeditions. "He was good at growing plants—discovering what was needed. For instance, he figured out how to grow ferns from spores," recalls Dorothy Blanchard. Kleinschmidt lived with his wife and daughter in a house on the grounds. He supervised about four other gardeners, who took responsibility for specific greenhouses. "The workers, Walter and his group, played pinochle in the boiler room every noon," recalls Peter Kaufman, who was hired as curator of the gardens in 1956.

The gardens closest to the greenhouse were arranged in a big oval and were dubbed "the graveyard," according to Kaufman, "because of their arrangement in horizontal beds divided by family and genus." The land beyond the graveyard was used for specific research projects, such as Eileen Erlanson's wild roses, Kenneth Jones's ragweed, and Stanley Cain's delphinium. Dow Baxter, a forest pathologist from the forestry department, grew Chinese chestnuts, trying to come up with a disease-resistant strain to replace the American chestnut.

Felix Gustafson's tomato plants loom large in everyone's memory, because he gave his extras to staff members. "I'd take them and eat them off the vine. They were marvelous," recalls local pediatrician Mark Hildebrandt, who worked at the gardens as a teenager. Blanchard, who rode her bike to work before getting a car, learned to ride no-handed so she could eat tomatoes on the way home.

THE GREENHOUSES PROVIDED a year-round source of plants for botany classes and faculty research. Flowers were also grown there for special university occasions, such as commencements or honors convocations or visits from dignitaries like Haile Selassie and the queen of the Netherlands.

The nucleus of the gardens' collection of cacti and other succulents was assembled by Elzada Clover, a botany professor who had done work in the Southwest and Central America. In January 1938 Bartlett recorded in his diary that "Elzada Clover has a wild plan for a trip through the can[y]on of the Colorado. She assures me it will be a truly scientific venture." Clover and a friend, Mary Lois Jotter, completed their "wild plan," earning the distinction of being the first women to make the trip by boat. In 1952 Clover added another first: being the first person to develop and teach an entire class at the botanical gardens. It was a very popular undergraduate course, and according to a history put out by the botanical gardens, "through it many students were led to concentrate in botany."

In 1955 Bartlett reached retirement age and was succeeded by A. Geoffrey Norman. Five years later the gardens moved to their present site on Dixboro. "We moved as many trees as we could," recalls Peter Kaufman. "Some spreading junipers didn't take, but most of what we moved did. We took all the rare stuff that we had collected." The new gardens were named after regent Fred Matthaei Sr., who donated the land.

The 350-acre Matthaei gardens are seven times as large as the Iroquois site and have more than twice as much greenhouse space—forty-four thousand square feet. The other main difference is that at the present gardens there is much more public involvement, with hiking trails, adult education classes, meeting space, and an active friends group.

The Iroquois site remained empty for most of the 1960s. Helen Corey, who lived on Iroquois in a house backing up to the gardens, used to walk her dogs on the deserted site, which she remembers as "an oasis in the middle of the city." Although the gardens were in ruins and the buildings falling apart, she recalls, there were still "nice trees, some fruit bearing."

In 1969 the first stage of the Woodbury Gardens apartments was built. In honor of the former use, the developers named the streets Aster and Wisteria. Residents still enjoy at least nine kinds of trees originally planted in the botanical gardens, including Dow's Chinese chestnuts.

# When Football Players
# Danced the Cancan

*The Michigan Union Opera's Cross-Gender Fun*

In 1949 U-M junior Jimmie Lobaugh landed a starring role in the Michigan Union Opera. He dressed up as a pregnant woman and belted out a showstopper entitled "I Want a Pickle."

The show was *Froggy Bottom,* a parody of the efforts of World War II veterans and their families to cope with the red tape of the GI Bill. "It was dreadful, horrible," Lobaugh laughs, "but we had a heck of a lot of fun."

A U-M tradition from 1908 to 1955, the Michigan Union Opera was created to raise funds for the Michigan Union building. Since the Michigan Student Union was then an all-male club, men made up the entire cast, playing both male and female roles.

The cross-dressing was always a source of much hilarity, especially among the friends of the "actresses." But some spectators were taken in. "After the shows, guys would wait outside to get dates with the 'girls,'" recalls Jim Graf, who as a child saw many of the pre–World War II shows because his dad built the scenery. "It was that good, their costumes and makeup."

There couldn't have been any question, however, about the gender of the burly football players who were recruited to form chorus lines in female costumes relevant to the plot. Depending on the year, they might appear as geishas, Egyptian temple dancers, or cancan girls.

The MUO's first show, 1908's *Michigenda,* set the tone for ensuing productions. The plot concerned efforts to keep a rich donor, Mr. Moneyfeller, from finding out that his nephew wasn't actually on the U-M faculty. The "real" professors—students impersonating well-known faculty members of the time—were hidden away in a tunnel, which eventually exploded from all the hot air. Meanwhile, the student characters were transported to the magic land of the title, a place where there were no professors and where Granger's, a then-popular dance hall on Huron Street, was open six nights a week.

*Michigenda* opened at the Whitney Theater downtown, a location chosen to encourage attendance by local residents as well as academics. On opening night the enthusiastic audience stood in the aisles and refused to leave until the cast had taken five curtain calls. All five performances were sold out, with special trains of U-M alumni coming in from Detroit.

The next year's show, *Culture*, was just as big a hit. The plot revolved around a ten-foot slide rule that could solve any problem. After the show, the slide rule was acquired by the engineering department, where for years afterward it was a fixture of the annual Engineers' Ball.

THE MICHIGAN UNION, the first such organization in the country, was formed in 1904. In 1907 the group purchased the State Street home of law professor Thomas Cooley. The rest of the site of the present Union was purchased with the proceeds of the first two Michigan Union Operas.

The custom of using football players in the chorus originated with the fourth production, *The Awakened Ramses*. Two weeks before the show opened, the dean of students announced new eligibility rules that prevented half the cast from taking part. The production could have been doomed but for the timely intervention of football coach Fielding Yost, who convinced his players to fill in.

The players had recently concluded their season and showed up with "bruised shoulders, bandaged knees, and clumsy feet," recalled Earl Moore, the show's student conductor (later the U-M music school dean). But "there was no question of the dedication and zeal that these new 'actors and dancers' put forth in Whitney Theater to match the same qualities in their performances on Ferry Field." The athletes caused such a sensation that from then on, no MUO performance was considered complete unless it included a chorus of football players dressed as women.

Planning for the MUO productions started with a campuswide competition for scripts. The director usually reshaped the material, and often cast members had ideas to make it funnier, so it would turn out to be a group effort.

The MUO became so popular that many more students tried out than there were roles available. The men who were cast came from all over the university. "You crossed paths with people you wouldn't otherwise know—premed, athletes," recalls Jack Felton, who appeared in several 1950s productions and wrote some of the music for one. "I wanted to do it for an extracurricular activity, to do something besides grind away at books," recalls Jerry Gray, who danced in the chorus for 1953's

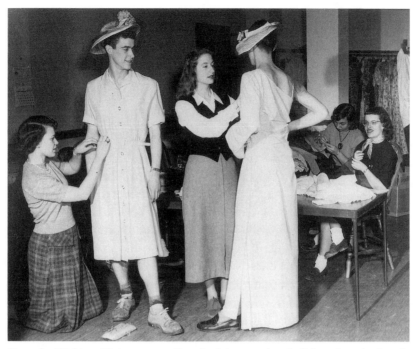

Since the Michigan Union was an all-male club, men played all the roles—both male and female. *(Courtesy of Bentley Historical Library.)*

*Up 'n' Atom* wearing a woman's dancing outfit complete with a stuffed brassiere. Although Gray claims he wasn't much of a social dancer, he had no trouble learning the steps, which he often practiced going home through the Law Quad.

The MUO went on the road for the first time in 1914, when both the Detroit and Chicago alumni associations offered to sponsor shows. That year's opera, *A Model Daughter*, took place in Paris and so seemed well suited for export. There had been talk of touring before; questions about whether out-of-town audiences would catch the U-M humor, and if so whether it would paint an unflattering picture of the campus, had made the producers hesitate. But the first road trip was such a success that it became a yearly tradition.

CONSTRUCTION ON THE PRESENT Union building started in 1916, and subsequent operas helped pay off the bonds that financed it. But the tradition nearly faltered when the United States entered World War I the following year. By 1918 so many men were off fighting that Union manager Homer Heath asked, "Which shall it be: an opera with Michigan girls or no opera?" That was the only year in which women appeared in the MUO.

A turning point came with the arrival of Broadway director E. Mortimer Shuter in 1919. Unable to get into the army during World War I, Shuter was doing his bit for the war effort by directing USO shows when MUO general chairman F. C. Bell met him in Philadelphia and convinced him to come to Ann Arbor for a year.

The 1919 show, *Come On, Dad*, featured elaborate scenery, fancy costumes, and new dance styles. (Shuter's good friend Roy Hoyer, a Broadway singer and dancer, helped coach the students.) Earl Moore praised Shuter's "ability to create almost professional results with average amateur materials." The show was such a triumph both in town and on the road that Shuter was persuaded to stay instead of returning to Broadway.

In 1921 Shuter produced *Top o' th' Mornin'*, with prelaw major Thomas Dewey playing the male lead. As Patrick O'Dare, an evil pretender to the Irish throne, the future New York governor and Republican presidential candidate stopped the show with a number called "A Paradise of Micks." Reviewers raved about the "velvety texture" of Dewey's baritone voice, and he toured eight cities when the show went on the road. But according to Dewey's biographer, Richard Norton Smith, "usually on these train trips, he could be found alone, often in the last car, uncomfortable with the camaraderie and alcohol" shared by the rest of the cast.

Shuter reached his peak with 1923's *Cotton Stockings (Never Made a Man Look Twice)*. Lionel Ames, described by a reviewer as "a clever actor and mimic," played the female lead so successfully that he later went on to a vaudeville career as a female impersonator. That year the MUO invaded Ivy League territory, playing in Philadelphia, New York, and Washington and receiving rave reviews wherever it went. Several female characters "looked astonishingly real as pretty fixtures of feminine grace," reported the *Washington Times*. "Others, chorines notably, were such virile masculines that all fashion's fripperies and layers of cosmetics couldn't disguise razored chins or stalwart underpinning." The cast met President Coolidge in Washington and went on to New York, where they set the record at the Metropolitan Opera for the highest box office of an amateur production.

By then there were complaints that the MUO was straying too far from its roots, so Shuter chose *Tickled to Death* for the next production, with a plot that revolved around U-M archaeologists in China. The set contained a temple reputed to be a replica of an actual Chinese one, but the characterizations were evidently less authentic—a Chinese graduate

Star Jimmie Lobaugh mugs
with audience member Gov-
ernor G. Mennen Williams.
*(Courtesy of Bentley Historical
Library.)*

student wrote a letter to the *Michigan Daily* complaining that the production was "a gross misrepresentation of Chinese."

ALTHOUGH THE SHOWS originally made a lot of money, the productions
were always financially risky because of the high costs of sets, rented
costumes, and travel. On New Year's Eve 1929, shortly after the stock
market crash, the MUO suffered a major loss, playing to an empty theater in New York during a blizzard. The next year the opera suspended
production.

In the mid-1930s the MUO was revived in a lower budget form, with
students doing more of the work. The plot of the 1934 show, *With Banners Flying*, had athletic director Fielding Yost taking over as university
president and featured scenes in the *Michigan Daily*, the Arb, student
boardinghouses, and the Union. It was followed by *Give Us Rhythm* in
1935. But neither show was a big financial success, so the operas were
suspended again.

The next revival, in 1939, went in the opposite direction, returning
to the days of full-scale productions. Plans even called for Shuter to
direct, but he died that November. His death delayed the premiere of
*Four out of Five* (based on the gibe that four out of five girls were pretty
and the fifth went to the U-M) until February 1940. Football players,
including Forest Evashevski and Bob Westfall, again formed a chorus,

Star Lionel Ames went on to a vaudeville career as a female impersonator. *(Courtesy of Bentley Historical Library.)*

while Heisman Trophy winner Tom Harmon played a lead: as Jimmie Roosevelt, the president's son, he helped a freshman become a Big Man on Campus by fixing him up with movie star Hedy La Tour. The MUO returned to its usual December dates later that year with *Take a Number.* It featured a date lottery, modeled on the draft lottery, which set up boy-girl meetings in the Arb. The last show in this series, *Full House,* opened four days after Pearl Harbor and was hardly noticed.

The MUO resumed in 1949 with *Froggy Bottom* (a takeoff on Foggy Bottom in Washington, D.C.), which dealt with the problems of veterans and their families on campus. "Congress didn't understand academic requirements, universities couldn't understand the red tape to make them work, and the GIs were caught in the confusion," Jack Felton recalls.

Some of the lyrics for *Froggy Bottom* were actually written by a woman student, Ann Husselman (now Rusanoff). Edward Chudacoff, an MUO composer, had come up with a tune but had no words for it; Husselman suggested some, and he asked her to write more, which she did. Although she never came near the all-male set, one of the songs she wrote, "Till the Dawn," was picked up by Fred Waring and played on his radio show.

Jimmie Lobaugh, the lead in *Froggy Bottom,* helped publicize the show by cohosting a reception at the Women's League with the "male" star of the Junior Girls' Play. He recalls getting into wig, makeup, black dress, black hat, and black high heels and riding from the Union to the League in a horse-drawn carriage. His counterpart was a short woman dressed as a farmer, wearing a hat with a big brim. The two stayed in character through the reception. When it was over Lobaugh went back downstairs, but to his dismay the horse and carriage were gone. His costume didn't include a purse, so he had no money to call a cab. He describes the walk back in high heels as "no treat."

Lobaugh went on to play leading-woman parts for the next four years, alternating with roles in productions of the Gilbert and Sullivan Society, of which he was a founder. He played a Mae West character in the 1951 *Go West, Madam* and a former vaudeville star the next year in *Never Too Late*. "Gosh, I was beautiful," he laughs.

Lobaugh's parents would come by train from Bartlesville, Oklahoma, to attend the opening nights, sitting in the orchestra next to such dignitaries as then-governor G. Mennen Williams. Lobaugh once posed for a photo sitting on the governor's lap. After graduation Lobaugh was asked to come to Broadway as a female impersonator, but he didn't want to spend his life playing women, opting instead for a career as a high school music and drama teacher. Even there, though, he found his MUO experience valuable: "I could direct both males and females," he says. "I could help the girls walk, talk, act, and behave in style."

THE POSTWAR MUO stuck to the original formula but with up-to-date subjects such as the atomic bomb (*Up 'n' Atom*), labor unions (*Lace It Up*, set in a lingerie factory), and radio giveaway shows (*Never Too Late*). Football players continued to form chorus lines in costumes appropriate for each play—in *Go West, Madam* they were cancan girls.

The postwar plays also toured, traveling by bus around Michigan and to nearby states. If not quite as glamorous as playing Manhattan, the experience was still memorable. "We had so much fun, it's a wonder we had any voice left," recalls Felton. Arriving and playing at important theaters was always awe inspiring. Lobaugh remembers performing in a theater in Buffalo where Mae West had appeared the week before.

At the parties after the out-of-town performances, alumni were often more interested in meeting the football players than the stars in the cast. Robert Segar, who played a male cheerleader in 1954's *Hail to the Victor*, recalls football players "taking an empty wine bottle to show the plays. The center would put it between his legs and toss it a few feet to the quarterback. The alumni loved it."

Cast of the 1914 *Junior Girls' Play. (Courtesy of Bentley Historical Library.)*

*Four years before male students began the Michigan Union Opera, female students were putting on the Junior Girls' Play (JGP), with women cross-dressing to play men's roles. For the first show, in 1904, dean of women Myra Jordan lent her husband's clothes to the "male" characters.*

*Like the MUO, the JGP was written, composed, and directed by students. The story lines also were similar—takeoffs on campus events, satires of classic books, or fun in exotic locales. After the men produced their first show,* Michigenda, *the women responded with a parody called* Michiguse. *One of the male leads in the 1914 production (discussed earlier) was played by future dean of women Alice Lloyd—better remembered today for giving her name to a postwar dormitory.*

*Originally most of the performances were open to women only. But in the 1920s the JGP took a page from the men's book and opened the plays to the general public as fund-raisers for the Michigan League building. After the building was completed in 1930, the JGP moved into its new Lydia Mendelssohn Theater.*

*The JGP not only predated the MUO, it outlived it as well—the last JGP show was in 1962.*

In the 1950s the cross-dressing was still considered risqué by some. From the first there had been accusations of vulgarity, partly due to suggestive ad-libbing by cast members. "The humor was slightly naughty," admits Jack Felton. And of course, the gay implications were also there. Lobaugh recalls that one of his leading men would bring a girlfriend to rehearsals. "He told me, 'I don't want anyone to get the idea you and I are a pair.' I was so naive I hadn't thought of it."

In 1956, the year the Union finally opened to women (before that they could come in only through a side door and, with a few exceptions, had to be accompanied by a male), MUO was absorbed into MUSKET—"Michigan Union Show and Ko-eds Too"—ending almost half a century of same-sex casting.

But even though it ended almost half a century ago, the MUO is not forgotten. Besides raising money for the Union building, the shows created a treasury of U-M songs, the tours were great publicity for the university, and the productions provided a start for many show business careers. Among the long list of notables coming out of the MUO are Billy Mills, who was the bandleader for the *Fibber McGee and Molly* radio show; Jay Gorney (Gornetzky), who wrote the music of "Brother, Can You Spare a Dime?"; and Valentine Davies, who wrote the story for the movie *Miracle on Thirty-fourth Street*.

At the Michigan Union centennial in January 2004, the Union acknowledged its debt by making the Michigan Union Opera the centerpiece of the celebration. The Union invited MUO alumni back, had present music students sing MUO songs, and rechristened a room the Union Opera Lounge. Located on the first floor across from the Anderson Room, the lounge is a treasury of MUO pictures and memorabilia.

# Lane Hall

*From the YMCA to women's studies*

If the walls of Lane Hall could talk, they might recall discussions on ethical, religious, and international topics and distinguished visitors such as Bertrand Russell, Reinhold Niebuhr, and the Dalai Lama. The elegantly understated Georgian colonial revival building on the southwest corner of State and Washington has been an intellectual center for student discussions since it was built. From 1917 to 1956 all varieties of religious topics were examined; from 1964 to 1997 it changed to an international focus. In October, after a major expansion and renovation, it was rededicated as the new home for women's studies at the U-M.

Lane Hall was built in 1916–17 by the U-M YMCA. Within a few years it came under the control of the university's Student Christian Association (SCA), which included the campus branches of both the YMCA and the YWCA. In addition to organizing traditional religious activities, SCA published a student handbook, ran a rooming service, and helped students get jobs.

Funded in part by a $60,000 gift from John D. Rockefeller, Lane Hall was named after Victor H. Lane, a law professor and former judge who was active in SCA. When it opened in 1917, students could read books on religion in the library; listen to music in the music room; meet with student pastors in individual offices; or attend functions, either in the 450-seat auditorium upstairs or the social room in the basement.

SCA cooperated with area churches and also provided meeting places for groups that didn't have a home church, such as Chinese Christians and Baha'is. But Lane Hall is most remembered for its own nondenominational programs, which were open to all students on campus. Some, like Bible study, had an obvious religious connection, but the programs also included the Fresh Air Camp (which enlisted U-M students to serve as big brothers to neglected boys), extensive services for foreign students, and eating clubs.

Lane Hall became one of the most intellectually stimulating places on campus. "While the university was, much more than now, organized in tightly bounded disciplines and departments, our program was working with the connections between them, and particularly the ethical implications of those interconnections," recalls C. Grey Austin, who was assistant coordinator of religious affairs in the 1950s. "Religion was similarly organized in clearly defined institutions, and we were working, again, with that fascinating area in which they touch one another."

With the coming of the Great Depression, many students struggled financially. In 1932, looking for a way to save money, a local activist named Sher Quraishi (later an advocate for postpartition Pakistan) organized the Wolverine Eating Club in the basement of Lane Hall. The club's cook, Anna Panzner, recalled in a 1983 interview that they fed about 250 people three meals a day. She was assisted with the cooking by John Ragland, who later became the only black lawyer in town. About forty students helped with the prep and cleanup in exchange for free meals, while the rest paid $2.50 a week.

Lane Hall itself had trouble keeping going during the Depression, often limping along without adequate staffing. Finally, in 1936, SCA gave Lane Hall to the university. The group didn't stipulate the use of the building but said they hoped it might "serve the purpose for which it was originally intended, that is, a center of religious study and activities for all students in the university." The university agreed and, while changing the name to Student Religious Association, kept and expanded the SCA programming.

"THE OFFICIAL HEAD of Lane Hall would be a minister hired by the university, but the work was done by Edna Alber," recalls Jerry Rees, who worked there in the 1950s. "Alber ran Lane Hall like a drill sergeant," agrees Lew Towler, who was active in Lane Hall activities. "You'd try to stay on her good side."

The first university-hired director of Lane Hall was Kenneth Morgan. The high point of his tenure was a series of lectures, The Existence and Nature of God, given by Bertrand Russell, Fulton Sheen, and Reinhold Niebuhr.

Morgan left during World War II and was replaced by Frank Littell. "He was a dynamic man who you either liked or didn't," recalls Jo Glass, who was active at Lane Hall after the war. "He made changes and left." After Littell, DeWitt C. Baldwin, who had been Lane Hall's assistant director, took over. Called "Uncle Cy" by many, he was an idealistic former missionary who also led the Lisle Fellowship, a summer program to encourage international understanding.

Although social action was important, religion as the study of the Bible was not ignored. For instance, Littell led a seminar for grad students

Postcard view of Lane Hall when it was still the YMCA. *(Courtesy of Bentley Historical Library.)*

on aspects of religion in the Old and New Testaments. Participant Marilyn Mason, now a U-M music prof and the university organist, compares the seminar to a jam session, saying, "They were very open minded."

Other Lane Hall activities were just plain fun. Jerry Rees enjoyed folk dancing on Tuesday evenings in the basement social hall. Jo Glass has happy memories of the Friday afternoon teas held in the library. "You'd go to religious teas and meet people you met on Sunday, or go to international teas and meet people from other countries," she says, "but you'd go to Lane Hall and meet a mixture of everybody—all kinds of people wandered in."

Doris Reed Ramon was head of international activities at Lane Hall. She remembers that in addition to providing room for international students to meet, the building had a Muslim prayer room and space for Indian students to cook meals together. After World War II, with the campus full of returning servicemen struggling to make it on the GI Bill, a new eating co-op was organized, called the Barnaby Club. Member Russell Fuller, later pastor of Memorial Christian Church, recalls that the group hired a cook but did all the other work themselves, coming early to peel potatoes or set the table or staying afterward to clean up.

THE LANE HALL PROGRAMMING came to an end in 1956, when the religious office was moved to the Student Activities Building. The niche that Lane Hall held had gradually eroded as more churches established campus centers and the university founded an academic program in religious studies. Also, according to Grey Austin, there were more questions about the role of religion in a secular school. "The growing consensus was that the study of religions was okay but that experience with religion was better left to the religious organizations that ringed the campus."

In the 1960s, centers for area studies began moving into Lane Hall—Japanese studies, Chinese studies, Middle and North African studies, and South Asian and Southeast Asian studies, all of which were rising in importance during the cold war. Many townsfolk, as well as students, remember attending stimulating brown-bag lunches on various international topics, as well as enjoying the Japanese pool garden in the lobby. During this time visitors ranged from President Gerald Ford and Governor James Blanchard (who was delighted with the help the center gave him in developing trade with China) to foreign leaders such as the Dalai Lama and Bashir Gemayel, who became president of Lebanon, and famous writers such as Joseph Brodsky and Czeslaw Milosz.

One of the people who passed through Lane Hall during this period was Hugo Lane, great-grandson of Victor Lane. In response to an e-mail query, Lane recalled that he had an office in Lane Hall when he worked as a graduate assistant for the East European Survey, a project of the Center for Russian and East European Studies. "Needless to say, I took great pleasure in that coincidence. . . . On those occasions when my parents visited Ann Arbor, a stop at the hall was obligatory."

The centers for area studies eventually joined the U-M International Center in the new School of Social Work building across the Diag. After they left, Lane Hall became a temporary headquarters for the School of Natural Resources and Environment while its building was renovated. Then Lane Hall was vacated for its own extensive addition and renovation.

Today, the new and improved Lane Hall is home to the U-M's Women's Studies Program and the Institute for Research on Women and Gender. "It's wonderful space to the occupants, very affirming," says institute director Abby Stewart. "It feels good to be here."

# Inglis House

*The U-M's elegant retreat was built with a fortune based on factory fans.*

At one time or another early in this century, all six children of Detroit physician Richard Inglis lived in Ann Arbor. An interesting bunch, they included Agnes, the first curator of the U-M's Labadie collection of social protest literature; Frank, a Detroit pharmacist; David, a pioneer neurologist; Will, a Detroit businessman; and Kate, who owned a fruit and chicken farm that stretched all the way from Geddes Avenue to the Huron River.

But the sibling who left the most imposing legacy was James, a wealthy industrialist. He and his wife, Elizabeth, built Inglis House, an elegant French-chateau-style mansion that since 1951 has been owned by the U-M. The university uses it to house and entertain its many visiting dignitaries in suitable style. During her fourteen-year tenure, former facilities coordinator Sandra Simms amassed a collection of thank-you notes extending from former president Gerald Ford and his wife, Betty, to the exiled Tibetan religious leader the Dalai Lama. (An aide wrote to say that "His Holiness very much enjoyed His stay.")

The Inglises built the secluded mansion, which occupies an 8.5-acre plot at 2301 Highland Road, as a retirement home. Its formal, traditional style belies the mundane business that paid for it.

James Inglis was ten when his father died. The family was left a legacy of $3,000 a year from real estate holdings, enough to live comfortably at that time, but James left school at age fourteen. According to family legend, it was because his mother wouldn't give him enough money to get his hair cut as often as he liked. Starting out as an office boy at $2.50 a week, Inglis advanced to become owner of American Blower Company, where he developed fans for cooling Detroit's burgeoning auto factories. The company was immensely successful and respected—so much so that during the Depression, the National Bank of Detroit asked Inglis to serve on its board to help raise public confidence in the institution.

In 1903, when he was thirty-nine, Inglis married Elizabeth Hughes, a Presbyterian minister's daughter fourteen years his junior. They moved to Ann Arbor about 1918, living originally on Baldwin Street.

The Inglises' stately home, designed by local architect Woody Woodburn to resemble a French chateau, has hosted visitors ranging from Gerald and Betty Ford to the Dalai Lama. *(Courtesy of Bentley Historical Library.)*

They had become familiar with the town during frequent visits to Inglis's sister Kate, who had moved to the farm on Geddes with her husband, Frank Smith, in 1901. The Smiths' big white farmhouse still stands, looking much the same, at 2105 Geddes, near Concord. During the city's building boom in the 1920s, the Smiths started subdividing the farm into residential lots on what are now Highland, Concord, Lenawee, and Lafayette Streets. James Inglis saved his sister the job of platting the bottom of her farm by buying the land that ran down to the river as a site for his dream home.

Architect Lilburn "Woody" Woodworth designed a French chateau house of stones and irregular bricks, with a slate roof and elegant accoutrements. Though large (twelve rooms on four levels), it worked well as a family home. Inglis's niece, travel writer Carol Spicer (daughter of brother Will), remembers the house as the natural gathering place for the extended family. She recalls "lots of jokes and laughter in the house."

The gardens, designed by Elizabeth Inglis, were quintessentially English, with a formal garden, a cutting garden, a meadow, an orchard, and wildflower areas. The grounds also included a tennis court and a three-hole golf course and even, at one time, peacocks. (They eventually had to be banished because of their noise.)

Elizabeth and James Inglis (*top center*) with their children and grandchildren sit under the wisteria-covered arches at the back of their house in 1945. (*Courtesy of Bentley Historical Library.*)

James Inglis died in 1950, leaving the house to his wife for her lifetime and then to the university. But Elizabeth Inglis did not wait that long. She gave the house to the U-M less than a year later when she moved to Kalamazoo to be with her daughter.

THE NEW U-M PRESIDENT, Harlan Hatcher—like all incoming university presidents since—was given the choice of living in Inglis House or in the president's house on South University. In a 1982 seminar on the evolving role of the president's wife (published by the Bentley Library), Hatcher's wife, Anne, recalled thinking that "in many ways, it would have been nice, for the children particularly, to be in a neighborhood rather than in the middle of a campus with no little kids around to play with. But we really felt that it was important to maintain the central location."

Inglis House stood empty until 1964, when the university decided to use it as a guest home for important visitors and out-of-town regents. They refurbished it, filling it with a mixture of modern, traditional, and French Provincial furniture and hanging some original paintings by Courbet and Turner borrowed from the U-M art museum.

It took horticulturist Chuck Jenkins five years to restore the gardens to their former glory after fourteen years of neglect. He says he "got a good sense for the major elements" by looking at pictures and talking to Walter Stampflei, the Inglis's gardener, who still lived in the gatehouse; he also corresponded through a third party with Elizabeth Inglis, who lived until 1974.

Inglis House can accommodate forty people at a formal dinner and more for a reception or meeting. The Inglis family's unusual combination living room/dining room now serves well as a big dining room. Guests easily make do without a living room by beginning their evenings in the paneled downstairs library with hors d'oeuvres and cocktails. Carol Spicer, speaking of the house's present use, says, "If my aunt and uncle came back, they would be pleased."

# Transportation

## Orange Risdon's 1825 Map

*Michigan captured in its infancy.*

The U-M's Clements Library was delighted to receive in 1999 the gift of a very rare 1825 map: one of the few remaining copies of Orange Risdon's map of southeast Michigan. "It is the first map of Michigan that shows serious surveying and settlement," explains Brian Leigh Dunnigan, the library's curator of maps. Risdon, best known in this area as the founder of Saline, is also famous in Michigan history as the chief surveyor of the Detroit-Chicago Road, now U.S.-12.

Though Risdon's surveys were done under government contract, the map was a private venture. Risdon drew it himself and paid to have it published, planning to sell copies to pioneers trying to pick out places to settle. Unfortunately for him, a former employee came out with a competing map and grabbed most of the market. But though it failed to make its creator rich, Risdon's map today gives us a wealth of information about what our area looked like just one year after Ann Arbor was founded.

Officially called "Map of the Surveyed Part of the Territory of Michigan," it measures forty-three by twenty-nine inches. It shows the area from Toledo north to Saginaw Bay and includes Washtenaw County and a corner of Jackson County.

Surveyors hired by the federal government started working in southeast Michigan when it was still a territory in 1818, since precise demarcation was a necessary prelude to selling the land. They divided the state into counties, the counties into six-mile-square townships, and the townships into square-mile (640-acre) sections. The grid allowed buyers, when they went to the land office to buy land, to clearly identify their purchase.

Although a few intrepid settlers came earlier, serious settlement in Washtenaw County did not begin until the 1820s. Ypsilanti was founded in 1823 or 1825, depending on how the city is defined. Ann Arbor, Dexter, and Dixboro were all founded in 1824.

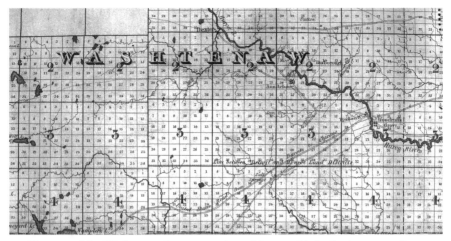

Close up of the Washtenaw County portion of Orange Risdon's 1825 map. *(Courtesy of Clements Library, University of Michigan.)*

The Risdon map, although strictly a factual document, reveals two historic transitions, one long past at the time it was published, the other still to come. The long, narrow lots Risdon mapped along the rivers in Detroit and Monroe were legacies of the French who were the state's first white inhabitants. "They all had access to the water," explains Dunnigan.

Risdon's map also shows Toledo, then called Port Lawrence, as part of Michigan. Though Toledo/Port Lawrence was indeed within Michigan Territory as defined by Congress, Ohio made a strong claim, and the issue was further muddied by years of contested surveys. The conflict briefly turned violent in the "Toledo War" of 1835 and would not finally be settled until 1836, when Michigan accepted a federal ultimatum to cede the city to Ohio in exchange for the Upper Peninsula.

The handful of roads shown all lead from Detroit to surrounding towns: one to Saginaw (now Woodward Avenue) and one to Port Huron (now Gratiot Avenue), as well as the road to present-day Chicago. Tepees mark the location of American Indian settlements, but there are none in Washtenaw County (the closest ones are in Macon and Wyandotte). Near Detroit, Hamtramck has already been established; Dearborn also is there but not under that name—Risdon calls it "Bucklin."

The Washtenaw County shown on the map is larger than it is today, because it includes two townships that are now part of Jackson County. Ann Arbor is spelled "Ann Arbour," which is how founders John Allen and Elisha Rumsey spelled it when they platted their 640-acre parcel the year before. Dixboro is also spelled the old-fashioned way, "Dixborough." All of the county's townships, with the exception of present-day Lyndon Township, are sectioned off, but none is yet named.

The map contains practical information for would-be settlers, such as the location of inns and where to register land purchases. In Washtenaw County, the only inn outside of the towns was labeled Sutton, in today's Northfield Township. Settlers had to go to Detroit to buy property in Washtenaw County, except for those acquiring land in the southern tier of townships—today's Manchester, Bridgewater, Saline, York, and Augusta—who were directed to Monroe.

Only five settlements are shown in Washtenaw County: besides Ann Arbour, Dixborough, and Dexter there are Ypsilanti and Woodruff's Grove. Showing the last two as separate places adds fuel to a continuing debate between Ann Arbor and Ypsilanti over which was settled first. It is clear that Ann Arbor was founded in 1824 and Ypsilanti in 1825—but Woodruff's Grove was founded in 1823, and it was later absorbed by Ypsilanti. Saline is not shown on the map; by the time Risdon drew it he had bought the land for his own settlement, but he would not get around to laying out the town until 1832. The only marking is a salt spring nearby.

ORANGE RISDON was particularly well qualified to make this map, being a trained surveyor who had already made two trips to Michigan. Risdon was born in 1786 in Vermont and moved with his family to Saratoga County, in eastern New York, when he was three. He attended local schools until age thirteen. Afterward, according to the 1881 Chapman *History of Washtenaw County, Michigan,* "he was dependent on his own efforts."

Risdon studied surveying under a Mr. Rice of Ballston Spa, New York. In 1807, when he was twenty-one, Risdon got a job assisting the noted surveyor Elisha Johnson, who had a contract to survey one hundred thousand acres in the new counties of Allegany and Genesee. "His duty was to carry the chain, for which he was to receive $16 per month, but scarcely a week had passed when his skill in surveying was discovered, and with the consent of the land agent, the work was divided, and his wages increased to about five times the amount of the first stipulation," says the county history. Two years later Risdon was hired to assist in laying out the infant cities of Lockport, Brockport, and Buffalo.

During the War of 1812 he worked for the federal government as an assistant surveyor. After the war he met Sally Newland, and the couple married in 1816. Risdon bought land with his earnings, eventually owning 1,000 acres on New York's Genesee River. Risdon resolved to move to Michigan Territory after suffering losses in the 1817 commercial crisis, but he did not arrive in Michigan until 1823, when he spent a month traveling on foot through Washtenaw and other nearby counties. He returned the next year, this time spending four months on a two thousand–mile exploring trip on horseback with Samuel Dexter. After their trip Dexter bought land on Mill Creek, just off the Huron River, and began the work of establishing the village that bears his name. Risdon bought 160 acres on the Saline River and the Indian trail that what would soon become the Detroit-Chicago Road, land that would later be the nucleus of the city of Saline.

How Risdon and Dexter met is lost to history. They could have known each other from New York, since Risdon's parents still lived in Sarasota County and Dexter resided in Athens, two counties south, or they may have met while traveling.

Their backgrounds were very different: Risdon was six years older and had been supporting himself since he was thirteen, while Dexter had both a bachelor's and a master's degree from Harvard. (Dexter's father had served in the cabinets of both Adams and Jefferson.) But both have gone down in history as town founders who went well beyond land speculation and worked to improve their towns. They both offered free land to any church wishing to get established, and they were both abolitionists who were rumored to be part of the Underground Railroad. It is easy to imagine that they discussed these issues during their long hours of travel together.

RISDON'S REPUTATION as a surveyor followed him to Michigan, and in the same year he bought his land he was hired to direct a survey for a road connecting Detroit and Pontiac. In fall 1824, when he must have been almost done surveying for the season, he began work on his map. From his two exploring trips, plus his surveying work, Risdon would have known much of the area firsthand, and for the rest he could rely on work done on earlier surveys.

Risdon advertised in the *Detroit Gazette* on October 1, 1824, seeking advance subscriptions to pay for the cost of producing the map. He promised that "the work will be put into the hands of the engraver as soon as a sufficient number of subscribers is obtained to warrant the expense of publication."

The ad pitched the map as useful to emigrants and explorers: "The first thing necessary to an immigrant is a general knowledge of the surveyed portion of the territory, of the course of its streams and the relative situation of its different parts. The publisher, having spent some time in exploring that junction of the territory embraced in his map, will be enabled to locate the most important Indian paths, which as they were made by those who were acquainted with every part of the country will be an important guide in the future location of our roads." Risdon promised that the map also would include Indian reservations and villages and would "embrace the lines of counties, townships, and sections, regularly numbered according to the surveys."

Although the mapping of Michigan had been going on for six years, settlement had been slow, both because Michigan was off the beaten path (easterners going west overland were more likely to pass through Ohio and Indiana) and because the territory was rumored to be all swamp. The first problem would be solved a year later when the Erie Canal opened, making it easy for easterners to reach Buffalo, where they could board a Lake Erie steamboat for Detroit. Risdon addressed the swamp story head-on in his ad: "The country which was formerly believed to be uninhabitable excepting on the river and lake shores, abounds in lands of the most fertile and healthy description." Even the climate, he claimed, "is particularly adapted to our eastern constitution."

The maps were to be "engraved in an elegant style and published on Super Royal paper." Risdon offered his map in three formats: in two sheets that could be stored flat in a drawer, for $2.50; cut into twenty-four sections and pasted on linen—so that the map could be folded without losing detail—and supplied with a leather carrying case, for $3; or varnished on rollers, perfect for land agents and lawyers who would be consulting it in their offices, also for $3. The Clements Library's copy is of the last type.

The next year, 1825, Risdon started the job for which he is most famous: chief surveyor for the great military road from Detroit to Chicago, today known as Michigan Avenue or U.S.-12. Work on the survey no doubt showed him features to include on the map but left him little time to work on it. He hired a helper named John Farmer, finished the map, and sent it to Rawdon, Clark, and Company in Albany, New York. On November 13 he paid them $400 for engraving the two copper plates. Five weeks later he paid to have 472 copies printed. After printing, each copy was hand painted. By the time they were ready to deliver, however, winter had shut down shipping on Lake Erie. Risdon's subscribers had to wait until May 1826 for an announcement in the *Detroit Gazette* that their copies were ready.

That delay proved fatal to the map's commercial prospects. Later in the summer of 1826, Farmer published his own rival map. It was basically the same as Risdon's but with added details that had been learned in the interim. Farmer's map, being more up-to-date, overshadowed his employer's. "It was bad luck that Orange didn't get the map in time to get it promptly to the subscribers," says Brian Dunnigan. By examining both maps, Dunnigan can tell that Farmer had probably done most of the hand coloring on Risdon's map. "John Farmer dominates after this— he becomes 'the' Michigan mapmaker," says Dunnigan. "He is probably the best known Michigan mapmaker of the nineteenth century."

Risdon moved on from the failure of his map, earning a good living as a surveyor. He surveyed at least seventy-five townships and the city of Saginaw, and he reexamined or resurveyed forty-five more townships. He continued working for the government until 1856, when he was seventy.

By then his own village was well established. In 1829 Risdon had returned to his property south of Ann Arbor and built a twelve-room house on a hill overlooking his Detroit-Chicago Road. He brought his family out from New York and began building up his new town. His house was used as Saline's first inn, post office, general store, and polling place. Risdon himself served as postmaster and magistrate, officiating at the first marriage in the township. After Michigan became a state in 1837, he was elected to the Michigan House of Representatives.

Risdon's "advice was often sought in the selection of lands," the county history records. "Very many miles were traveled by him to point out desirable locations, yet [he was] ever unwilling to receive a reward." Although there is no evidence that he made any other maps, his contemporaries knew of his pioneering effort. L. D. Norris, in an address to the Washtenaw County Historical Society in 1874, said, "The first general map of the surveyed part of this territory of which I have any knowledge was published in 1825 by Orange Risdon, then and now a pioneer of Washtenaw."

Risdon died in 1876 at age ninety, a well-regarded member of the community. "He was genial in his disposition, unselfish, benevolent, and liberal almost to a fault," said the county history. At his funeral, "great numbers of people from neighboring towns and cities were in attendance." His home passed to his daughter after his death. In 1948 the house was moved to Henry Street to make room for expansion of Oakwood Cemetery. Still standing, it has been divided into apartments.

THE CLEMENTS COPY of Risdon's map was a gift from the Michigan Map Society, purchased to honor Frank Kerwin, a founding member of the society who had recently died. The Michigan Map Society meets at the Clements and works closely with the library, so members knew that although the Clements had a large collection of Great Lakes maps, it was missing this very important one. Since Kerwin, a Grosse Pointe resident and sailor, was himself a collector of Great Lakes maps, the Risdon map, a copy of which had gone on the market, seemed a logical choice. Of the 472 copies originally printed, only thirteen are known to have survived. Kerwin lived long enough to learn of the purchase but died before the formal presentation in May 1999.

The map society has about seventy members; most are from the Ann Arbor and Detroit areas, but some come from more distant places, such as Lansing and Grand Rapids. Although mostly amateurs, they are a very knowledgeable group; many are serious map collectors. Several of them volunteer their expertise to help the Clements staff. They meet four times a year to hear map-related lectures; including a talk by Dunnigan on his book *Frontier Metropolis: Picturing Early Detroit, 1701–1838,* before it was published.

Since the Clements is a research library, people cannot just come in and casually look at Risdon's map. "Serious researchers may study the map once they have completed our reader registration process, which is relatively simple," explains Dunnigan. The map itself will also be exhibited from time to time, but at the moment, no public exhibition is scheduled.

# The Michigan Central Depot

*When the railroad was the city's lifeline, it was Ann Arbor's grand entrance.*

The elegant 1886 Michigan Central Railroad Station at 401 Depot Street, now the Gandy Dancer restaurant, testifies to the importance of train travel a hundred years ago. No expense was spared to make this massive two-towered stone building what the *Ann Arbor Register* called "the finest station on the line between Buffalo and Chicago."

Access to a railroad line could mean the difference between life and death for a struggling young town in the mid-nineteenth century. Before the Michigan Central reached Ann Arbor in 1839, a trip to Detroit was a difficult all-day affair on horseback. On the train, it could be done comfortably in two and a half hours. The movement of freight improved even more dramatically. The depot swiftly became the funnel through which virtually all traffic in and out of the city passed.

The Michigan Central was putting up new depots all along its route when the Ann Arbor station was built, but each had its own unique design. Ann Arbor's was designed by Detroit architect Frederick Spier (who also designed the Kelsey Museum and St. Thomas Catholic Church) in the then-popular Richardson Romanesque style. It was built by Gearing and Sons of Detroit of glacial stones quarried from Four Mile Lake between Chelsea and Dexter and cut at Foster's Station on Huron River Drive near Maple Road.

The inside was elegant, with stained-glass windows, red oak ceilings and trim, French tile floors, and even separate waiting areas for men and women. Ivy grew up the side of the building, petunias and carnations were planted around it, and a fountain spurted at the point of a triangular garden just east of the baggage shed, where the Gandy Dancer's valet parking lot is now. In the 1880s, gardens were considered an important element in railroad station design—after all, the station was the first impression visitors received of the town.

The Railway Express office was in the smaller stone building to the west of the main station. In those days, before trucks, trains carried goods of every description, from food (for instance, bread from the Ann

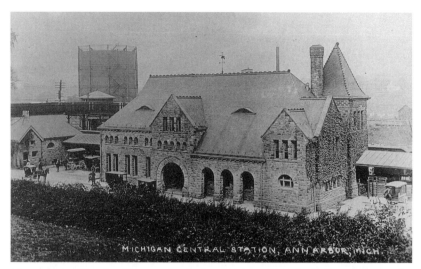

No amount of fine detailing—stained-glass windows, French tile floors, or even the garden and fountain—could mask the depot's location in what was then a gritty industrial district. The dark mass looming on the left in this early postcard was the huge illuminating gas plant on Broadway. *(Courtesy of Bentley Historical Library.)*

Arbor Home Bakery was delivered to the western part of the state) to kit houses. Whole train cars were devoted to mail, which was sorted as the train moved and then thrown out onto station platforms as the train whizzed by. Mail service was often faster than it is today: a letter mailed at the Ann Arbor station in the morning could be delivered in Chicago that afternoon.

EVEN AFTER THE AUTOMOBILE came into general use, people took the train for most long trips. In 1915, there were thirteen Detroit to Chicago passenger trains a day, plus other, shorter runs. Many Ann Arborites commuted daily to jobs along the route. Others used the train for excursions. Kathryn Leidy recalls day outings with friends to Hudson's in downtown Detroit. And of course the beginnings and endings of university semesters found the train station crowded with students, the more adventurous of whom had slid down State Street on their trunks.

Celebrities and artists arrived by train and were met at the station by committees of dignitaries. Alva Sink, whose husband, Charles Sink, was head of the University Musical Society, greeted countless musicians, including Ignacy Paderewski, who arrived in 1933 in his own sleeping car. Former U-M bands director William Revelli often provided the escort as they left; among those he saw off at the depot were Victor Borge, Meredith Willson, Gene Krupa, Benny Goodman, and Pablo Casals.

As late as World War II, when rationing of gas and tires made car travel difficult, the depot hummed. Betty Gillan Seward, who worked as the station's accountant during the war, remembers it as a very busy time. In addition to the regular trains, there were extras for troop transport. Art Gallagher, retired editor of the *Ann Arbor News*, remembers traveling to Kalamazoo during the war to visit his father and often having to stand the whole way because the train was so crowded with soldiers and civilians.

The depot's last hurrah came in 1960, when both John Kennedy and Richard Nixon addressed rallies from their campaign trains. They were the last in a long line of politicians to make whistle-stops in Ann Arbor, running back to William Howard Taft, Teddy Roosevelt, Grover Cleveland, and William Jennings Bryan.

IN 1970, THE DEPOT was sold to Chuck Muer, a restaurateur with an interest in historic restoration. By then the trickle of passenger traffic that remained was easily accommodated in the former freight building to the west and later in a small station built by Amtrak west of the Broadway Bridge. Muer, who was ahead of his time in restoring old buildings for new uses, later did similar remodeling of a historic fire station in Cincinnati and a railroad station in Pittsburgh. He kept the Ann Arbor depot building intact. The original stone walls, slate roof, stained-glass windows, red oak ceilings, fireplace, and baggage scale are still there. He added a kitchen in the open area between the baggage building and waiting room, windowed in the platform area, and changed the color of the outside trim from green to dark mauve. Muer named his restaurant the Gandy Dancer, after the laborers who once maintained the tracks.

# Ann Arbor's "Other" Railroad

*Though it was overshadowed locally by the Michigan Central, the little Ann Arbor Railroad once carried the city's name all across lower Michigan.*

A century ago, railroads were Ann Arbor's lifeline. Just about everyone who came to the city, and virtually everything they needed to live here, arrived by train. Though most of those passengers and goods were carried by the Michigan Central Railroad, the route more closely identified with the city elsewhere in the state was its namesake, the little Ann Arbor Railroad.

The Michigan Central ran east-west, linking Ann Arbor to the big-city worlds of New York and Chicago. Known affectionately as "the Annie," the Ann Arbor Railroad ran south to Toledo and northwest to Frankfort, Michigan, stopping along the way at small towns such as Whitmore Lake and Owosso.

Ann Arbor's two train stations, built just three years apart, testified to the Annie's junior status. In 1886, the Michigan Central spent $33,000 to build a grand station on Depot Street. As the Gandy Dancer restaurant, the elaborate stone building remains an Ann Arbor landmark to this day. By comparison, the Ann Arbor Railroad spent only $4,400 to build its new station in 1889. Today, few people even realize that the Doughty Montessori School at 416 South Ashley Street was once one of the gateways to the city.

Though modest, the Ashley Street station possessed a simple elegance. The waiting room had a fireplace, detailed woodwork, and pew-like wooden benches on wrought-iron frames. A telegraph operator and a stationmaster, both wearing green eyeshades, sat in a bay window overlooking the tracks, where they could see trains coming and going. Originally, a baggage shed stood to the south of the station, across an open stretch of platform; the two buildings were connected in the 1920s.

Until the station was built, Ashley Street was known as East Second Street. Even today many people are puzzled that Ann Arbor has Fourth and Fifth *Streets*, on the Old West Side, and Fourth and Fifth *Avenues*, downtown. But the original names were even more bewildering: the

Horse-drawn carriages met trains coming into the station in this 1896 view. The Old West Side, discernible in the background, was still sparsely settled. *(Courtesy of Bentley Historical Library.)*

avenues were also called streets, and the only way to tell them apart was to specify "east" or "west." The new name eliminated the confusion with West Second Street, just two blocks away, while simultaneously recognizing the Ann Arbor Railroad's builder, "Big Jim" Ashley.

BORN IN 1822, Jim Ashley was a flamboyant character with strong opinions. He was described by Henry Riggs, a chief engineer of the Annie who went on to become dean of the U-M's Engineering School, as "a very large man, probably six feet tall and very heavy. His abundant white hair was worn long, down nearly to his coat collar in the style affected by Henry Ward Beecher." Like Beecher, Ashley was a passionate abolitionist. He was elected to Congress from his home state of Ohio in 1858 and helped to guide the Thirteenth Amendment, abolishing slavery, through Congress in 1865.

After serving five terms, Ashley was defeated for reelection because he had supported the attempt to impeach President Andrew Johnson. Fortunately, he had ties to Ulysses Grant, who was elected president the same year. Grant appointed Ashley governor of the Montana Territory. He was known as "Governor Ashley" for the rest of his life, long after he retired from politics and returned to Toledo to invest in the burgeoning railroad industry.

Ashley's inspiration to build a railroad north into Michigan came after he discovered that the only way he could visit his sons attending the U-M was to travel via Detroit. Even before the Civil War, some people in Ann Arbor had tried to create a north-south railroad that would compete with the Michigan Central, but the attempt had folded before any track was laid. Ashley bought up the stock in the defunct company, gaining control of the right-of-way it had acquired to the city. Then he turned around and resold stock to Ann Arbor business leaders to raise funds for construction.

The new railroad reached Ann Arbor at noon on May 16, 1878. After the workmen laid the track across South State Street, they were escorted by a band and a procession of citizens to Hill's Opera House, where the Reform Club served them a temperance supper—Ashley, a deeply religious man, strongly opposed drinking. (During his tenure as president of the railroad, he also insisted that no trains run on Sundays.)

The railroad passed west of downtown along Allen's Creek. Chosen because it was relatively flat, the route also turned out to be a good source of freight traffic because many factories had located along the creek to take advantage of its water. The tracks crossed the Michigan Central near Main Street and then spanned the Huron River on a wooden bridge (replaced twice since) and continued north toward Whitmore Lake.

Over the next decade, Ashley gradually kept building northwest, town by town. For all of his show of religious piety, Ashley was no more scrupulous than other capitalists of the freewheeling Gilded Age. He once hijacked a shipment of rails being transported on the Annie for his own use and was briefly jailed before he paid for them. Other lawsuits filed against his business to collect unpaid bills were fought out in the courts clear into the twentieth century. And he sometimes resorted to quasi-legal shenanigans to secure rights-of-way. In one case, when a property owner refused to sell, Ashley sent him a notice to appear in court in another city—and then built the tracks while he was out of town.

In a talk given to the Washtenaw Historical Society, Dan McClary, who has done extensive research on the railroad, commented that "except for Ann Arbor, [Ashley] missed every major city in the state. The reason he did [this] was [that] Toledo was a major port. They shipped a lot of [raw] commodities down there. He was tapping into Michigan's products, especially grain, produce, livestock and timber."

Finally, in 1892, at the age of seventy, Ashley purchased a small local line that connected the Ann Arbor Railroad to Lake Michigan at Frankfort. Such a move wasn't the dead end it seemed. The resourceful Ashley had picked Frankfort for its excellent harbor, and he had already cut deals with railroads across the lake in Wisconsin and in Michigan's Upper Peninsula. He launched the world's first open-water rail ferry service, hauling loaded freight cars back and forth across the lake. To

Ann Arbor R. R. Bridge and Sunday Excursion, Ann Arbor, Mich.

The Ann Arbor Railroad crosses the Huron River at Argo Dam. *(Courtesy of Bentley Historical Library.)*

attract even more traffic to Frankfort, he built a large tourist hotel, the Royal Frontenac, which drew vacationers from as far away as southern Ohio and Chicago.

CLOSER TO HOME, Ann Arborites often took the Annie to Whitmore Lake to spend the day at the beach or to attend dances at the town's two major hotels. Families who owned summer places in the area could get off at Whitmore Lake or Lakeland (near Zukey Lake, which connects to the Huron River chain of lakes) and transfer to a commercial launch that would take them right to their cottages. Vacation traffic was so heavy that in the summer, the railroad scheduled eight trains a day between Ann Arbor and Whitmore Lake, dubbing the run the "Ping-Pong Special."

Passengers also rode the train south to Ohio. George Koch remembers as a boy taking the train to Toledo, back when "you really were traveling when you'd go fifty or sixty miles from home." People often came by train when they were referred to University Hospital for complex medical problems—it was fairly common to see a patient taken off the train on a stretcher. And as Ashley had hoped, U-M students from Ohio used the Annie to get to school. Football Saturdays were an especially busy time for the railroad; when Michigan played Ohio State, the line carried fans from all over the Midwest.

Football fans—and everybody else—began to drive their own cars in the first two decades of the twentieth century. But while passenger traffic on the railroad gradually declined, freight service took up the slack. In Ann Arbor, the track was lined with businesses that relied on it for deliveries of coal (from West Virginia, Kentucky, and Tennessee), lumber (from up north), or block ice (from the same lakes where people vacationed). Other firms used the railroad to ship their finished products, including organs, furniture, and flour.

The busiest shippers had their own rail sidings, where freight cars could be parked off the main track for loading and unloading. Cars bound for these sidings would be delivered to the railroad's roundhouse behind Ferry Field and then delivered by a small switch engine the next day. All other cars were dropped at the freight house at William and First Streets (now a parking lot) to be unloaded.

George Koch remembers that, to get the best price on shipping, several construction companies would order building supplies together. Paul Lohr recalls that farm implement companies would send a single shipment destined for retail outlets in several towns; the owners would all go down together and help one another load their trucks. The late Frank Braatz recalled that he once ordered a Sears kit house that was delivered to the freight house on several cars; he went down with a horse-drawn wagon to pick it up.

ONE OF ASHLEY'S ORIGINAL GOALS had been to make Toledo more of a rival to Detroit, and to some extent, he succeeded. Enough Ann Arborites were interested in what was happening in Toledo to provide a customer base for the *Toledo Blade*. In the late 1920s, Sam Schlecht used to meet the train from Toledo to pick up bundles of the paper, which he then delivered to the Ann Arbor drugstores and cigar stores that sold them. Before Prohibition, the Annie also delivered two Toledo-brewed beers, Buckeye and Green Seal. Distributor Fred Dupper would go down to the freight house with his horse and wagon to pick up the beer, along with the ice to keep it cold.

In the 1940s, the Annie carried oranges from Florida. A group of local investors owned an orange grove there and would sell their crop from a boxcar parked near the Ann Arbor Implement Company on First Street. They built a little orange-painted shed near the tracks to store leftover fruit for later sale.

The railroad also had spin-off effects on the local economy. For instance, train engineers provided jeweler John Eibler with extra business by coming in at regular intervals to have their watches cleaned and cal-

The station today as the Doughty Montessori School. *(Courtesy of Stan Shackman.)*

ibrated. Eibler's grandson, also John Eibler, worked at the store and re-members the watches as "big, heavy things." He explains, "By law they had to be cleaned regularly, whether they needed it or not, like airplanes today."

Passenger service enjoyed a reprieve during World War II, when railroads were used extensively to transport troops. The Annie's last passenger train ran in 1950. Freight traffic also declined after the war, as more and more shippers switched to trucks.

America's railroads went through a wave of bankruptcies and re-organizations in the 1960s and 1970s. The former Michigan Central eventually emerged as part of Conrail, the government-backed freight line; Amtrak also uses the east-west track to carry six daily passenger trains between Detroit and Chicago.

The Ann Arbor Railroad ended up in the hands of the state govern-ment. The state still owns the northern section, which now runs only as far as Yuma, near Cadillac. In the 1980s, however, a private company bought the track from Ann Arbor to Toledo. The reconstituted Ann Ar-bor Railroad currently runs two daily freight trains carrying auto parts, finished autos, sand, cement, grain, lumber, produce, and agricultural products. By 1997, the only Ann Arbor stops were at Fingerle Lumber and Burt Forest Products, on Felch Street.

When passenger service ended, the Ashley Street station stood empty for a few years and then was used for short periods by various businesses: a beer distributor, a teenage nightclub, a counter shop. None lasted very long. In 1984, teacher Lyn Law bought the building for her Montessori school. Law did a sensitive remodeling, keeping the best parts of the waiting room and also restoring the original bay window. The school is now owned by Sherry Doughty, who has done more work on the building, carefully preserving the original look.

Not all of the Annie stations fared as well. Don Wilson, of the Ann Arbor Technical and Historical Association, says at one time every town along the route had a station but that today there are only a handful left. A few others also have found new uses: the one at Shepherd is now a museum, while Mount Pleasant's is a microbrewery and restaurant. The advantages of saving an old building are apparent at the Doughty Montessori School, where the children enjoy the railroad motif inside, while outside they climb on a slide made from an old caboose.

# Ann Arbor's Streetcars

*Linking town and campus at the turn of the century*

Streetcars and interurbans appear in many photos of old Ann Arbor, moving along tracks down the middle of major streets and powered by overhead wires. The smaller streetcars, called "dinkies" or "Toonerville Trolleys" (after a comic strip), were used within the city limits. The beefier interurbans used streetcar-type tracks to carry passengers and freight between towns.

Ann Arbor's first streetcar track was laid in the summer of 1890. The system was originally designed to be horse powered, but just a few months before opening it, the developers switched it to electric power. (The first successful electric-powered streetcar system had opened only two years earlier, in Richmond, Virginia.) A year later, in 1891, the state's first interurban began operating, running down Packard between Ann Arbor and Ypsilanti.

Ann Arbor had two streetcar routes. The Depot Line ran from the Michigan Central Railroad station (now the Gandy Dancer) to downtown and then east on William to State Street. There the line divided to encircle the U-M campus. The north branch went up North University to Washtenaw to Hill and then to the car barn on Lincoln Avenue near Burns Park. The south branch went on Monroe to East University to Hill and then to the car barn. The second route, the Packard-Huron Line, ran from what is today Vets Park to downtown and then southeast on Packard to the city limits (then Brooklyn Street) near Burns Park.

Dr. Karl Malcolm recalled that when he lived at the corner of Cambridge and Martin Place, he could catch either the north or south branch of the Depot Line on Lincoln Avenue when he was headed downtown, since either one would get him there. Malcolm remembers the streetcars being heavily used: when he went shopping with his mother, the cars would often be full, with people standing, especially near five o'clock or in bad weather.

Bertha Welker sometimes took the streetcar to Forest Hill Cemetery, where her family had a burial plot. Elsa Goetz Ordway usually walked from her home on First Street to the high school on State Street

An open summer trolley car pauses to pick up a passenger at the corner of Main and Washington early in the century. (The old courthouse tower is in the background.) The large white sign on the back of the car advertises a 10¢ round-trip fare to a baseball game at the county fairgrounds (now Burns Park). *(Courtesy of Bentley Historical Library.)*

(now the Frieze Building) but would catch the streetcar on William in really bad weather. Morrie Dalitz generally relied on his bike for transportation but sometimes caught a streetcar at Hill and Washtenaw, near his home on Vinewood.

The trolley cars were the same on both ends; front and back were defined by the direction they were going. At the end of the line, the motorman would get out and reverse the trolley attached to the overhead wires and then remove the control wrench from the accelerating switch at one end of the car and connect it to the switch at the opposite end. The detachable headlight was moved from one end of the car to the other. Inside, the conductor would walk down the central aisle flipping the seat backs down so they faced the other way. In summer, the trolley companies switched from closed cars to open ones with running boards, which the conductor used to collect fares since there were no aisles on the summer cars.

Except in rainy weather, the open cars were more enjoyable. On hot summer nights, the lines offered special 3¢ runs (the usual price was 5¢) that people would take just to cool off. Malcolm says they were a great treat. "We would beg our parents to take us," he recalls. The special rides also provided a pleasant, inexpensive date.

The first car barn was on Detroit Street between Division and Kingsley. After a fire in 1894 destroyed the building and five of the six cars, the barn was rebuilt at the edge of town, on the corner of Wells and Lincoln across from the county fairgrounds (now Burns Park). The new barn faced Lincoln but ran along Wells, with an empty lot in back where the summer cars were stored. Malcolm remembers the car barn as "just an old shed sort of thing, wooden, open most of the time, with a couple of tracks running into it." The car barn was managed by Theodore Libolt, who lived across the street.

Two of the most famous streetcar employees also lived in the neighborhood: motorman James Love lived on Wells and conductor Marion Darling on Olivia. Milo Ryan, in *View of a Universe*, wrote, "Everyone enjoyed the joke of [their names], even they. When the car was ready to start up, leaving a switch or whatever, the motorman would sometimes call out, 'Ready, Darling?'

"'Yes, Love.'

"It alone was worth the nickel. But it startled newcomers fresh off the train in this college town."

Carol Spicer remembers Love as a very friendly driver. When his streetcar was forced to wait while another passed in the opposite direction, he would announce a "rest stop" and pass the time entertaining the riders with stories. He was willing to pick up people between official stops or to let them off right in front of their houses as he passed by.

The system reached its full extent by 1900, with six and a half miles of track and ten cars—two on each route and four spares—and covered most of the town that then existed. The Depot Line was cut back slightly in 1902, when the brakes on one trolley failed going down Detroit Street and it ran into the train station. From then on, the trolleys stopped at High Street, and train passengers had to walk down the hill to the station carrying their luggage. In 1913, to cut costs, the conductors were eliminated. The company bought new cars with only one entrance and a fare box near the driver.

Male U-M students seem to have considered the streetcars fair game. Stories abound about their neglecting to pay, or riding the fenders, or starting fires, or derailing the trolleys by jumping up and down or by lifting them off the tracks. But motormen got their revenge after the trolleys were finally equipped with air brakes: they could stop the car fast enough to send a rider sprawling off.

In early January 1925, a fire destroyed the Lincoln-Wells car barn. Although the trolleys were saved, the fire hastened a civic discussion already in progress about switching to buses. The city was growing, and as more townsfolk acquired cars, streetcar ridership was falling off. Margaret Sias, who lived on a farm on Traver Road, remembers that on the last day the streetcars ran, her mother took her for a ride from downtown to her aunt's house on Hill Street. On January 30, 1925, the streetcars, displaying banners that proclaimed, "Goodbye Folks! The Scrap Heap for Me," led a parade that included twelve new buses. In the first bus, a band played funeral dirges.

The interurban stopped running in 1929, but for many years the tracks that the trolleys and the interurbans shared remained. Finally, toward the end of the Depression, WPA work crews began removing them. But every now and then, when road work is being done, remnants of the track will be found and puzzle younger workers who don't know that Ann Arbor ever had a trolley system.

# 109 Catherine—Car Age Services

*From humble garage to elegant office*

Many buildings are changed as new uses are found for them, but the building at 109 Catherine has gone through a more dramatic transformation than most. The simple tile block structure was built around 1918 and in its first four years was used as an auto livery, a junk store, an agricultural implement store, and a harness factory. In 1922 it became the City Garage, and for the next forty years, it bore the stamp of its energetic, promotion-minded owner, Ed Kuhn. Kuhn's own life was rife with career changes—he was variously a policeman, a mechanic, the owner of a taxi service, a restaurateur, and a mail contractor—and he found uses every bit as varied for his building.

Ed Kuhn was born in Ann Arbor in 1882. According to his son, Bob, and his widow, Josephine, he was an inveterate tinkerer who became involved with automobiles early in his career. In 1910, he joined the Ann Arbor Police Department, where he was the first police officer to drive a patrol car. He pursued and caught up with Robert W. Kempfert, whom he suspected of surpassing the ten-mile-per-hour speed limit. The case never got to court because the chief of police, Frank Pardon, refused to believe that the REO Kempfert was driving could surpass eight miles an hour.

In 1917, Kuhn left the department to become a partner at the City Garage, then at 300 North Main. He kept the name when five years later he bought the building next door at 109 Catherine. Kuhn evidently had a taste for promotion; the motto on his business letterhead was "Comes In All Shot/Goes Out 'Red Hot.'" The City Garage offered "general automobile repairing and storing" as well as oils and supplies and tire and tube repairing. Kuhn also operated a Dodge taxi service out of the shop. In 1927 he remodeled the building, adding a second story to be used as living quarters.

During the Depression, Kuhn started to diversify. He began in 1935 by leasing some of his garage space to the post office to store their vehicles. He also worked out a contract with them to deliver mail to the Ann Arbor and New York Central railroad stations and to make special

The City Garage as it looked after a second story was added in 1927. The zigzag pattern on the second level remains today, although the tile blocks are covered. *(Courtesy of Bob Kuhn.)*

The inside of the garage. *(Courtesy of Bob Kuhn.)*

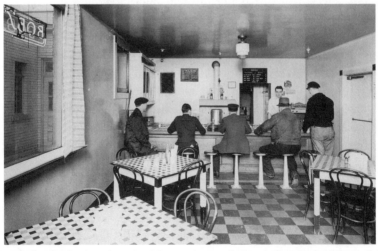

The inside of Bob's Lunch, 1936. The customer at left is unidentified. Next are John Schumacher, an employee of Crippen Drug Store; a postman; Pat Hickey, a foreman at Snyder Excavating Company; and Pat Hickey's son, Jim Hickey, owner of Hickey's Standard Service next door on Main Street. Behind the counter is cook Frank Petrick. *(Courtesy of Bob Kuhn.)*

The building at 109 Catherine today. *(Courtesy of Bob Kuhn.)*

runs to the Ann Arbor Airport to pick up and deliver the airmail that was transported in open cockpit planes.

In 1936, Kuhn turned part of the front of the building into a small restaurant, which he named Bob's Lunch after his son. He himself was the manager and dishwasher. Josephine waited tables, with her sister, Helen Roy. Bob Kuhn was the all-around helper. One of his jobs was delivering meals, by foot, to people who could not get away from their jobs. Bob's Lunch had its own matchbooks that urged people to come "for a light lunch" of "tasty . . . toasted sandwiches" and bragged about the "delicious coffee."

In the 1920s and 1930s, Catherine Street was closer to the hub of downtown Ann Arbor than it is today. Lunchtime customers were mainly people who worked in the area as employees of the post office across the street, the Ann Arbor Dairy next door, the White Swan Laundry, Godfrey Moving and Storage (later the Workbench), and nearby stores on Main Street, as well as customers from Hickey's Service Station, the City Garage's successor at 300 North Main. Farmers' Market days would bring additional diners.

By 1939, Kuhn had given up the garage operation entirely. He rented the remaining street frontage to Charles J. Morgan for a barbershop known as Charlie's. It remained in operation until 1970, and then the space was occupied for a few years by Marti's Card and Candy Shoppe, run by Bob Kuhn's wife, Bobbie, and daughter, Marti. The rear garage area was successively rented to Ben Burkhardt Typesetting, Stern's

Printing Service, Ann Arbor Glass, Wolverine Glass, Arbor Lite, and Hohlenkamp Plumbing. In the front of the building, Kuhn continued running Bob's Lunch until 1946. Kuhn retired after the war but continued to keep busy. He was a deputy sheriff and a member of the Ann Arbor Elks. He died in 1959.

The restaurant was run by others under various names until 1975, when the whole building was transformed into the Cafe Creole. The cafe's owner removed the wooden siding and cedar-shake awning that had been added in the 1960s and covered the front and sides of the building with a putty-colored coat of stucco. After working more than a year on the transformation, they opened in 1979, only to close two years later. They were replaced in 1983 by Lovejoy-Tiffany Travel. Since 1991 the building has been occupied by Q Ltd, a design and communications firm, further expanding the diversity of one modest building.

# The Ann Arbor Cooperative Society

*Argiero's restaurant was once one of the Midwest's busiest co-ops.*

Argiero's, the cozy Italian restaurant on the corner of Detroit and Catherine Streets, was from 1936 to 1939 the site of a social experiment: a co-op gas station and grocery store. They were run by the Ann Arbor Cooperative Society, a group that organized during the Depression to seek alternatives to capitalism to distribute the necessities of life.

The co-op was started by a small group meeting in the Hill Street living room of Harold Gray, the millionaire idealist who started the utopian Saline Valley Farms. Their first project, in 1933, was to purchase coal in bulk, thus eliminating the middleman. At the time, coal was a necessity of life, since it was used to heat most homes. Neil Staebler, who with his father, Edward, ran the Staebler and Son Oil Company, was very sympathetic to their cause. (He later became chair of the Michigan Democratic Party and served a term in Congress.) Staebler helped arrange for the co-op to buy coal by the train carload. One of the founding members, William Kemnitz, an attorney who had lost his job at a Detroit bank during the infamous bank holiday, served as the co-op staff person, calling all the members and taking their coal orders by phone. At about the same time, the group also began buying food in bulk.

In 1936, the co-op expanded into a full-time enterprise. Neil Staebler rented the group his Detroit Street gas station, as well as the brick barn behind it on Fifth Avenue. Bill Kemnitz became general manager, with his office in the gas station. Kemnitz's three sons, Bill Jr., Milt, and Walt, all worked there as gas station attendants at various times. Walt, then in high school, remembers his salary was 29¢ an hour. Milt, now an artist well known for his pictures of local scenes, painted the sign, the first in a long career.

The co-op grocery store was set up next door in the old barn, which dated to 1887. An extensive remodeling included installing indoor plumbing and adding plate glass show windows to the Fifth Avenue side. The goal of the grocery store, according to manager Abe Rosenkrantz,

Employees posed proudly outside the Ann Arbor Cooperative Society's gas station in the late 1930s. *Left to right:* Milt Kemnitz, Zilpha Olson, Bill Kemnitz Jr., Bill Kemnitz Sr., and Winifred Proctor. *(Courtesy of Bentley Historical Library.)*

was "honest consumer value." Rosenkrantz, who had worked in retail as manager of an office supply business before coming to Eastern Michigan University as a student, walked a tightrope, trying to offer the best products available, such as oranges without coloring, while keeping prices competitive with the chain stores, which could afford a low profit margin.

Charter co-op member Helen McCluskey chaired the board of directors' store committee, leading tasting sessions where prospective store items, such as canned peas, were opened and sampled, with the group voting on which brand they thought best.

Rosenkrantz says that to the casual consumer "the store looked like other supermarkets of the day except for labels they wouldn't recognize." He says in some ways the store was like a Meijer, in that it also offered nonfood products such as aspirin (Consumers Union had recently reported that Bayer was no better than off-brand aspirins) and some appliances. In 1937, the group also started a credit union.

Members felt they had a personal stake in the co-op. Says Bill Kemnitz Jr., "Everyone who bought owned the place. There were not many dissatisfied customers. If there were, we would work it out to everyone's satisfaction." Mary Hathaway, daughter of members A. K. and Angelyn Stevens, remembers, "It was our store. We felt very proprietary. Even as a small child you sense where your parents feel connected."

THE ANN ARBOR CO-OP soon became the second largest in the Midwest, with Chicago's the only bigger one. In 1939, pressed by a shortage of parking, needing more room, and wanting its own building, the organization moved to 637 South Main Street. It stayed there until 1955, when a Kroger opened across the street and put the co-op out of business.

The Detroit Street gas station reverted to a for-profit station during World War II. In the late 1940s and 1950s, it and the store buildings housed a used-car dealership. In 1965 Tony Argiero bought both buildings; he rented the gas station to a fish market and the store to an air-conditioning shop. In 1977, Argiero decided to use the buildings himself for an Italian restaurant he would run with his wife, Rosa. Tony had met Rosa in 1960, on a visit to his mother's village, Castelsilano, in the southern Italian province of Calabria. Rosa, obviously an authentic Italian cook, got her professional start cooking at Perry Nursery School.

Tony and Rosa enclosed the overhanging drive-in part of the gas station and built an addition on the back. They later put an addition on the west side. In 1985, they sold the restaurant to their four children. Amelia dropped out after two years, but today sons Sam, Carmin, and Michael still run it.

The Ann Arbor Cooperative Society still exists. Though it no longer has a gas station or a grocery store, its credit union is still thriving as part of the Huron River Area Credit Union, located on West Stadium. Member number 2 on the membership list is Helen McCluskey.

# Industry

# The Rise & Fall of
# Allen's Creek

*The stream that flows through Ann Arbor's Old West Side hasn't been seen above ground since 1926, but you can still see its influence.*

Allen's Creek, the site of the city's first settlement, still runs through Ann Arbor's west side. Named for Ann Arbor's cofounder John Allen, it has a romantic sound to it, bringing to mind pictures of Potawatomi following its course, settlers camping and picnicking on the banks, livestock drinking from it, and children playing in it. That idyllic picture has some truth in it, but Sam Schlecht, who knew it well in the years before it was put in a pipe below ground in 1926, says the creek was by then more like a "ditch in the road." Historically, its value to Ann Arbor had more to do with urban development than natural beauty.

The main branch of Allen's Creek runs northward roughly parallel to the Ann Arbor Railroad tracks, starting at Pioneer High and spilling into the Huron River just below Argo Dam. Three tributaries flow east into it from the Old West Side. Eber White starts on Lutz, crosses Seventh Street, and flows into the main stream at William; Murray-Washington rises at Virginia Park, crosses Slauson Middle School playground, and joins the creek near West Park; and West Park–Miller drains the ravine between Miller and Huron.

Ann Arborites who were born after 1926 or who came to town after the creek was interred would probably not even know it exists except that it surfaces periodically as a political issue. In 1983, the voters approved a bond issue to repair it. And in recent years it has been part of an ongoing discussion about a possible greenway that may include opening it up again.

Allen's Creek must have been named immediately after John Allen and Elisha Rumsey founded Ann Arbor in 1824. It is referred to by that name in all the early accounts and shows up on the map of "Ann-Arbour" that they registered in Detroit in May 1824.

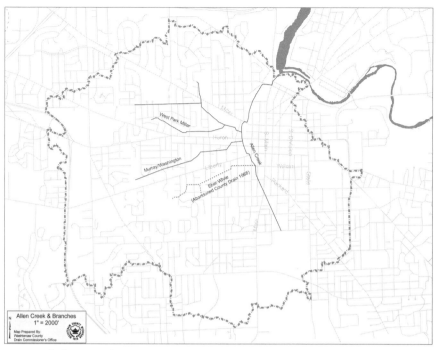

Map of Allen's Creek. *(Courtesy of Janis Bobrin, Washtenaw County Drain Commissioner.)*

Allen and Rumsey arrived here in February, looking for government land to buy as a town site. After returning to Detroit to pay for one square mile of property, they came back and set up camp on what is today the corner of First and Huron, with the creek right behind them as a water source. Rumsey and his wife, Mary Ann, later built a house on the site.

As Ann Arbor developed in the 1850s and 1860s, many businesses located along the creek. The creek apparently did not have a current strong enough to furnish real water power—the only industry that used it in that way was the Ward Flour Mill, at the mouth where the creek joined the Huron—but many businesses used its water for processing. Four tanneries on or near the creek used its water to soak cowhides and pelts of wild animals trapped in the surrounding forests. A foundry, Tripp, Ailes, and Price, on Huron Street where the Y is today, used the creek's water for its sand casting. And two breweries, the Western, later called the Michigan Union, on Fourth Street (today Math Reviews) and the City Brewery on First Street (today the Cavern Club), used the creek water to cool their beer.

In 1878, when the Ann Arbor Railroad reached town on its way between Toledo, Ohio, and Michigan's north, its developers chose the land beside Allen Creek to lay their track. Not only was it flat, but it was already the location of many of the industries they wanted to serve. Putting the tracks there guaranteed that the area would remain industrial even after water supply was no longer crucial.

As INDUSTRY GREW, so did the population. In 1846 William Maynard laid out the first section of the Old West Side, from First to Fourth Streets. He added more streets in 1858 and 1861. But unlike today's subdivisions, with houses built one after another down each street, the area took shape slowly, with the higher land being built on first. The most desirable streets were Liberty, Huron, and Miller because they were high and dry. The three streets, which were originally Indian trails, fanned out to avoid crossing the creek tributaries that ran between them.

Cross streets going down into the valleys between those main arteries weren't developed until years later. Murray and Mulholland Streets, which cross the creek, were not laid out until 1911 and 1916. And some of the lowest parts of the creek bed were never built on at all—today they are West Park, Slauson playground, and the second Bach School playground.

A few west side home owners took advantage of having the water nearby. David Allmendinger, owner of the downtown organ factory, built a house in 1890 at 719 West Washington, just in front of the creek. He dammed the creek to create a series of ponds, incorporating natural springs that were found on the property. He brought in soil to plant a rose garden and added a rustic bridge across the pond and a gazebo for family gatherings (he had thirteen children).

Allmendinger planted water lilies and stocked the pond with carp, one of which, according to family legend, answered to the name of Billy. But the carp were endangered when the city water pump station next door began drawing more water from the springs: the pond level fell so low that the family cat could catch fish by just reaching in.

Some west siders used the creek more practically—to water their livestock. In the nineteenth and early twentieth centuries, the line between city and country wasn't as sharply drawn as it is now. Many people kept chickens, or even a horse or a cow, on their city lots. (There are still a number of barns around the Old West Side, used today as garages.) Sam Schlecht remembered his grandparents telling him of cows drinking from the creek near their Seventh Street house. Marty Schlenker's family told him that their livestock used to drink from the creek at First Street behind their Liberty Street hardware store.

Allen's Creek going by the Dean and Company warehouse near the Ann Arbor Railroad tracks between Liberty and Washington. *(Courtesy of Bentley Historical Library.)*

ALTHOUGH THE CREEK INFLUENCED the location of industry, houses, and the railroad its importance had shrunk to almost nil by the early 1900s. Water was piped indoors after 1885, when the Ann Arbor Water Works Company was set up, so the creek was not necessary for industry, and homes and the railroad tracks had already been established. The only use for the creek was for recreation.

A stream running through a residential neighborhood can be a beauty spot and a play area, as the Allmendingers proved. But people around today who were children before the creek disappeared say that was the exception. Many interviewed said they didn't remember playing in the creek at all, while others remembered it as simply not important.

On hot days, Geraldine Seeback and her sister used to wade in the branch of the creek that ran by the east side of their parents' fluff rug factory on Huron, which replaced the foundry where the Y is today. Asked if her parents worried about her safety, Seeback laughs and says, "It wasn't dangerous." She remembers the water as about four feet wide but only ankle deep.

Allen's Creek flood
in 1902 as it crosses
Washington Street.
*(Courtesy of Bentley
Historical Library.)*

Karl Horning, who grew up on Third Street around the same time, has similar memories of the creek. He says, "It was nothing of significance; it didn't add anything to the city." He remembers that he and his friends could see the creek running under the Ann Arbor Railroad freight house on William and Ashley. The freight house was built right over the creek: evidently the creek was so small that builders just ignored it. Marty Schlenker remembered that the Feiner glass warehouse across the street from the freight house was also built over the creek.

Perhaps the person still around who is most familiar with the creek back then is Sam Schlecht, an inveterate explorer who lived in several different Old West Side houses as a boy and saw the creek from different vantage points. Between Seventh and Eighth Streets, near Slauson Middle School (now Waterworks Park), the creek widened into a little pond. Schlecht and his friends made a burlap swing and attached it to a tree so they could swing out over the pond. If they fell in, they were in no danger of drowning—only of getting very dirty. Schlecht describes the pond as "slop water covered with algae," not deep enough for swimming.

Invisible for most of its course, Allen's Creek emerges to join the Huron below Argo Dam. *(Courtesy of Stan Shackman.)*

Although the creek was low most of the time, it could overflow in the spring when the snow melted. Horning remembers that it would back up into gardens on First Street. That was a problem, since the water was polluted from outhouses and years of industrial use. In 1921, the city pumping station on Washington Street, which drew water from the springs that fed the Murray-Washington branch of Allen's Creek, was closed because of contamination from surface water.

In 1923, eighty-seven of the hundred property owners along the main branch of the creek petitioned city council to make it into a storm sewer. At a joint meeting that July, the city council and the Ann Arbor Township board agreed to the request. Alderman Herbert Slauson (for whom the school is named) said, "We do hereby determine that said proposed drain is necessary and conductive to the public health, convenience, and welfare."

IT TOOK THREE YEARS to do the engineering and to enclose the main creek in underground cement pipes. The pipes taper from eleven feet in diameter at the mouth to four feet at the headwaters near Pioneer High. In 1925, property owners along the West Park–Miller branch petitioned to have it put into a storm drain, and in 1927, residents along the Murray-Washington and Eber White branches followed. The tributary pipes range from four feet to about eighteen inches in diameter. In 1969 the creek and its tributaries were consolidated into the same drain district.

Sam Schlecht remembers when the creek was being put underground. The section near Keppler Court was on the path he followed to walk downtown, and he often stopped to watch the workmen. He remembers that although they had a primitive backhoe, a lot of their work was done by hand. When he got too close, the workmen would shoo him away. At the time, he remembers, Mulholland Street ended at the creek, with a cement wall to stop cars from going farther. After the creek was put into the pipe, Mulholland was extended across and turned west to end at Seventh Street. Later it was moved east and turned to end at Washington.

The main section of the drain was finished in 1926, just after the city celebrated its hundredth anniversary. The *Ann Arbor News* wrote, "Planned as a part of the city's permanent sewerage to take care of the drainage from the creek's watershed for all time to come, it is probable that the concrete house for John Allen's creek once it is completed, will remain intact on the two hundredth anniversary of the founding of Ann Arbor."

That was optimistic—it was more like fifty years later that Allen's Creek again needed attention. The Allen Creek drain, as it is now known, flooded in 1947 and 1968. Putting a creek in a drain was no guarantee it would stay there—the pipes, of course, hold a finite amount of water—and as Ann Arbor continued developing to the west, filling in more land with buildings, houses, and parking lots, the amount of runoff channeled into the drain kept increasing. By the mid-1970s, it became obvious that the Allen's Creek drain needed a fresh appraisal.

A study commissioned by the city in the early 1980s offered a choice of several solutions. The most effective options—replacing the pipes with larger ones or building a second drain parallel to the first—were rejected as too expensive. Instead it was decided to repair the present system to make it as efficient as possible. Ann Arbor voters approved a $1.1 million bond issue, and in 1983 the city set to work repairing deteriorated culverts, relocating other utilities' pipes that crossed the drain, and resurfacing bottom areas that had eroded.

The bond money covered the most critical work. Since then, the Washtenaw County drain office and the city's engineering department have continued to work together on drain maintenance. The county is responsible for routine upkeep of the main line of the drain, while the city takes care of the tributaries going into neighborhoods. Major projects are financed using the county's full faith and credit and with the city's storm water utility fees.

In 1993 the last two sections identified as needing work—an area near the Salvation Army headquarters on Arbana and another on Seventh

Street near West Park—were completed. Both the city and county agree that Allen Creek drain is, at least for now, in good shape, even if under-sized to serve its drainage area. Drain commissioner Janis Bobrin says there are "no visible areas of concern" but that the county "will continue to evaluate and maintain the drain."

Periodically people talk about opening up portions of the drain and returning it to a natural creek. Current discussion is focusing on the po-tential of creating a greenway along the creek corridor. Whether Allen's Creek stays underground or not, its importance to the city has, if any-thing, continued to grow over the years. For instance, when Michigan Stadium was returned to natural turf in 1991, a tributary of the drain that ran right under the fifty-yard line was directed around the field and large pumps were installed to permanently lower the water table. The pumps allowed the U-M to lower the playing field itself by more than three feet below the level at which it otherwise would have been covered with water. Without Allen's Creek, Michigan Stadium would be a lake.

# Henry Krause's Tannery

*It was the forerunner of Hush Puppies shoes.*

In the late nineteenth century, Henry Krause was one of the city's biggest taxpayers. The leather-making factory he built on Second Street stood into the twenty-first century, and his name lives on in Krause Street nearby. But his real claim to fame is that his Ann Arbor tannery was the forerunner of Hush Puppies shoes.

Krause was born in Treffurth, Prussia, in 1820, to a family who had been tanners for two centuries. He learned the trade from his father and traveled over the greater part of Germany on foot as a *Handwerkebursche*— a journeyman—before immigrating to America at age twenty-four. Krause worked briefly in New York and in Liverpool, Ohio, before coming to Ann Arbor in 1845. With its large German population and several tanneries, Ann Arbor was a natural choice for an immigrant with his skills.

Krause's first Ann Arbor job was with Emanuel Mann, who also had been born in Germany and learned tanning from his father. The next year Krause went to work for another German tanner, C. Kusterer, whom he soon bought out. In 1850 he moved the business to Second Street between Liberty and William, where he built a wood frame tannery next to a tributary of Allen's Creek.

A source of water was essential for a tannery. Tanners soaked hides in water to clean them, then in a solution of water and lime to loosen the hair, and finally in water and tannin to preserve and soften the leather. The tannin came from oak bark, and in addition to using water for soaking, early tanneries used water to power the mills that ground the bark.

Krause prospered, and in 1868 he replaced his wooden tannery with a brick one, 30 by 120 feet. A separate storehouse held 225 cords of oak bark, and a third building housed a steam engine for grinding it. By now, Krause was selling leather throughout the state, principally for harnesses. His factory used seven thousand hides a year, and its annual sales were about $45,000.

Three other nearby tanneries competed with Krause. The Weil Brothers tannery was on the southwest corner of First and Huron, on

Tannery building shortly before it was torn down. *(Courtesy of Stan Shackman.)*

land that was once the home of Elisha Rumsey, Ann Arbor's cofounder. The five Weil brothers, Jacob, Solomon, Moses, Leopold, and Marcus, were the nucleus of Ann Arbor's earliest Jewish community, but they moved on to bigger cities in the 1870s. Jacob Heinzmann, another German immigrant, set up a tannery in 1851 on the corner of William and Third, on the same Allen's Creek tributary as Krause's. (Its site is now a parking lot for the Argus Building.) On the other side of the tributary, also on Third but closer to Liberty, Christian Duttenhofer, a former Weil Brothers employee, started his own tannery in the 1860s. Duttenhofer's was probably a smaller operation, since the address was also his home.

Krause also built up a retail operation. In 1849 he built the first brick building on the block of Main Street south of Washington, adding to it in 1861. (In the nineteenth century, most businesses were still clustered around the courthouse to the north.) Besides selling his leather there, he made shoes and boots.

Krause married Catherine Hirth in 1846, just a year after he arrived in Ann Arbor. As his business prospered, they were able to move to a seventeen-room house on the corner of Third and Liberty, now the location of St. Paul's. (They used the house as a parsonage and school before razing it in 1929 to make room for the church.) The Krause property ran well north of their home down to Washington and west to what is today a U-M parking lot.

IN 1881 THE KRAUSE TANNERY was incorporated with $40,000 in capital and was subsequently outfitted with new equipment. But by then, Krause and Heinzmann were the only tanners left in town. Local tanners were probably beginning to feel the competition of large industrial tanners with lower prices and national distribution. Wildlife in Michigan was also becoming scarce, and both Krause and Heinzmann included in their ads offers to buy pelts. Krause's ad claimed that he paid "more for hides and pelts, furs and tallow than any other man in the state." He also began selling other brands besides his own custom-made shoes.

Krause was a respected tanner. In 1850, early in his career, he won a first place at the Michigan State Fair. The *Ann Arbor Register Weekly* said of Krause at the time of his death in 1893, "As a tanner of superior leather he had a wide reputation," adding, "Although meeting with financial reverses in later years his integrity was unquestioned."

The city directory hints at the rest of the story. Krause seems to have given up control of the company in the 1881 incorporation, apparently the price he paid for the capital to finance the tannery's final renovation. Beginning that year, others are named as the company's officers, while Krause is identified only as the plant superintendent. The Krause tannery disappears entirely from the directory in 1888. In the 1890 directory, Henry Krause is listed as a clerk for Samuel Krause, his son, at the Main Street store.

The store closed a few years later, ending the Krause family's fifty years in the leather business in Ann Arbor. But by then, another of Henry and Catherine's sons (they had seven children) was flourishing in western Michigan. In 1883, G. Adolph Krause, known as G.A., had bought a leather shop in Grand Rapids in partnership with his mother's brother, Fred Hirth, also a tanner. In 1901 the Hirth-Krause Company, as it was then known, moved to Rockford, a small community close to Grand Rapids, and expanded their tanning and manufacturing. G.A.'s sons, Victor and Otto, and his grandson Adolph continued in the firm. Today the company is Wolverine World Wide, Inc., the world's largest tanner of pigskin and the makers of Hush Puppies, the shoes with the sad-eyed basset hound trademark. Henry Krause's 1850 award from the Michigan State Fair is prominently reproduced in the company's official history.

MEANWHILE, THE KRAUSE TANNERY building in Ann Arbor continued to be used as a factory, first to manufacture brass goods and then car accessories, vapor lamps, and windshields. In 1925 the newly formed King Seeley Company moved in to begin manufacture of gas gauges, using the tannery building but adding a modern factory in front of it. Purchased by Chrysler in 1968, it became GT Products, manufacturer of diesel governors and fuel vapor valves, in 1982 and ended its life as Eaton Corporation. The tannery building was razed in 2005 to make room for an adaptive reuse condo project in the newer factory building.

# The Athens Press on Main Street

*From hand-set type to desktop publishing in five generations*

In 1933, when Adam Goetz moved Athens Press to 308 North Main Street, the technology he used was not much different than it had been in Gutenberg's day. The simple brick-fronted building was essentially one big room. The printing press was in front, while in the back, Goetz stood at a desk setting lead type by hand, one letter at a time.

By then, Goetz had already been a printer for fifty years. Although he'd been a part owner in the business since 1900 and sole proprietor since 1907, the 308 North Main shop was the first plant built specifically for his company. It would not be the last. Now known as Goetzcraft, Ann Arbor's oldest job printer currently employs eighteen people at its twelve thousand–square foot plant on the south side of town.

Born in Germany in 1866, Goetz came to the United States with his family at age five. At fifteen he began working in the print trade, no doubt learning on the job. He started at the *Washtenaw Post*, a German-language newspaper, and then worked at the Register Publishing Company and the Inland Press before joining with three fellow workers to form Athens Press. The name came from their location, a room on the second floor of the Athens Theater on North Main.

The Athens Press took all sorts of small assignments. An early scrapbook passed down to Larry Goetz, Adam's great-grandson, includes letterhead and business cards, party invitations, political literature, and jobs for the university. Those items are still familiar to job printers today, though many of the clients memorialized in the scrapbook, such as the Germania Club and the Ann Arbor Boat Company, are no longer in existence. There's also not much demand anymore for such once-popular items as commemorative ribbons, restaurant meal tickets (bought in advance for a certain number of meals, they were often used by single men or immigrants here without their families), and advertising blotters (a common freebie when people wrote with pens dipped in ink).

In 1906, the press had to move because the theater was being remodeled and expanded (a process that included a name change to the

The Athens Press second home was a storefront at 208 North Main. *(Courtesy of Larry and Paulette Goetz.)*

Whitney). They ended up across the street and one block north, in a now-gone storefront at 208 North Main.

Larry Goetz was told by his great-aunt Hermina that her father was often razzed by his partners for working too hard and earning all of the money. Athens Press's original account book bears out her story. There are countless references to Goetz getting extra pay for working nights or on Sundays. Not surprisingly, soon after the move, Goetz was able to buy out his two remaining partners, Clyde Kerr and Alfred Schairer. Both men opened their own printing companies; Schairer teamed up with Oswald Mayer to form Mayer-Schairer office supply store (they got out of printing in the 1950s).

ADAM AND PAULINE GOETZ's children, Herbert and Hermina, helped in the shop from an early age, pulling their red metal wagon down Main to make deliveries. Adam was happiest working in the back setting type, and so when Herbert got old enough to work full-time, he took over the business end, talking to customers and doing the books.

After 1938 the shop sent out big typesetting jobs to Ben Burkhart, who had one of the city's only Linotype machines in his shop on the other side of the alley in what had been the City Garage. The Linotype, named for its ability to set a full line of type at a time, was very expen-

In 1933 the press finally got a building of its own at 308 North Main, now Eureka Cleaners. *(Courtesy of Larry and Paulette Goetz.)*

sive and hard to operate, but Burkhart had taught himself to use it by fooling around with one while a student at Ann Arbor High. Much like computer companies do today, in the 1920s, manufacturers would sell typesetting machines to schools at very reasonable prices so that students could learn how to operate them. Burkhart, who is still in business today, thinks he is now the last working Linotype operator in the Midwest.

Herbert Goetz was interested in modernizing the business, but his dad refused to retire. As he always had, Adam Goetz continued to set type by hand, chewing tobacco as he worked (he sent his grandson, John, to buy it for him at the cigar store on Huron). Finally, in 1943, Herbert threatened to enlist in the army unless his dad let him buy the business. It was an empty threat (Herbert had a health condition that made him ineligible), but his father finally agreed to sell. Adam Goetz never retired, however, continuing to work until two months before he died at age seventy-seven. According to his obituary, he had been the oldest living member of the typographical union, which he'd joined in 1885.

In 1944 Herbert Goetz changed the name of the Athens Press to Goetzcraft, since by then it had been thirty-six years since the business had been in the Athens Theater. Five years later he built a new, larger building across the street, at 307 North Main, adding new machinery and

The press moved across the street, to 307 North Main, in 1949. *(Courtesy of Larry and Paulette Goetz.)*

doubling the staff to about ten people. While his father never changed his way of working, Herbert kept up with the evolving industry. In the 1950s, the company bought its own Linotype machine, and later, when they came out, photo offset printing presses.

Like his father and grandfather, John Goetz started working at the press at a young age, coming in after school when he was a student at Slauson Junior High. He started out sweeping, feeding hand-fed presses, and baling. As soon as he got his driver's license he was sent on deliveries, and he came to work full-time when he graduated from high school.

Since his dad had firm control of the business end, John concentrated more on the machinery, learning how to run and repair the presses, the bindery, and—especially challenging—the Linotype. Herbert retired more gracefully than his father had, moving to Florida in 1962 and leaving John in charge. A workaholic like the rest of the family, Herbert opened a liquor store in Florida, where he worked the rest of his life.

John's son Larry, like the previous three generations of Goetz men, started working at a young age, riding his bike to the shop after school to help out. Although he studied printing at Ferris State University, he says he really learned on the job. He joined the company full-time in 1971, in time for the next printing revolution: computer typesetting. His father, guessing this was the way to go, invited his foreman and wife to dinner and, over a good meal that his wife, Evelyn, had cooked, suggested that Evelyn and the foreman's wife work together to find out whether photo composition (a then-new technique for setting type on film) could replace the Linotype. "It drove us nuts, but we mastered it," Evelyn recalls. Goetzcraft was the first printer in Ann Arbor to offer the new technology.

Five times faster than the Linotype, photo composition "was the hottest thing in town," John recalls. "Other machines became obsolete while people still owed money on them." By the mid-1980s, Goetzcraft sold its Linotype to a man in Charlevoix for $3,000. According to John, "It was a fraction of what we paid, but we were lucky to get that." By then, Goetzcraft was already moving into desktop publishing.

Since 1979, Goetzcraft has been located in the Ann Arbor Industrial Park at 975 Phoenix Drive. They do fancier work than Adam Goetz could have ever imagined: brochures, catalogs, and posters, printed in an array of colors. But one thing hasn't changed. The family continues to make up about half of the workforce. Larry Goetz, now president, is assisted either full- or part-time by ten family members: his father and mother, John and Evelyn Goetz; his wife, Paulette; his sisters, Julie Trevino and Lee Ann Haynes; his brothers-in-law, Jeff Haynes and Jeff Swanson; and his three children, Britton, Bryan, and Brooke.

The original plant that Adam Goetz built at 308 North Main became a dry-cleaning business after Goetzcraft left. Eureka Cleaners is now owned by Steve Hur, who also owns College Cleaners on North University. Like Adam Goetz, Steve Hur is an immigrant, and his craft, too, runs in the family: he bought the business from his sister, who originally had bought it from their brother.

# 439 Fifth Street:
# From Drinking Spot to Play Yard

*Bach School's playground was once a west side bar.*

Children playing on the Bach School playground probably have no idea that it was once the location of adult recreation. From 1901 to 1919, a beer distributorship and popular west side drinking spot was located behind Jacob Dupper's home at what was then 439 Fifth Street, now the north end of the playground. In those pre-zoning days, he ran several businesses from outbuildings on the property. His barn was the Ann Arbor distributorship for Buckeye and Green Seal beers, both made by a Toledo brewery. And a small structure usually called "the shop" was the neighborhood bar.

The shop stood across the driveway from Dupper's house and farther back from the street. Neighborhood men came in the evening to share a companionable drink, to chat, and to play cards. Dupper's grandson, Henry Velker, from whom most of this information was obtained, remembers that the clientele came from all over the Old West Side, then known as the city's Second Ward.

The building (sometimes called "the caboose") was furnished with tables and a short bar. It had room for about thirty or forty people, who could buy beer, wine, or whiskey. Velker remembers that customers came in all seasons, although in the summer they usually came later in the evening after their chores were finished. In the winter, when darkness descended sooner, they came earlier and stayed longer.

The customers were all men. Erna Steinke Jahnke, who grew up on nearby Jefferson Street in the years that Dupper's business was in operation, says that she never heard of any women going there. Parents also discouraged their children from hanging around the neighborhood bar.

Jacob Dupper was born in 1860 in Bondorf, a small town thirty miles south of Stuttgart. According to Velker, Dupper learned the brewery and distributing business while still in Germany. When he moved to Ann Arbor in his twenties, his first job was working for the Northern Brewery on the north side of town.

The Dupper family lived at 439 Fifth Street, now the north end of the Bach School playground, and ran a beer distributorship from their barn. *(Courtesy of Louis Velker.)*

George Voelker delivered beer with the aid of a horse named Sam. *(Courtesy of Louis Velker.)*

In 1901, Dupper obtained the Ann Arbor franchise for Buckeye and Green Seal beers. Although there were two local breweries, many local residents disloyally claimed that the Toledo brands tasted better. Dupper kept them supplied, delivering the beer to stores, restaurants, fraternities, and private parties.

As a sideline, he also delivered ice. He had his own icehouse on the

Fred Dupper behind the counter of his shop. *(Courtesy of Louis Velker.)*

property, stocked with ice cut and shipped in from Whitmore Lake. The barn served as his beer warehouse and also housed the horses and wagons he used for deliveries.

The beer was shipped from Toledo, in both bottles and kegs, via the Ann Arbor Railroad and was unloaded at the Ashley Street station on a First Street spur of the tracks. From there it was taken by horse and wagon the five blocks to the Dupper house.

When Dupper died in 1907, his son, Fred Dupper, took over the business with his wife, Minnie. Fred Dupper's brother-in-law, George Voelker, who lived across the street, worked as a driver for the company. (George Voelker was Henry Velker's father. Velker changed the spelling of the name to more closely match the pronunciation.)

Though the shop and the distributorship closed with the beginning of Prohibition in 1919, the Duppers continued to live in the house for many years. Sam Schlecht, who lived on Fifth Street in the 1920s, remembers the painted ads for Buckeye beer on the sides of Dupper's barn long after the beer itself had disappeared.

Fred Dupper died in the early 1940s. The house was used as a residence for about twenty more years, until it was torn down to make room for an expansion of the Bach School playground.

# The Artificial Ice Company

*Delivering coolness door to door*

Before the days of electric refrigerators, people kept perishable foods in ice chests cooled by blocks of ice. For most of Ann Arbor's early history, the ice was harvested from frozen lakes and rivers. But after 1909, natural ice was supplemented, and then totally replaced, by artificial ice, so named because it was manufactured rather than gathered.

The main sources of natural ice were the dams on the Huron River and Whitmore Lake. The ice would be cut at the end of January or the beginning of February—after it became thick enough to make the effort worthwhile but before the danger of a thaw. Using horse-drawn ice plows, harvesters would cut the ice into square slabs and then move it to an insulated icehouse for storage.

In 1909 Ann Arbor supported six ice dealers. They made home deliveries to icebox owners and also supplied butcher shops, restaurants, saloons, and beverage companies. Henry Velker, whose grandfather and uncle owned Dupper's beer distributorship on Fifth Street from 1901 to 1919, remembers that their ice came from lakes north of Ann Arbor. The ice was sent by rail, unloaded at the Ann Arbor Railroad depot on Ashley Street, and delivered to a barn on the back of their property that was devoted solely to ice storage.

Farmers, who needed ice to preserve their meat and dairy products, usually had their own icehouses and often filled them with ice harvested from ponds on their property. Ann Arbor's most famous farm, Cobblestone Farm, originally had a stone icehouse on the east side of the property near the smokehouse. Mary Campbell, granddaughter of the 1881 owner, William Campbell, remembers reading in her grandfather's diary about trips to the Huron River to collect ice.

RELYING ON ICE from natural sources had several drawbacks, including the vagaries of the weather (an early thaw could be a disaster), melting during the long summer storage season (dealers cut two pounds for every pound they sold), and the risk of infection from contaminated water. So in the late nineteenth century, inventors began experimenting

Horse-drawn wagons delivered the ice all over town. *(Courtesy of Bentley Historical Library.)*

with ways of manufacturing ice. By 1909, commercial ice making reached Ann Arbor with the formation of the Artificial Ice Company.

The company's first plant was located at 301–315 West Huron, running from the corner of First Street down to the railroad tracks. (In the 1990s an elegant restaurant named Robby's at the Icehouse was in that building but was located a floor above where the ice was actually made.) The company owned more land, on the north side of Huron just west of the railroad tracks, which they used for horse barns and for coal storage. In 1927 they moved the whole operation there, having built a larger, more modern plant at 408–416 West Huron.

Both plants had a production area, a storage room, a loading dock, a truck repair space, and an office. In the first plant, water took forty-eight hours to freeze, while in the newer one the time was cut to twenty-four hours. City water was poured into two hundred– or three hundred–pound molds. After it froze, the ice was lifted with cranes, removed from the molds with running water, and then stored upright in the storage area until needed.

A few customers came to the factory to get their ice, but most had it delivered. Walter Schlecht, who worked as a driver at the first plant, loaded his horse-drawn delivery wagon by hand, sliding the ice to the loading dock with the aid of ice tongs. Clarence Haas, a driver in the second plant, had it easier: he drove a truck, which he loaded by pushing the ice blocks onto a conveyor belt that automatically notched the ice into twenty-five-pound sections on its way down.

Schlecht had a longer day than Haas—he had to spend time each morning getting the horses from the barn and hitching them to the wagon—but he found that horses did have advantages. He was hired in the summer of 1918, while still a teenager, to replace a driver who had been fired when he showed up for work drunk. When Schlecht asked where to go, his boss answered, "Just follow the horses—they know the route."

Customers placed square cards in their windows, each corner differently colored to indicate orders for 25, 50, 75, or 100 pounds. The icemen would cut the desired amount on site, since carrying the ice around in large blocks reduced melting. Even so, some melting occurred during the day, and customers toward the end of the route sometimes complained that their 25-pound pieces were not as big as they should be.

Electric refrigerators were first seriously marketed for homes beginning around 1913, but it took them a long time to totally replace iceboxes. "The change was gradual," recalls Haas, who began work as a driver in 1929. He says the change was further slowed by World War II, when manufacture of refrigerators ceased so those factories could be used to make war supplies.

Because ice sales were heavily concentrated in the summer, the Artificial Ice Company developed a complementary business selling coal during the winter. But coal sales also were hurt by technological improvements, as people switched to oil and gas furnaces.

To eke out more money as the ice and coal business waned, the Artificial Ice Company changed the truck repair shop in the back of the factory into a cold storage area for keg beer used by area bars. This area has been remodeled into the kitchen for Say Cheese Cheesecake Bakery.

The last owner of the Artificial Ice Company was Carl Rehberg, son of Louis Rehberg, the brewmaster of Northern Brewery on Jones Street. Rehberg inherited the brewery and during Prohibition started Arbor Springs water company, selling the springwater formerly used for beer. A part owner and employee of the Artificial Ice Company from the early days (he was the immediate boss of both Schlecht and Haas), he worked out joint contracts with many local companies to have drinking water and the ice to keep it cool delivered simultaneously.

After the Artificial Ice Company was dissolved in 1965, Rehberg continued running Arbor Springs. After he died, his wife, Elsa, ran it a few years and then sold it to the present owners, Bill and Judith Davis.

# The West Side Dairy

*From creamery to music*

Two connected buildings at 722–726 Brooks, nestled at the back of a driveway in a residential neighborhood, are puzzling to people passing by unless they know it was once a family-run dairy. The front part was constructed in 1919 and the large part in back in 1940. Brothers-in-law Adolph Helber and Alfred Weber owned and operated the West Side Dairy for thirty-four years, delivering fresh dairy products to city residents until 1953.

Adolph Helber, born in 1886, grew up in a large family on a farm on Dexter Road in Scio Township. He left school in the seventh grade, not uncommon at the time, and worked as a hired farmhand until 1904, when he went to work delivering milk for Jake Wurster, a brother-in-law. Wurster's dairy was on the corner of Catherine and North Fifth Avenue.

When Helber started in the dairy business, milk was still sold "raw," or untreated, fresh from the cow. (Although pasteurization equipment, developed to kill milk-borne infections, was available in the 1890s, it hadn't yet been universally adopted.) The raw milk was stored in a big tank at the front of the horse-drawn delivery wagon and scooped out into a pitcher or milk can supplied by each customer on the route.

In 1912 Helber married Alma Weber, the sister of a fellow driver, Alfred Weber. The Weber family house was at 809 Brooks, then the last residential street off Miller. Alma and Alfred's father, Jacob, owned much of the land in the area. In 1914 the Helbers moved to 720 Brooks, and in 1919 Helber and Alfred Weber opened a dairy out of a small one-story cement-block building they built in the Helbers' backyard. Milk was supplied by Helber's brother Carl, who had stayed on the family farm, and also by the Seyfried and Hanselman farms.

Helber and Weber started their days at 4 AM, feeding and harnessing the horses. They delivered milk in the morning and in the afternoon pasteurized and bottled it for the next day. Because neither the farmers nor the customers had good storage, the partners accepted and delivered milk seven days a week. Their only time off was Sunday afternoon. Their

The West Side Dairy in the mid-1930s. *Left to right:* Henry Grau, Alfred Weber, Eddie Weber, Adolph Helber, and Leon Jedele. All are related by blood or marriage. The dairy had just switched from horse-drawn milk wagons to trucks and was experimenting with various models—three different makes are visible. *(Courtesy of Paul Helber.)*

wives, Alma Helber and Rose Weber, ran the office, did the bookkeeping, handled over-the-counter sales, and helped with production.

IN THE DAYS BEFORE cholesterol worries, dairies competed for the richest milk the farmer had. Before homogenization, customers could see at a glance how rich the milk was by the thickness of the cream on top. (Narrow-necked milk bottles were developed to exaggerate the visible cream.) The West Side Dairy made skim milk (or buttermilk) only as a by-product of butter making, selling it back to the farmers for a penny a gallon as feed for their pigs and chickens.

As the number of their customers grew, Helber and Weber were able to hire help, giving priority to relatives. The delivery men included Eddie Weber, Alfred's brother, whose route included what is now known as the Old West Side; Leon Jedele, Rose Weber's brother; and Henry Grau, who was married to Alma's sister Clara. After relatives, neighbors were hired. The employee who probably lived the farthest away was Fred Yaeger, who walked to work every morning from his home on Pauline.

The family employees built houses in the neighborhood near their work. Alfred Weber's neighbor, Will Nimke of 827 Brooks, built him a house at 730 Brooks. Eddie Weber lived at 727 Gott, where he grew

The West Side Dairy buildings today. *(Courtesy of Stan Shackman.)*

wonderful dahlias. When the Helbers' sons grew up, they lived in the neighborhood, too, Erwin at 706 Brooks and Ray at 725 Gott. Jacob Weber owned and rented other houses, one at the corner of Brooks and Summit and three others on Gott Street, right behind the dairy. Weber and Helber owned the house between their two houses and rented it to the Moon family. The Weber property also included a big field west of the house, where the horses sometimes grazed.

Making deliveries, the milkmen would walk along the sidewalk as the horses plodded alongside them in the street. Sam Schlecht, who helped out on the routes as a teenager, recalls that the horses "knew more about the route than the human beings." If milk was delivered on a dead-end street, the horses would turn around while the men delivered to the last houses. If the milkmen cut through a backyard to deliver milk on the next street over, the horses knew to meet them there. Schlecht remembers that at the end of the route, as they went down Chapin toward Miller, the horses would pick up their pace, eager to get home for their oats and hay. When Helber and Weber switched to trucks in 1934, the milkmen found them a mixed blessing. They no longer had to feed and harness the horses each morning, but their routes took them longer without the horses' help.

Deliveries were made every single day except Christmas and Thanksgiving. On the day before those holidays, the milkmen would go around twice, in case a customer had forgotten anything that morning. Henry Michelfelder, a relative of Leon Jedele's, remembered that if his family ran out of something during the day, they could call the dairy and it would be brought over.

The milk and cream delivered for sale by retail stores were very fresh, since every day the milkmen would take back any that wasn't sold. The day-old products were used to moisten the cottage cheese the dairy made. In the 1940s, when refrigeration had become common, the dairy scaled back to three deliveries a week. Marian Helber, Ray's wife, remembers that "people had a fit. They thought they needed fresh milk every day for their coffee or cereal."

Erwin and Ray Helber grew up working in the dairy part-time and summers. After graduating from Michigan State Normal College (now Eastern Michigan University), Ray worked bottling and also delivering. During World War II he left to work at King Seeley (he learned of the job opening because the plant was on his route) and ended up staying there until 1975, when he retired. Erwin stayed at the dairy, gradually taking over more of the responsibility from his father and uncle. In 1953, when the brothers-in-law retired and sold their business to United Dairies (later Sealtest), Erwin stayed with the new owners, eventually moving to Flint with Sealtest.

TODAY THE BUILDINGS look similar from the outside but have totally new uses inside, mostly related to music. Four Davids (Orlin, Sutherland, Collins, Peramble) between them teach or repair guitar, violin, pianoforte, and piano. The neighborhood is also filled with evidence of the dairy for people who know where to look: a four-car garage (used for delivery trucks) at the corner of Summit and Brooks, a barn at 809 Brooks (later used for a construction business), and a big lot at 827 (a horse grazing area, now a big private garden). After the dairy moved out, tenants included a sugar packing manufacturer and a bookbinding operation. In 1964, Robert Noehren, a U-M organist and a pioneer in the organ revival movement, rented it for a pipe organ factory, presaging its present use. The field behind the Weber house is now the site of the Second Baptist Church.

# Downtown Ann Arbor

# L. W. Cole & the *Michigan Argus*

*Ann Arbor's oldest photo opens a window onto the city's turbulent early journalistic scene.*

The oldest known Ann Arbor photograph is a daguerreotype that shows the staff of the *Michigan Argus*, the city's Democratic weekly newspaper, circa 1850. Editor and publisher L. W. Cole (he was always referred to by his initials, even in his obituary) is in the center of the picture in black suit and top hat, surrounded by his youthful staff in rolled-up shirtsleeves.

When Cole came to Ann Arbor in 1838, he got his first job at the *Michigan Argus*. By the time this photo was taken, he was the paper's co-owner and had already survived several politically motivated takeover bids.

In the nineteenth century, newspapers existed to support a party or position, and both ownership and readership could change quickly with the political winds. It was largely by chance that this particular moment from the city's journalistic history happened to be immortalized by an itinerant photographer.

"Most daguerreotypes were pictures of a single person," says Cynthia Read-Miller of the Henry Ford, where the *Argus* photo was part of an exhibit of early photography. "This one is rare because it shows a group of people and even rarer because it shows an occupation."

"Practical photography began with the daguerreotype, a process that formed a single image rather than the negatives and prints that are familiar to us today," explains Read-Miller. Invented by Frenchman Louis Daguerre in 1839, the daguerreotype was popular from that date through the 1850s, when it was displaced by the glass-negative ambrotype.

Ann Arborites could have daguerreotype photos taken as early as 1842, when Charles Rood set up a studio for a few days in the Bank of Washtenaw building, which now houses the Wooden Spoon bookstore, at the corner of Fourth Avenue and Ann. (Unfortunately, none of Rood's photos appear to have survived.) The Cole photo very likely was taken

*Argus* staff still in their work clothes. Only the editor, L.W. Cole, dressed for the photo, putting on his suit and tall hat, circa 1850. *(Courtesy of the Henry Ford.)*

by another itinerant daguerreotypist, A. M. Noble. An advertisement for Noble's curiously named "Not London Daguerrean Gallery" appeared prominently on the top left-hand corner of the front page of the *Argus* on June 4 and June 18, 1851. Possibly the picture was part, or all, of the payment for the ad.

IF NOBLE HAD CHOSEN instead to advertise in the *State Journal*, an entirely different scene might have come down to us. While the *Argus* supported Democratic politicians, the *State Journal* backed the Whigs, the other major party at the time.

The *State Journal* was the descendant of Ann Arbor's first paper, the *Western Emigrant*. Started by Thomas Simpson in 1829, just five years after Ann Arbor was founded, the *Emigrant* tried to be fair and even-handed. Simpson wrote that "it shall be the constant aim of the Editor . . . to exhibit impartial information relative to the merit and qualifications of candidates for important public offices." He also vowed that "the columns of the *Emigrant* shall, so long as under my direction, be open to a full investigation of Free Masonry and Anti-Masonry." This last statement was too much for John Allen, cofounder of Ann Arbor (with Elisha Rumsey), and Samuel Dexter, founder of Dexter Village, and after five issues they purchased the paper and ran it with an editorial policy of anti-Masonry (they objected to the group's secrecy) and endorsement of temperance. After several changes in name and ownership, the *Emigrant* became in December 1834 the *Michigan Whig* and in September 1835 the *State Journal.*

Two months after the *Michigan Whig* debuted, in February 1835, Earl P. Gardiner founded the *Michigan Argus* to give local Democrats a voice. Gardiner, who was born in Connecticut in 1807, settled in Michigan after serving in the army at Fort Gratiot, now Port Huron. Gardiner's office was in Lower Town on the north side of the Broadway Bridge, above G. and J. Beckley's general store.

Cole joined Gardiner three years later. Born in Palmyra, New York, in 1812, Cole was only twenty-six when he arrived in Ann Arbor. The 1881 *History of Washtenaw County, Michigan* says that Cole "learned the printing trade at an early age," which must mean he had gone through an apprenticeship in New York. Samuel B. McCracken, editor of the *State Journal* from 1845 to 1855, described in an 1891 paper in the Michigan Pioneer and Historical Collections how these early apprenticeships worked.

"The printer's apprentice usually boarded with his master and slept in a bunk in the office. He was required to do the office chores, to cut and carry the wood for the use of the office, and to carry the papers in town, and in many cases he was required to cut the wood and do other chores at the house also. If in addition to this he did what was expected of him in the way of legitimate office work, he underwent a discipline not without its results in the formation of character. The mental discipline necessarily connected with his calling, the opportunities for reading, if improved, were supposed to fit him for the editor's chair."

The next year, 1839, the *Argus* temporarily stopped publishing, and the *Democratic Herald* became the party's mouthpiece. In 1843 the *Argus* resumed publication under the ownership of E. R. Powell and Orrin Arnold, with Gardiner again as editor. But internecine warfare between the left and right wings of the party kept the paper's management in a state of flux for the next three years. McCracken, writing a short history of the press in the *Local News and Advertiser,* a paper he started in 1857, explained, "Powell and Arnold got on very well for a few months, but being but boys, they had a flare-up and Powell quit. The office passed through various hands, alternating between Cole and Arnold, Cole and Bennett, changing so often that it's doubtful whether a process issued after banking hours on one day would have been good against the existing firm on the next."

*Argus* masthead. *(Courtesy of Bentley Historical Library.)*

McCracken continued, "The original diversion of the *Argus* from the true faith was not relished by many of the influential members of the Democratic party . . . who went by the common name of 'old hunkers.'"

The "old hunkers" did eventually win out. On January 28, 1846, Gardiner returned to power, this time with Cole, who had bought shares in the paper, as a partner. They wrote in their premiere issue: "In defiance of numerous obstacles we have been enabled to revive the *Michigan Argus* and with that name for our caption we again unfurl the Democratic banner." They went on to state that they supported "measures of Reform which we may deem advantageous to the people" but "oppose[d] measures which may be ostensibly brought forward under the specious garb of Reform, but are really designed only for hobbies [hobbyhorses], upon which unprincipled demagogues may ride into popular favor and ultimately into power."

Cole and Gardiner located the new incarnation of the *Argus* in the upper village, "a few rods north of the Exchange." Early Ann Arbor pictures show the *Argus* in an upstairs office on the corner of Huron and Main. Subscriptions to the four-page weekly were "$1.50 per annum, if paid in advance, $2.00 if not paid within six months, $2.50 if not paid at the expiration of the year."

The fortunes of the *Argus* rose and fell with the political tides. The big issue dividing Michigan Democrats at the time was the structure of the

Main Street, circa 1861. Note the Argus Printing Press sign on the roof of the building on the corner of Main and Huron. *(Courtesy of Bentley Historical Library.)*

court system and the selection of judges. Supporters of change locally included not only young people but notables such as state senators John Allen (who had set aside his anti-Masonic views to join the Democratic Party in 1839) and Samuel Denton, an abolitionist physician active in local affairs. The *Argus* and most local circuit judges, including William Fletcher (1836–42), George Miles (1846–50), and Edward Mundy (1848–51), opposed the shift. Only Alpheus Felch, a circuit court judge from 1842 to 1845 and then governor from 1846 to 1847, supported it.

Looking back on this period in a letter quoted in the 1881 county history, Cole wrote, "The new series of the *Argus* began at the time with judicial reform, when the present circuit court system was completely set aside. I called it a 'Judicial Revolution,' which it was; and the *Argus*, from the first issue, fought it until it was wiped out and dead. I suffered some for the course I pursued, but I was amply rewarded for my firmness afterward. The thing that was established was no 'reform'; it was a senseless revolution. It took some nerve, I confess, to stand the pressure brought to bear upon me, and for several months my subscription list only numbered about 50. To see about 80 of my own party marching to the polls under the banner of 'reform,' instigated by Dr. Denton and John Allen, and vote against Judge Felch and the Democratic ticket, gave me serious thoughts of the course I was about to take . . . but good counsel, such as Judges Mundy, Miles, Fletcher, Wilson and others, and my own sense of what should be done, determined me to go ahead, and I did, to the end of the foolish thing."

The judicial dispute was largely resolved by the new state constitution of 1850, and the Democratic rift was mended—much to the benefit of the erstwhile outcasts. By 1854 *Argus* subscriptions had risen from a low of fifty to a robust eighteen hundred.

Cole and Gardiner stayed with their middle-of-the-road Democratic politics, even opposing what were then seen as "radical" efforts to abolish slavery nationally. For "the stability of our happy Union," they urged "the North to avoid all action and language in reference to slavery which will unnecessarily irritate the South."

Slavery may seem an unusual subject for a small-town paper, but in fact most of the *Argus* was devoted to state and federal politics. Even foreign news was given more coverage than local events, which were barely noted; at that time, because the town was so small (population forty-five hundred in 1850), it was assumed that everyone knew what was happening locally.

After putting out the paper for eight and a half years, Cole and Gardiner sold it to Elihu Pond, best known today as the father of Irving and Allen Pond, the architects of the Michigan Union and Michigan League. Cole and Gardiner said little about the reasons for the change. Their parting editorial on June 29, 1854, said only, "Circumstances that need not be enumerated now indicate that the connection between ourselves and our patrons must be terminated." They departed as they had arrived, as diehard Democrats: "Wishing prosperity to the party whose principles we have endeavored in a feeble manner to sustain and health and happiness to our numerous friends, we close this last set of public duties."

Gardiner finished his career as a printer for the *Ann Arbor Journal*. He died in 1866. In the county history, Cole praised the partner "whose memory I shall always cherish with the kindliest feelings. . . . He was the first to sign the Martha Washington [temperance] pledge in Ann Arbor, and so far as I know, he never in the least deviated from it. He died as he lived—an honest man, a Christian, and one of the best temperance men."

Cole moved to Albion and established the *Albion Mirror*, which he published for the rest of his life, remaining a staunch Democrat. Mc-Cracken described Cole in 1891 as "one of the oldest newspaper men in the state actively engaged in the business." Cole died three years later, in 1894, at age eighty-one, working until the end. According to his obituary, "his last editorial work [was] a few days before his last and fatal illness."

# John Haarer Photography Studio

*Continuity and change on Liberty Street*

John Haarer, one of Ann Arbor's early photographers, showed that his artistry went beyond photography when he built an elegant brick storefront studio and home at 113 West Liberty. After surviving an attempt to tear it down for parking in the 1960s, the 1888 building is today home to the West Side Book Shop, with the upper stories a wonderful urban apartment.

Haarer was born in 1840 in Öschelbronn, in the German state of Württemberg. The son of a farmer, he was educated from ages eight to fourteen in the village school, where he "became thoroughly familiar with his native tongue and also quite adept in Latin," according to his sketch in the 1891 county history. At age twenty-one he immigrated to Ann Arbor, where he worked as an agricultural laborer and then as a section hand on the railroad. In 1861 he opened a photography business on the third floor of Mack and Schmid's store on the corner of Liberty and Main.

Ann Arbor's first photos were taken by traveling daguerreotypists. Introduced from France about 1840, Louis Daguerre's process produced a direct, mirrorlike image on a polished silver surface. Although these instant portraits had to be held in certain ways to be discernible and images were reversed, they quickly caught on all over the country. By 1846 Ann Arbor had its first resident photographer: an ad that year announced that "L. C. Goodale, having furnished himself with a supply of the best Material, is now prepared to take Likenesses at his residence, corner of Catharine and Fifth street."

Haarer started out making ambrotypes, a newer type of photograph that replaced daguerreotypes in the mid-1850s. Ambrotypes were easier to view than daguerreotypes and cheaper to make. Working with collodion, a newly developed base, spread on a piece of glass, the photographer produced an image that yielded a positive view when turned over and mounted on a black background. But like daguerreotypes, each ambrotype was unique and could not be reproduced.

The next step, which Haarer soon took, was to expose the glass plate

Haarer moved his studio to this modest frame building (*left*) in the mid-1870s. He replaced it in 1888 with the Romanesque structure that still exists at 113 West Liberty. (*Courtesy of Bentley Historical Library.*)

longer and then use it as a negative to make paper prints. The photo still had to be taken when the collodion was wet, though, so the photographer had to stay close to the darkroom. That's why most early photographs are studio poses. (To get his wonderful Civil War photos, Mathew Brady built a portable darkroom in a horse-drawn wagon.) Haarer had several backdrops that he could use to vary his shots. One extant picture, owned by the former occupants of the upstairs apartment, shows palm trees in the background. Another one, owned by Carolyn and Joseph Arcure, owners and restorers of the apartment, has a woodland scene with trees and flowers.

Haarer took both carte-de-visite and cabinet photos. The carte de visite became popular after 1854, when a French photographer devised a multiple-lens camera that allowed a number of poses to be recorded on a single plate, thus reducing printing costs. These small individual pictures were mounted on stiff cards about four by two and a half inches and used as calling cards. People began collecting them and saving them in albums. Cabinet cards—larger mounted photographs, usually four by five and a half inches—were introduced in 1866. Both the Arcures' photo and an early self-portrait of Haarer at the Bentley Library are cartes de visite; the one owned by the former tenants and another owned by Jay Platt, the owner of the West Side Book Shop, are cabinet cards large enough for back drops to show.

John Haarer posed proudly in late 1880s in front of his impressive new photography studio and bookstore on West Liberty. *(Courtesy of Bentley Historical Library.)*

Sometime in the mid-1870s Haarer moved his studio from Main Street to a two-story wooden building on Liberty midway between Main and Ashley. As was common at that time, he worked downstairs and lived upstairs. He married for the first time in 1871, but his wife died a year later. In 1875 he married Katherine Zimmer, a native of Canada, and they had seven children.

IN 1888 HAARER BUILT a beautiful new building to house both his business and his growing family. The story that has been passed down is that Haarer and Martin Noll, a shoe repairman, chipped in to buy a German lottery ticket and won. (Noll used his share to build the gorgeous Queen Anne house at 921 West Huron.)

Haarer moved his existing building onto another lot and then spared no expense on the new one. It was built in the Richardsonian Romanesque style, then much in vogue, with rounded arches above the windows, multicolored brick in ornate designs, and a front gable. Transom windows and fancy brass hardware were used both inside and out.

The upper two stories, which formed the family living quarters, included two parlors (one for everyday and one for important visitors), a kitchen, and a dining room on the second floor. An impressive marble-faced fireplace dominated the front parlor, which was separated from the rear parlor by pocket doors and beadboard. On the top floor a front master bedroom had room for a nursery; five smaller bedrooms were used by the older children. "I'm amazed they could raise so many kids there," says Genevieve Haarer Vergari, the widow of the couple's grandson Ernest. "The streets were dirt then. So was the alley. They turned kids loose. You couldn't keep them cooped up—they had to go out and play ball. There were no cars, just horses and buggies."

Haarer ran his business on the ground level, locating his studio and darkroom in the back with a reception area in front. His darkroom, now the restroom for the bookstore, still has amber transom lights. A door led to the staircase going up, so Haarer didn't have to leave the building to get to the family quarters.

The new store was large enough that Haarer added books and stationery to his offerings, with German books a specialty—Platt found a window shade in the basement that reads "German Book Handler." The books quickly became central to the business, as Haarer's biographical sketch in the county history three years later indicates.

> *There is nothing more fascinating to a love of ideas than a bookstore filled with the choice works of ancient and modern writers. Within their uncut pages are the treasures of all the ages. One of the most popular resorts in the city of Ann Arbor to the man or woman who loves books is that of which Mr. Haarer is the proprietor, he having a fine book and stationery establishment in the college city of Michigan.*

Haarer was wise to develop this second line of business to fall back on, because the year he moved into his new building, the Eastman Company introduced a dry film that could be put in a camera and used anytime. It freed the professional photographer from staying so close to the darkroom—and also launched the mass market for amateur photography. In 1888 Eastman began selling Kodak cameras that came with a hundred-exposure roll of film inside. After the film was shot, the customer would send in the whole camera, and Eastman would develop the film and send it back with new film inside. Suddenly almost anyone who wanted to could take photographs.

By 1898 Haarer was still selling books but had given up photography. Instead, he had begun selling insurance—a business that would stay in the family for three generations.

Haarer died in 1916 at age seventy-five, five years after suffering a paralyzing stroke. Two of his sons took over the business—Julius handling the insurance sales and Ernest the bookstore. (Ernest was later joined by his son, also named Ernest.) Two other sons, George, a partner in a clothing store, and Oscar, a pharmacist with Eberbach and Son, also lived in town. Julius and Oscar never married and shared the former family quarters above the store for the rest of their lives.

Oscar may not have strayed as far from the family business as it appears; it is likely that he got interested in producing medicines by seeing his father mix photographic chemicals. He sold some of his own creations out of his brothers' store. Platt found a blue bottle bearing a Haarer label in the basement, and it appears to contain some type of liquid medicine. A box of tins of Wonder Salve was also found. According to the label it was quite a panacea, recommended to treat "burns, sores, cuts, eczema, piles, rheumatism, carbuncles, ulcers, and wounds."

LEROY EHNIS RECALLS buying his schoolbooks in the 1920s and 1930s from Haarer's. But the main business in the years that followed was insurance of all kinds. Ads say the Haarers sold fire, auto, and casualty insurance. Vergari recalls the setup in the days when her husband was involved. There were two desks in the front room, with Julius sitting closest to the door on the right and Ernest, her husband, at a desk farther back. The back rooms were used for storage; display cases took up the rest of the front room. "Julius used to put sayings in the window, and people would stop and read and chuckle," recalls Vergari. "I think he got them from an old book."

In 1964 the city bought the building with the intention of tearing it down for a parking lot but gave Oscar and Julius permission to stay there for the rest of their lives. Julius died in 1966 and Oscar in 1967. By 1974 the city still had not torn down the building, so the Sesquicentennial Commission established its headquarters there (Ann Arbor, founded in 1824, turned 150 that year). After a year of events, displays, and meetings in the building, the city dropped the plan to demolish the building and sold it to Carolyn and Joseph Arcure.

The Arcures rented the downstairs to Jay Platt for his bookstore and began work on restoring the upstairs apartment for themselves. They brought back the fine features, still there but run down by years of neglect. They also made a few changes to open the place up more, creating a two-floor atrium by taking out the ceiling above the dining room and making a new master bedroom on the third floor by combining two of the small bedrooms.

By the time the Arcures did their restoration, the custom of store owners' living above their businesses had been virtually forgotten. Up-

More than a century later, the restored storefront is home to Jay Platt's West Side Book Shop; in the back room, Doug Price (*right*) sells antique photographs. *(Courtesy of Adrian Wylie.)*

stairs space downtown was usually relegated to storage or sometimes offices. Proponents of a stronger downtown wanted to encourage renewed residential use of the area, arguing that it would make for a safer, more vibrant, urban environment. Habits and regulations stood in the way, but downtown living finally caught on in the 1990s. Today the numbers of downtown apartments—and the prices people are willing to pay for them—have soared.

Downstairs, Platt is equally enthusiastic about his space, appreciating its history and character. He hired artist John Copley to create a sign appropriate for the age of the building and also to paint the name of the store on the window in a form that mirrors the architectural features of the building. In the back room where John Haarer had his studio, Doug Price now sells antique photographs.

# Hoelzle's Butcher Shop
# & Metzger's Restaurant

*It returned to German hands when it became part of Metzger's restaurant.*

One German American family followed in the footsteps of another when Metzger's German restaurant expanded into 201 East Washington in 1991. The brick building with the eye-catching turret that overlooks the corner of Washington Street and Fourth Avenue was built in 1883 by butcher J. Fred Hoelzle.

Hoelzle (1859–1943) came to Ann Arbor when he was seventeen and went to work for butcher John C. Gall at his store at 217 East Washington. Hoelzle married a relative of Gall's named Alice and took over the business when Gall retired. In 1893 he moved down the street to the new building at Fourth Avenue and renamed his shop the Washington Market. A 1905 promotional booklet about Ann Arbor boasted that he "supplied the tables of Ann Arbor with the best meat that the world produces, makes the best sausage on the market, keeps poultry and fish in season, gives a clean cut and full weight, is impartial and obliging and has the confidence of the best citizens."

Hoelzle advertised as a "dealer in fresh and salt meats, lard, sausage of all kinds." The salted meat he treated right on the premises. The sausage he also made himself, probably from authentic German recipes handed down from Gall. The fresh meat, brought in whole or in halves, was slaughtered in a space dedicated to this activity on the banks of the Huron River, east of the Broadway Bridge, and stored in big walk-in iceboxes behind the store. It took strong delivery men to lift the huge ice blocks, ranging from twenty-five to three hundred pounds, into place almost at ceiling level.

When Hoelzle moved into his new building, his was just one of eighteen meat markets in downtown Ann Arbor. Without transportation or good home cooling, most people shopped daily for fresh meat, preferably at a store within easy walking distance of their homes or jobs. Saturday nights were especially busy, with farmers coming into town to

Washington Street and Fourth Avenue in 1893. *(Courtesy of Bentley Historical Library.)*

stock up on supplies and townsfolk buying meat for their big Sunday dinners.

Cal Foster, who as a teenager worked at Merchants' Delivery, a horse-drawn delivery service, remembers picking up orders from the Washington Market. They were packed in wooden crates—which he describes as "heavier than the devil"—and delivered to student rooming houses, sororities, and fraternities.

Hoelzle sold his business in 1926 but continued to work at other meat markets as long as he was able. The building continued as a meat market under a succession of owners until the late 1940s. In the 1950s it was Sun Cleaners, then Martin's Gems and Minerals, and then Harry's Army Surplus, until Metzger's expanded from next door in 1991.

METZGER'S WAS FOUNDED in 1928 and moved to 203 East Washington in 1936. Founders William Metzger and Christian Kuhn both grew up in the village of Wilhelmsdorf, in southern Germany. They left to escape the inflation that wracked Germany in the 1920s. At Metzger's father's bakery in Wilhelmsdorf, customers needed a bushel of money just to buy a loaf of bread.

Metzger's first Ann Arbor job was at the bakery of his sponsor, Sam Heusel. (Heusel, the grandfather of radio personality Ted Heusel, sponsored most of the bakers who came during those years.) Metzger went on to work at the Michigan Union as a pastry chef (his pot washer was

Fred Hoelzle's butcher shop on Christmas Day, 1909. The staff had worked all night cutting fresh meat for their customers' holiday celebrations. *(Courtesy of Walter Metzger.)*

Bennie Oosterbaan). Meanwhile, Kuhn worked on a farm near Saline, then as a janitor at the U-M Hospital, and finally as a cook at Flautz's restaurant at 122 West Washington (at one time home of the Del Rio).

When Kuhn's boss, Reinhart Flautz, decided to go back to Germany, Kuhn and his friend Metzger rented the space and started their own restaurant, the "German American." Kuhn was the cook, and Metzger ran the dining room. The German American was right next door to the Old German restaurant, then still being run by founder Gottlob Schumacher. (Fritz Metzger, William's brother, bought it in 1946. A third brother, Gottfried, who also came over in the 1920s, ran the Deluxe Bakery, and, until he retired, made the dark pumpernickel bread served by both the Old German and Metzger's.)

Business was booming when Kuhn and Metzger started in 1928, but a year later the Depression hit. To survive, the partners had to serve three meals a day, 364 days a year (they closed for Christmas). Metzger's wife, Marie, helped with waitressing, cleaning, cooking, and public relations. Their workday started at 6 AM and ended at midnight. Luckily, the Metzgers and Kuhn, a bachelor, lived above the restaurant at both its locations, so they could usually go upstairs midafternoon to take a nap.

Post–World War II students enjoying a night out at Metzger's. Note the formality of their dress. *(Courtesy of Walter Metzger.)*

The building today. *(Courtesy of Stan Shackman.)*

In 1936, Flautz returned to Ann Arbor and wanted to reopen his old place. Metzger and Kuhn moved two blocks down, to 203 East Washington, and reopened as "Metzger's German American." By 1937, the business was doing well enough that the family decided they could close on Sundays. When World War II came, they further decreased their hours, opening only for dinner because help was so hard to find. Food was also scarce, and meat was rationed. Even after the war, Walter Metzger, William's son, remembers people waiting to buy meat at the next-door butcher shop in a line that went all the way down to Huron Street.

When Walter Metzger returned from World War II, he began working full-time at the restaurant. (He had started at age ten, washing dishes, cutting beans, peeling potatoes, and even pouring beer and wine at the bar.) In 1959, Kuhn and William Metzger retired, and Walter bought his father's share. Kuhn sold his share to his nephew, Fritz Kuenzle, who stayed until 1974. Walter's son, John, joined in 1975, becoming sole owner in 1986. Walter, although retired, still helped.

It was John who arranged for the expansion next door into the old meat market. His goal was twofold: to preserve the historical appearance of the building and to make the two parts work together. He redid the outside to match old photographs, while inside he continued the decorating scheme of steins and other German memorabilia from the original restaurant.

The most dramatic change, at least to passers-by, is the cow weather vane on the turret. In Hoelzle's day, a cow weather vane proudly indicated what he sold, but it had long ago disappeared. John and Walter Metzger had been looking for a replacement for some time when relatives found a perfect one in Boston and gave it to them to celebrate the opening of the expanded restaurant.

In 1999 Metzgers closed in Ann Arbor and later reopened in Scio Township, thus continuing the family tradition another generation. Their Washington Street store has been used for several different restaurants, but one thing has remained; the cow is still on the roof, demonstrating the history of the first two occupants.

# Prochnow's Dairy Lunch

### Grub for the workingman

**B**ack in the days when Courthouse Square was the center of town, Prochnow's Dairy Lunch, at 104 East Huron, was strategically placed as a casual eatery for the many workingmen in the area. "Everyone in town ate there," according to Derwood Prochnow, second cousin of Theodore Prochnow, the owner of the restaurant from 1902 to 1929 and 1937 to 1940.

The county's Victorian courthouse (1887–1955) sat in the middle of the block, surrounded by grass and trees, and it had identical entrances on all sides—Main, Ann, Fourth, and Huron. Anyone leaving from the Huron Street door could see Prochnow's Dairy Lunch right across the street. An interurban stop, a row of busy stores sandwiched between the Allenel Hotel and the Farmers and Mechanics Bank, and the courts and other government services all drew people to that block. Morrie Dalitz, driver for and later owner of the Varsity Laundry (on Liberty where the Federal Building now stands), remembers Huron Street between Fourth and Main as "busy and vibrant."

Prochnow's Dairy Lunch was tucked in behind the Farmers and Mechanics Bank in a building so narrow that there was no room for tables, just a horseshoe-shaped counter. However, the restaurant boasted many accoutrements that today are de rigueur for fancy yuppie restaurants: pressed-tin ceiling, ornate cash register, marble counters, wainscoting on the lower wall, and fancy mirrored coat racks.

Theodore Prochnow is remembered by his cousin as "not tall, about five-nine or five-ten. He walked with a limp because he was crippled in one leg, but he was a strong man. He ran the Dairy Lunch for years as the number-one operator." The kitchen was in the back. Daiitz remembers the sight of Prochnow cooking away, a cigar hanging out of his mouth.

Prochnow opened the restaurant in 1902, when he was only twenty-seven years old. He began in partnership with Otto Schaible, but by 1909 he was the sole owner. He operated the restaurant until 1929, when, tired of the daily grind, he sold it and started the Prochnow Food Specialty

For almost four decades, Theodore Prochnow's lunch counter was part of a "busy and vibrant" block opposite the old courthouse. This photo was taken near the end of World War I; Prochnow is probably the man third from left. *(Courtesy of Doug Price.)*

Company. But in 1937 he was back at the restaurant. The interim owners, first Fred Slade and then Raymond Smith and Thomas Fohey, weren't able to make a go of it during the Depression.

Prochnow served full meals, mainly breakfasts and lunches, but nothing fancy. There was no liquor, and it was not the sort of restaurant people went to in the evenings or on dates. In fact, it was "men only," according to Bertha Welker, who remembers the restaurant well because her older sister dated an employee, Ben Oliver. "It was a men's luncheon place," Welker explains. "Women didn't go out much in those days."

Derwood Prochnow describes the fare as "food the workingman wanted, food that filled his ribs"—meat, potatoes, gravy, and vegetables. He reports that Prochnow "didn't monkey with salad." Dessert was homemade pies. Overall, he rates the food as "good grub."

Dalitz gives a dissenting opinion: he remembers once finding a cigar butt in his oatmeal. Feeling sick but not wanting to offend Prochnow (who was a good Varsity Laundry customer), Dalitz just stepped out for some air until he felt better. "I couldn't eat oatmeal for a long time after that," he recalls.

Dalitz remembers that pancakes, both regular and buckwheat, were Prochnow specialties. He also remembers revolving specials according to the day of the week—for instance, "terrible liver on Thursday." According to Dalitz, the draw of the restaurant was the low prices.

Of course, a mainstay of this kind of casual restaurant was coffee. Derwood Prochnow says that the Dairy Lunch was famous for having "the best coffee east of the Mississippi." His cousin bought it in barrels from a supplier in the East and put his own label on it. One of the main offerings of Prochnow's specialty food business was the coffee.

The Dairy Lunch customers were mainly people working or doing business in the area—at the courthouse, the Farmers' Market (then located on the Fourth Avenue side of the courthouse), or the many businesses on Prochnow's side of the block. These included two telegraph offices, two cigar stores (one reputed to run a betting operation on the side), a photography studio, real estate offices, a barber, a tailor, and a cab company.

Dalitz remembers other customers: farmers coming to town for the day, truck drivers, milk wagon operators, construction workers, and policemen who worked nearby in the old city hall at Huron and Fifth (kitty-corner from the present one). While there were other food places on the block, they were not in direct competition. Court Cafe served more snack-type food, like sandwiches and hamburgers, while Candyland's specialties were sweets and ice cream treats like banana splits and tin roofs.

Prochnow finally left the business for good in 1940. He died four years later. During the years he was feeding Ann Arbor, other Prochnows were also making their marks. His cousin David, father of Derwood, owned the Prochnow Grocery Store at 208 South Ashley, next to Hertler Brothers farm supply store (now the Downtown Home and Garden). Another relative, Walter Prochnow, started Ann Arbor Buick in 1923.

Today, the block where Prochnow's Dairy Lunch was once part of a busy business district has been swallowed up by two monumental buildings, the First of America Bank, facing Main, and the Courthouse Square Senior Apartments, facing Fourth. The small gap between them where Prochnow's once stood is now First of America's parking lot.

# Justin Trubey *&* the Ice Cream Trade

*His Main Street parlors and west side factory were summer favorites.*

In the days before home refrigeration, ice cream was a rare delicacy. Available at only a few places in town, it was usually consumed right where it was made, either at an ice cream parlor or at summertime ice cream socials. "We didn't have ice cream much," recalls senior citizen Florence Haas. "It was a treat for us when we were kids."

When Ann Arbor's senior citizens were children, an important purveyor of this treat was Justin Trubey. He was proprietor of Trubey's Confectionary, first at 116 South Main (1909–16) and then at 218 South Main (1917–23) and later owned the wholesale Trubey Ice Cream Company, 438 Third Street (1923–32).

Justin and Sarah Trubey moved to Ann Arbor in 1909, probably to be near good medical care, since their son, Harold, was sickly as a child. They came from Jewell, Ohio, where Justin had run a grocery store and Sarah had been postmistress. Trubey's brother, Barevius Trubey, owned a creamery in nearby Sherwood, Ohio, which was most likely where Trubey learned to make ice cream.

Trubey took over an existing ice cream parlor on Main Street. Assisted by his wife and son, he made ice cream and candy on the premises and also served light lunches. At the time, ice cream was steadily gaining in popularity. Although known to Europeans since Marco Polo brought a sherbet recipe home from the Far East in the thirteenth century, ice cream was rarely consumed by the general population until the middle of the nineteenth century. That was when a string of inventions—first the hand-cranked ice cream freezer and later electricity and commercial refrigeration units—made ice cream quicker and cheaper to produce.

As ice cream became more available, various methods of serving it were devised. Most innovations started as the solution to a problem. In 1880 the ice cream soda was invented by Detroit's Fred Sanders when he substituted ice cream for plain cream in a carbonated drink because his cream supply had turned sour. The sundae followed in 1890 as a re-

Justin Trubey (*foreground*) and his son and daughter-in-law, Harold and Elsa Trubey, in Trubey's Confectionary, 116 South Main Street, 1910. *(Courtesy of Doug Trubey.)*

placement for sodas, which some responsible citizens considered too stimulating for Sunday consumption. The ice cream cone surfaced at the 1904 World's Fair, when an ice cream vendor ran out of bowls and began wrapping the ice cream in waffles.

TRUBEY'S ICE CREAM PARLOR met all these tastes, selling cones, sodas, and sundaes as well as plain ice cream. Its main competitor was the Sugar Bowl restaurant across the street. The Sugar Bowl was fancier and sold a larger variety of food, but many of Trubey's customers, especially children, felt more comfortable in the simpler establishment. According to Edith Kempf, "Trubey's was not fancy, but it was thought to be very clean. And the ice cream was very good."

Frieda Saxton remembers that she "lived for" visits to Trubey's. On Sunday afternoons her dad would give her a dime. Then, accompanied by girlfriends, she would walk to Trubey's from her family's home on First Street and order a bowl of tutti-frutti ice cream—a multicolored, multiflavored concoction of vanilla ice cream and candied fruit.

After fourteen years of operating the ice cream parlor, Trubey decided to concentrate on the manufacturing end. In 1923 he moved his equipment to a factory he had built behind his home at 438 Third Street. The confectionary on Main was taken over by Mack and Company, the department store next door, which used the space to expand its dry goods department.

Trubey's ice cream factory was a very primitive operation by today's standards. Its equipment consisted of two ice cream machines and a sink. The only employees were Trubey and his son, Harold, who by that time had married Elsa Aprill, an employee of the ice cream parlor.

Harold Trubey's son, Bob Trubey, remembers watching his father and grandfather make the ice cream. He says they used a liquid mix to which cream, sugar, and flavoring were added. Vanilla, strawberry, and chocolate were the mainstays, although in later years they experimented with more exotic flavors like pistachio. After the ice cream was made, it was placed in the cold storage room, which the Trubeys had insulated with four-inch-thick cork. Ammonia coolant was piped through coils

### Summertime Ice Cream Socials

*In the early years of the century, ice cream socials were eagerly anticipated by children seeking to supplement their meager ice cream consumption. Bertha Walker remembered that before she was old enough to go to ice cream parlors her main source of ice cream was ice cream socials held at the German Park off Madison, near her family's home on Sixth Street. Her dad gave each of the kids in the family a nickel, and they would line up to buy the confection at a shanty set up for the purpose. They found the ice cream quite satisfactory, although vanilla was usually the only choice.*

*Frieda Saxton remembered going to wonderful raspberry socials out on Dexter Road, just past Maple. The annual event was a fund-raiser for the Masons, hosted by a Mr. and Mrs. Johnson, raspberry growers who were very active in the group. Eating fresh raspberries over ice cream was a treat she looked forward to all year.*

*Edith Kempf remembered that Ann Arbor churches did not host ice cream socials but left that activity for the country churches. Her favorite was one that is still going, as of this writing, at Bethel United Church of Christ, near Manchester.*

in the room from a compressor in the basement. An office in front also served as a retail outlet, mainly for neighbors.

Harold Trubey's other son, Dorwin Trubey, remembers that after classes got out at Bach School on Fourth Street, groups of his classmates would sometimes follow him over to his grandfather's factory two blocks away. Justin Trubey would welcome the young delegations by giving each child a freshly made "smile," today called a Dixie cup.

Most of Trubey's ice cream was sold wholesale. Using Dodge trucks, which he said always started best, he delivered ice cream all around town, to stores and restaurants, sororities and fraternities, traveling as far afield as Groomes Beach at Whitmore Lake. The trucks weren't refrigerated, so the ice cream was packaged in heavy five-gallon galvanized metal containers placed inside a wooden crate and surrounded by ice with rock salt sprinkled on top.

In 1932 Trubey's merged with McDonald's Ice Cream, a Flint firm with a branch on Main Street near the stadium. Two years later, Justin Trubey died of cancer, but Harold continued with McDonald's for the rest of his working life. The Trubey factory building continued to be used, either for small manufacturing operations or for storage.

In 1978, when John and Elsa Stafford bought the building and remodeled it, they found the four-inch cork insulation in the cold storage room still intact and one of the walk-in coolers still there—remnants of the building's original use.

# Recreation and Culture

# Otto's Band

*Playing "The Victors" in manuscript and sending soldiers off to war, they gave the city its sound track for half a century.*

On a temporary stage illuminated by gasoline lamps, Otto's Band gave summer concerts on the county courthouse lawn in the early decades of the twentieth century. The audience, who in the days before radio and record players had few opportunities to hear music, was very appreciative of all the pieces, but the highlight was always "The Holy City." Everyone was quiet as bandleader Louis Otto rose and played the sentimental religious solo on his cornet. When Otto finished, he was answered by Ray Haight, playing his trumpet from the Allenel Hotel across Huron Street. "It was the most beautiful thing I ever heard," Ralph Lutz, who played in the band, recalled in a 1974 interview. "I'll never forget it."

Otto's Band, under slightly varying names, entertained townsfolk and commemorated important events for almost fifty years. Henry Otto Sr. started the band in 1875, and his son Louis took over in 1895. The musicians, numbering about twenty, marched in parades, provided music for dances, gave concerts, and sent soldiers off to the Spanish-American War and World War I. Under Louis's leadership they became a professional band, the first local members of the musicians' union. Among their many accomplishments is the honor of being the first to play the U-M fight song, "The Victors."

Music was a vital part of German American culture. Marion Otto McCallum, niece of Louis Otto and daughter of band member Henry Otto Jr., recalls that "a good share of the population" came out to see the band whenever it played. "There were other little bands, but Otto's was *the* band as far as I can see," McCallum explains. "It was a good part of our living at that young age."

ACCORDING TO FAMILY STORIES, Henry Otto Sr. left Germany because he was tired of fighting for the king. He first came to North America during the Civil War era and lived in New Hamburg, Ontario, near Strat-

Henry Otto's band in front of the old courthouse. *(Courtesy of Bentley Historical Library.)*

ford. In 1870 Henry moved to Ann Arbor with his brothers, Valentine and Jonas. He returned to Canada in 1872 but came back here for good in 1875 after receiving an offer to join Jacob Gwinner's band.

Henry and his wife, Margaret—also a German immigrant who'd initially settled in Canada—built a house at 558 South Fifth Avenue. Today, Fingerle Lumber takes up most of the neighborhood, but at the time it was still pasture and swamp. When he wasn't playing music, Henry Otto was a blacksmith who specialized in shoeing horses. He carried on his trade at 215 South Ashley, later the site of the Schwaben Halle, with his sons Jonas and George.

Otto played many different instruments, but the violin was his favorite. He taught all of his six children to play instruments and formed his four sons into a youth marching band. After Jacob Gwinner died, Otto formed his own group with son Jonas, then fifteen, as one of the players. He led the Ann Arbor City Band for twenty years before passing the baton to another son, Louis. Henry Sr., who by then was fifty-five years old, was probably quite willing to give up marching, and Jonas, thirty-five, was also willing to leave it to younger members of the family. Louis, who was just sixteen years old when he took over, played the cornet and trombone; another brother, Henry Otto Jr., played the tuba in the new group.

WHEN LOUIS OTTO took over, the band was a small group that played primarily for fun. Under his leadership it grew into a highly skilled, professional organization.

The younger Otto initially named his group the Washtenaw Times Band, presumably after a newspaper sponsor. In 1901 he found a long-term sponsor—the Masonic lodge to which most of the players belonged —and renamed the group Otto's Knights Templar Band.

Both Louis and Henry Jr. lived near their father and could easily consult him on music matters. Louis lived at 402 Benjamin Street; he had a day job as a painter at the Walker carriage factory on Liberty. Henry Jr. lived at 818 Brown and worked at Sauer Lumber Company, just west of his parents' house on Fifth, doing finish carpentry, such as trim work on doors. The Sauers must have been understanding bosses: McCallum remembers that her dad had no trouble getting off work to play engagements.

McCallum's family had one of the first telephones in the neighborhood, because her dad had to know about practice sessions and performance dates. "He practiced a couple nights a week," she recalls. "He'd come home from work and get dressed for practice and walk into town." If a concert was scheduled, "he'd leave the house with perfectly pressed pants [and] shined shoes. He'd be dusty or snowy when he returned, but when he left, he was perfect." In rain or freezing cold, Otto's musicians always met their commitments. "All that walking, carrying all those heavy instruments—how did they ever get around without collapsing in the heat or cold?" she wonders today.

After a performance, band members sometimes gathered in Henry Jr.'s living room to continue playing. "My brother Nelson and I would sit on the staircase," McCallum recalls. "We didn't dare bother them. It was very serious, professional playing."

Townsfolk celebrated most holidays with the help of Otto's Band. On Memorial Day the band paraded to and from Forest Hill Cemetery to honor soldiers of past wars. Louis Otto played taps, which another musician echoed from farther away. A 1914 picture shows the band returning from the cemetery, marching down North University toward State, with a boy riding a bike alongside. The rider is Henry Jr.'s son Jonas—who later got into trouble with his dad for riding so close.

On the Fourth of July the band played at Island Park. It was credited with making the island a popular picnic spot. Once, when band member Julius Weinberg was preparing to set off fireworks, a prankster beat him to it, causing much consternation among the band members, some of whom had to hide behind trees to escape injury. On Labor Day they

Louis Otto's band marching down North University, returning from playing at a Forest Hill Cemetery Memorial Day program. Note Jonas Otto, son of one of the band members, riding his bicycle near the band. He was later reprimanded. *(Courtesy of Bentley Historical Library.)*

marched from downtown to the Schwaben Park at Madison and Fifth for the annual picnic of labor union members. In between were the summer courthouse municipal concerts, which sometimes included group singing led by the band. After automobiles became popular, some attendees listened from cars parked around the courthouse and added to the applause by honking their horns.

During the winter the band played indoors at weddings and at the Masons' ball, held yearly at the armory. A smaller group, about half the band, also played for the skaters at Fred Weinberg's ice rink at Fifth and Hill (Weinberg was married to Henry Otto Sr.'s daughter Mary; Julius was his son). The players sat in a little hut in the middle of the ice, closing the windows periodically so they could get warm.

OTTO'S BAND WAS COMPOSED of townsfolk, and all were Germans or of German ancestry. At that time, town and gown generally kept to themselves—but they would come together to make music. Thanks to such a collaboration in 1898, Otto's Band was the first to play "The Victors," composed by U-M music major Louis Elbel.

Elbel and Louis Otto were friends. "I remember my father telling of Louis Elbel writing 'The Victors' and coming down to our [house] and playing it for father's comments," Louis's son Ferdinand recalled in a written reminiscence. Working from Elbel's manuscript, Otto's Band played "The Victors" at the very next U-M football game, and the song became part of the band's concert repertoire.

Otto's Band played frequently at early U-M football games, either on its own or supplementing the U-M band when there were not enough student players. "In nineteen two, three, four, townspeople made up about a quarter of the band," says Bob MacGregor, who has done extensive research on the history of the U-M band. In 1905 Otto's Band and the U-M band both went to Chicago for a game. A section of the stands collapsed, and the musicians ended up helping with first aid more than playing music.

In 1914 Ann Arbor musicians organized a branch of the American Federation of Musicians, Local 625. Otto's became the first union band in the city, and Louis Otto was elected the union's first president.

Three years later the United States declared war on Germany and entered World War I. If the German American band members felt any misgivings, they gave no public sign. Otto's Band played a prominent role in Ann Arbor's public commemorations of the war. On August 15, 1917, the *Ann Arbor News* reported that an estimated ten thousand people gathered to say good-bye to a group of recruits leaving for training at Camp Grayling. "Hundreds walked to the station alongside the marching troops," the paper wrote, "headed by Otto's Band, and keeping step to martial music."

When the war ended in 1918, Otto's Band was again out in full force. After parading through Ann Arbor, the band was asked to come to Chelsea to help the village celebrate.

Otto's Band is believed to have played for the last time on June 30, 1922, at the laying of the cornerstone for the Masonic Temple on Fourth Avenue (replaced in the late 1970s by the Federal Building parking lot). Though only in his forties, Louis Otto died two years later, in 1924.

No recording was ever made of Otto's Band, but people who played in or heard the band remembered it and talked of it the rest of their lives. Robert Steeb recalls how his father-in-law, band member Ernest Bethke, used to chuckle about a mistake he once made when marching south on Main. The band turned smartly onto Packard—all except for Bethke, who missed the turn and, to his chagrin, found himself marching alone down Main Street.

# Ann Arbor's Municipal Beach

*When thousands swam in Argo Pond*

"It was a lot, *a lot*, of fun," says Barbara Hepner Preston, remembering the summers she hung out at Ann Arbor's municipal beach in the late 1930s and early 1940s. Now the boat launch at Argo Park, the beach was on the banks of the Huron River, just north of the canoe livery. Preston and her sister, Gerry Hepner True, lived on Pontiac Trail and would go to the beach every day in the summer. "We'd walk down in the morning, go home for lunch, then go back. Sometimes we'd even go back in the evening."

The beach was a gift from Detroit Edison, which had bought the present Argo Dam in 1905 to generate electricity. In 1917, the company offered to develop the beach if the city would pay for its upkeep. The city accepted the offer, and Edison trucked in loads of sand and built a pier, three docks, and a beach house. The city paid a nominal rent of $1 a year before eventually buying the facility in 1938 for $100.

"On hot summer days you'd have to stand in line to get in," recalls True. Former lifeguard Dick Tasch adds, "On a good Sunday or holiday you could have more than a thousand [people]. There was not that much room for sunbathing, but lots of room in the water. Some would come for half an hour or an hour. There was a continuous flow."

Many of the regulars were from the north side (Lower Town), but kids from all over the city swam there. Some cut across Argo Dam from North Main, while others crossed the Broadway Bridge and came up along the millrace. Although hoboes camped along the millrace, Tasch remembers only one bad incident. "Once a little girl came running out screaming with a hobo behind. We called the police and Red Howard showed up in a car." Howard made sure the perpetrator and his closest cohorts were on the next train out of town.

The docks were placed in increasingly deeper water—the first at four feet, the next at about eight feet, and the last at twelve feet. Swimmers had to pass proficiency tests to go out to the deeper docks. "They could do any stroke—crawl, breaststroke—as long as they got out there and back," recalls Bob Ryan, lifeguard in the summer of 1942. The last dock

Collage: Bob Ryan, muncipal beach lifeguard in 1942, from his commanding view at the end of the pier, could see swimmers all the way out to "Clever's Folly," the artificial island. *(Courtesy of Bob Ryan.)*

had a tall tower, about ten feet. Getting the courage to dive from it was a real rite of passage.

Regulars fondly remember the beach manager, parks department employee Joe Bowen. "He was a nice, pleasant man," says Ryan, adding, "He didn't take any guff from kids. If they acted up, they couldn't come back for maybe a week."

Bowen must have worked incredible hours; people remember him being there whenever the beach was open, seven days a week. He kept an eye on the whole operation but was usually at the front desk, giving out lockers and renting towels and suits ("cotton with purple stripes that you'd not be caught dead in," Tasch remembers). Sometimes the Hepner girls helped at the front desk, just for fun.

Lifeguard Tasch usually sat at the end of the pier with the rowboat next to him, but on really busy days he would stay in the boat between the second and third docks. "Deep water is where the most trouble was," he recalls. Although Tasch was a parks employee and the swimming teachers were hired by the recreation department, they worked together.

The teachers spelled him every few hours, and he in turn coached the kids on their swimming when the beach wasn't too busy.

The lifeguards and the kids who came regularly got to know each other pretty well. "They were a fine bunch," Tasch recalls. "I had no trouble with rowdy or bad kids." He dubbed them the "hillbillies" because most of them lived up the hill on Longshore (then called "Cedar") or on Pontiac. Tasch sometimes brought his lunch, but often "the hillbillies would fight over who would go home and make me a sandwich. I liked that better."

When people wanted a break from swimming, the beach had a volleyball court, horseshoe courts, a slide, and a grassy place under a willow for picnics (the tree is still there). Gerry True remembers bonfires on the beach, where she and her friends would roast marshmallows and hot dogs and drink Kool-Aid. The high point of the summer, remembered by almost everyone who used the beach, was the swimming races. True still has some of the ribbons she won.

No food was sold at the beach, probably because Bowen already had enough to do. For a time Ryan's half brother, Don Blair, and Herb Wetherbee, who owned the land directly across the street from the beach, ran a pop and candy stand. But most of the time the kids went next door to what was then the Saunders Canoe Livery for pop, potato chips, or candy. Owners William and Gladys Saunders got to know the regulars so well that once a year they treated them to a cookout breakfast. "We'd take several, maybe six, canoes down the river about a half or two-thirds of a mile and build a campfire, and Mrs. Saunders would cook us bacon and eggs," True recalls. "It was something to look forward to."

In 1936, when Detroit Edison drained Argo Pond to repair the dam, the city took the opportunity to improve the beach, cleaning the river bottom of debris, deepening it, and bringing in clean sand. The next winter the city built an island dubbed Clever's Folly after alderman Arbie Clever, who had pushed for the beach improvements. "They hauled sidewalk cement, sand, and gravel, and put it on the ice," recalls neighbor Laurie Howley. "It dropped when the ice melted." A lawn was planted on the island, and the older kids loved swimming out to lie on the grass in the sun. "An old gentleman mowed it," recalls Tasch. "I'd take him out in the boat with a hand mower."

When the beach closed for the season, employees would take down the docks and store them for the winter. Tasch remembers that the deepest dock was the hardest to put up and take down. He recalls almost losing Bowen one time. "Joe was on the third dock holding a crowbar when he slipped and fell in. When he didn't come up, I dove in. I found him standing on the bottom, holding the crowbar. I told him, 'If you'd let go of the crowbar, you'd have come right up.'"

Tasch recalls that in his time the water was pretty clean. If present standards had applied then, though, the beach would probably never have opened. Pollution control efforts have cleaned up the river tremendously in the past few decades, but even now there are times when the Huron's bacteria count is too high for swimming.

Council minutes show that questions about water quality were raised in 1940, when the city was considering plans for a new beach house. The new structure was never built, and the beach closed for good at the end of the 1948 season. The buildings were demolished four years later.

Today, a small island in Argo Pond is all that remains of the municipal beach. Clever's Folly is now totally overgrown, and birds nest where local teens once sunbathed.

# The Roy Hoyer Dance Studio

*A taste of Broadway in Ann Arbor*

Performers tap dancing on drums or flying out over the audience on swings, women in fancy gowns and plumes floating onto the stage to the strains of "A Pretty Girl Is Like a Melody." A Busby Berkeley musical on Broadway? No, it was right here in Ann Arbor at the Lydia Mendelssohn theater: *Juniors on Parade*, a Ziegfeld-style production created by Broadway veteran Roy Hoyer to showcase the talents of his dance students and to raise money for worthy causes.

Hoyer came to Ann Arbor in 1930, at age forty-one. With his wrap-around camel hair coat, starched and pleated white duck trousers, open-necked shirts, and even a light touch of makeup, he cut a cosmopolitan figure in the Depression-era town. For almost twenty years, his Hoyer Studio initiated Ann Arbor students into the thrills of performance dancing as well as the more sedate steps and social graces of ballroom dancing.

Born in Altoona, Pennsylvania, Hoyer appeared in many hometown productions before a role as Aladdin in a musical called *Chin Chin* led him to a contract with New York's Ziegfeld organization. His fifteen-year Broadway career included leading roles in *Tip-Top*, *Stepping Stones*, *Criss Cross*, *The Royal Family*, and *Pleasure Bound*. Movie musical star Jeanette MacDonald was discovered while playing opposite Hoyer in *Angela*. But Hoyer himself by the end of the 1920s was getting too old to play juvenile leads. When the Depression devastated Broadway—in 1930, fifty fewer plays were produced than in 1929—Hoyer, like many other actor-dancers, was forced to seek his fortune elsewhere.

HOYER CAME TO Ann Arbor because he already had contacts here. In the 1920s he had choreographed the Michigan Union Opera, a very popular annual all-male show with script and score by students. His Roy Hoyer Studio taught every kind of dancing, even ballet (although the more advanced toe dancers usually transferred to Sylvia Hamer). On the strength of his stage career, he also taught acrobatics, body building, weight reducing classes, musical comedy, and acting.

The Floradora Sextette takes a bow. *Left to right:* Nancy Cory, Tommy Moore, Jean Reynolds, Douglas Wilson, Barbara Barr, Freddie Nickels, Beverly Tupper, Bobby Kuhn, Dolly Vlesides, Lauren Wolf, Patricia Riley, and Dickie Gauss. *(Courtesy of Bob Kuhn.)*

His sales pitch played up his Broadway background: "There are many so-called dance instructors, but only a few who have ever distinguished themselves in the art they profess to teach," he wrote in his program notes for *Juniors on Parade*. "Mr. Hoyer's stage work and association with some of the most famous and highest paid artists in America reflects the type of training given in the Roy Hoyer School."

Pictures of Hoyer on the Broadway stage lined his waiting room, and former students remember that he casually dropped names like Fred and Adele, referring to the Astaire siblings. (Fred Astaire did know Hoyer but evidently not well. When Hoyer dressed up his 1938 *Juniors on Parade* program with quotes from letters he'd received from friends and former students, the best he could come up with from Astaire was, "Nice to have heard from you.")

Hoyer's first Ann Arbor studio was in an abandoned fraternity house at 919 Oakland. He lived upstairs. Pat Bird Allen remembers taking lessons in the sparsely furnished first-floor living room. In 1933 the Hoyer Studio moved to 3 Nickels Arcade, above the then–post office. Students would climb the stairs, turn right, and pass through a small reception area into a studio that ran all the way to Maynard. Joan Reilly Burke remembers that there were no chairs in the studio, making it hard for people taking social dancing not to participate. Across the hall was a practice room used for private lessons and smaller classes.

Back then, young people needed to know at least basic ballroom steps if they wanted to have any kind of social life. John McHale, who took lessons from Hoyer as a student at University High, says that for years afterward he could execute a fox trot or a waltz when the occasion demanded. Dick DeLong remembers that Hoyer kept up with the latest dances, for instance, teaching the Lambeth Walk, an English import popular in the early years of World War II. (DeLong recalls Hoyer taking the boys aside and suggesting that they keep their left-hand thumbs against their palms when dancing so as not to leave sweaty handprints on their partners' backs.)

Hoyer's assistants were Bill Collins and Betty Hewett, both excellent dancers. Burke remembers that when the two demonstrated social dancing, their students were "just enchanted." Several ballroom students remember the thrill of dancing with football star Tom Harmon. As a performer in the Union Opera, Harmon came up to the studio for help in learning his dance steps and while there obliged a few of the female ballroom students. "I'll never forget it," says Janet Schoendube.

WHILE BALLROOM DANCING was mostly for teens or preteens, tap and ballet students ranged from children who could barely walk to young adults in their twenties. (Helen Curtis Wolf remembers taking her younger brother Lauren to lessons when he was three or four.) Classes met all year round, but the high point of the year was the annual spring production, *Juniors on Parade*.

The show was sponsored by the King's Daughters, a service group that paid the up-front costs and then used the profits for charity—medical causes in the early years and British war relief later. The three evening performances and one matinee were packed, and not just with the parents of the performers. During the drab Depression, people looked forward to Hoyer's extravaganzas all year long. Hoyer "jazzed us up when we needed it," recalls Angela Dobson Welch.

*Juniors on Parade* was a place to see and be seen. In 1933 the *Ann Arbor News* called it a "social event judging by the list of patrons and patronesses and the list of young actors and actresses whose parents are socially prominent." But the show's appeal wasn't limited to high society. Even in the midst of the Depression many less well-to-do families managed to save the money for lessons or worked out other arrangements in lieu of payment. Allen's mother helped make costumes; senior dance student Mary Meyers Schlecht helped teach ballroom dancing;

Roy Hoyer as he was pictured on the programs. *(Courtesy of Mike Collins.)*

Rosemary Malejan Pane, the acrobat who soloed in numbers that included cartwheels and splits, was recruited by Hoyer, who offered her free lessons when he learned she couldn't afford to pay.

The first act of the show featured younger children, wearing locally made costumes, while the second act showcased the more advanced students, who wore professional costumes. Every year Hoyer and Collins traveled to Chicago to select the dancers' outfits. For one 1935 number, the girls wore gowns that duplicated those worn by such famous stars as Ruby Keeler, Dolores Del Rio, and Carole Lombard. Live piano music was provided either by Georgia Bliss (on loan from Sylvia Hamer) or Paul Tompkins.

Sixty-some years later, students still remember such Hoyer-created numbers as "Winter Wonderland," a ballet featuring Hoyer and Betty Seitner, who stepped out of a snowball; "Floradora," six guys pushing baby buggies; "Sweethearts of Nations," eight girls in costumes from different countries, including red-haired Doris Schumacher Dixon as an Irish lass and Angela Dobson Welch as a Dutch girl. In "Toy Shop," dancers dressed like dolls; in another number, five girls, including Judy Gushing Newton and Nancy Hannah Cunningham, were done up in matching outfits and hairdos as the Dionne quintuplets.

*Juniors on Parade* ended with a high-kicking Rockettes-style chorus line of senior students. Then the stars returned home to their normal lives. Although some of them became very good dancers, none went on to careers in dance. (Doris Dixon later worked at Radio City Music Hall and was offered a job as a Rockette, but she turned it down when she saw how hard it was.)

The last big show was in 1941. When the war started, Hoyer cut back on his studio schedule and went to work at Argus Camera, where they were running two shifts building military equipment. He worked in the lens centering area and is remembered by former Argus employee Jan Gala as "a lot of fun, full of jokes." Another employee, Catherine Starts, remembers that "he was so graceful. He took rags and danced around with them."

AFTER THE WAR Hoyer kept his studio open, but people who knew him remember he did very little teaching in those years. His health was failing, and his former cadre of students and stars had moved on to college and careers.

In 1949 ill health led him to move back to Altoona. He worked as assistant manager at a hotel there and then as a floor manager and cashier at a department store. He was still alive in 1965, when an Altoona newspaper reported that he was back home after a nine-month hospital stay.

ALTHOUGH IT HAS BEEN forty-five years since Hoyer left Ann Arbor, he is not forgotten. Hoyer Studio alumni say they still use their ballroom dancing on occasion, and even the tappers sometimes perform. Angela Welch remembers a party in the 1980s at which the Heath sisters, Harriet and Barbara, back in town for a visit, reprised their Hoyer tap dance number. And years after the studio closed, accompanist Paul Tompkins worked as a pianist at Weber's Inn. Whenever he recognized a Hoyer alumna coming in, he started playing "A Pretty Girl Is Like a Melody."

# The Broadway Bridge Parks

*The area around the Broadway Bridge was once home to factories, junk-yards, and hoboes. Its transformation into three riverfront parks is one of the city's longest running sagas of civic improvement.*

The Broadway Bridge, connecting the central part of Ann Arbor with the north, spans the Huron River at a historically busy spot. Potawatomi trails converged to ford the river there. When John Allen and Elisha Rumsey came west from Detroit in 1824, looking for a place to found a town, they, too, crossed the river at this spot. The first bridge was built just four years later. Replaced and widened several times since, it was most recently redone in 2004. In 1830, Anson Brown, a pioneer who settled in Ann Arbor after working on the Erie Canal, dammed the river upstream from the bridge. Brown; his brother-in-law, Edward Fuller; and Colonel Dwight Kellogg used the flow from the dam to power a flour mill located just west of the bridge. Brown had grandiose ideas about turning the north side into the center of the city, but he died in the cholera epidemic of 1834, before his dreams could be realized. In 1839 William Sinclair purchased the property, repairing the mill and in-stalling new machinery. His new setup worked so well that after the 1841 harvest he shipped to New York, via the Erie Canal, 8,112 barrels of flour—a record for Ann Arbor up to that time.

SINCLAIR'S MILL WAS DESTROYED by a fire in 1860, but he quickly re-built it and was back in business the next season. The next owners were the Swift family, first Franklin and then his son John Marvin. In 1892 the mill became part of a conglomerate. The Ann Arbor Milling Com-pany, later called the Michigan Milling Company, bought it, along with several other mills in the area, and renamed it Argo. In 1903 they improved the mill and built a new dam, but again, fire claimed the mill. They rebuilt the mill, but with the development of cheaper steam power, water mills were increasingly hard put to compete. The dam and mill were sold in 1905 to the Eastern Michigan Edison company (later Detroit Edison), which was buying up all the water power along the river to generate electricity. Edison built a generating station that is still

A hobo cooks dinner near the Broadway Bridge during the Depression. For years, the city park behind the railroad station was known as Hobo Park. *(Courtesy of Bentley Historical Library.)*

there; though it no longer produces power, it is still used as a transmission substation.

Beginning in 1866, the Sinclair mill also powered the Agricultural Works, on the east side of the bridge (power was transmitted through a tunnel under the bridge). Founded by Lewis Moore, the Agricultural Works made all kinds of farm implements—plows, seed drills, mowing machines, hay tedders (machines used in drying and curing hay), rakes, straw cutters, corn shellers—and shipped them all over the country.

Finding a ready market in the days when most of the country's population was farmers, the Agricultural Works expanded throughout the century until it covered three acres, with a main building, a wood shop, a machine shop, a painting building, a lumberyard, and a foundry near the river. As it grew, it supplemented water power with steam power; by 1896, the promotional *Headlight* magazine declared it "one of the most important manufacturing enterprises of the city." But national manufacturers gradually took over the agricultural market, and the company closed in 1903. The Ann Arbor Machine Company, which made hay presses, occupied the premises for the next twenty years, using the same buildings. In 1924 Detroit Edison bought the site to build the garage and storage yard that are still there today.

Mills and factories weren't the only industries drawn to Lower Town, as the area north of the river was known. In the nineteenth century and into the twentieth, six slaughterhouses were built on the floodplain between the river and Canal Street. (Canal, although called a street, was "really an alley," according to Thelma Graves, who grew up nearby on Wall Street; residents of Wall used Canal to reach their back entrances.)

Though the last slaughterhouse closed in 1915, the floodplain remained heavily industrialized. In the 1920s, it was home to a concrete company, David A. Friedman's junkyard, a wire products company, the Leever and Leever lumber company, and Otto Earth's tin and upholstery shops.

Meanwhile, the south bank of the river was dominated by the railroad. The Michigan Central reached Ann Arbor in 1839, and the first train station was built on the west side of the bridge, near the present Amtrak station. In 1886 a new stone station, now the Gandy Dancer restaurant, was erected on the east side. But the handsome station had some less-than-attractive neighbors. In 1898, the land between the river and the original railroad station was purchased by the Ann Arbor Gas Company to build a new plant and storage tank. The plant heated coal (or, in later years, oil) in a vacuum to create a flammable gas that was piped into homes for cooking and lighting. The foul-smelling gasworks remained in operation until natural gas pipelines reached Michigan in 1955. Purchased by MichCon in 1938, the gas plant site is now the company's service center for Washtenaw County and parts of Wayne and Oakland Counties.

By the turn of the century, manufacturing industries were being replaced by power industries, but all four corners around the bridge were still given over to commercial and industrial uses. By then, however, Ann Arborites were beginning to think that parks would be a more enjoyable use of the riverside—and present a better picture to the outside world.

Mayor Royal S. Copeland, in a 1902 address to city council, bemoaned the fact that "to enter Lower Town it is necessary to cross the smoky Detroit Street bridge [today the Broadway Bridge], [and] traverse a long dusty street with the gas tanks on one side and foul smelling dump heaps on the other." The junk-strewn field east of the bridge was a particular sore point, because it was the first view of Ann Arbor to greet passengers arriving at the train station. Calling it "a blot upon an otherwise fair page," Copeland went on to paint a more attractive alternative: "How different it would be if the ground east of the street were a green

Before Eli Gallup created Riverside Park, now Broadway Park, in the 1930s, the river's north bank was a maze of small workshops and impromptu dumps. *(Courtesy of Al Gallup.)*

sward, garnished with flowers and shrubs! How much more convenient for the Fifth Ward [Lower Town] if they could follow a gravel footpath through that Riverside park, climb a flight of steps to a narrow bridge over the tracks and find themselves at the foot of State Street."

Copeland appointed a committee, including the city attorney, empowered to negotiate with the property's owners. He also announced that an anonymous donor had offered to pay half the costs of condemnation and purchase of the land. The donor, he said, "believes our city is damaged in the eyes of the traveling public by the unsightly and disgraceful outlook from the [train] car windows." Copeland was confident that the $1,000 appropriated in city funds would finish the job and the rest could be used to improve the park.

The committee had meetings, met with property owners, and had the city attorney write letters, but in three years it did not make much progress in obtaining the land, which was owned by eight different people. In October 1905, the committee reported that "some of the persons interested in said lands refused to name any price for the same and others have placed a value upon their lands far in excess of what your committee is willing to recommend the council to accept. Your committee is of the opinion that said lands can only be acquired by condemnation proceedings." With the exception of some land near the station that the Michigan Central Railroad donated, the properties were obtained by condemnation. Pleased with their work, the committee reported that "by removing the unsightly and ill-smelling dump heap of tin cans and dead cats, the traveling public will form a better opinion of our city." On April 30, 1907, the site was formally named Riverside Park.

Although the acquisition of Riverside Park was touted as a major accomplishment, little was done to develop it. Ann Arborites who were around before World War II say that Island Drive Park and West Park were the places to go; they remember using Riverside Park only as a cut-through, especially from Lower Town to campus. Jack Bauer Sr., who grew up in Lower Town, scoffs at the idea that it was ever even a park, saying, "No one ever went there. It was nothing but an opening." Indeed, it was so little used that when the park across the river on the north side was developed, it appropriated the name Riverside Park and Mayor Copeland's creation became known as Hobo Park.

HOBO PARK GOT ITS NAME because, as the closest public land to the railroad station, it was a favorite place for hoboes to hang out. Hoboing—riding the rails without benefit of a ticket, looking for work—probably started as early as railroading itself, but it became a real phenomenon in the 1890s and peaked in the Depression. Hoboes separated themselves from tramps by their willingness to work. Ann Arbor was a likely destination because the presence of the university meant work was somewhat easier to find here than in most Michigan cities.

Hoboes arrived by train, mostly in the warmer months, and fanned out all over the city. Older Ann Arborites, wherever they lived, remember hoboes coming to their doors and being given some food, sometimes in exchange for odd jobs, such as shaking out rugs, cleaning out furnace ashes, spading the garden, or mowing the lawn. Although some hoboes were tough characters, many were well mannered and clean. Some reportedly even had college educations. They were rarely invited inside but ate their food on the back steps or in the backyard.

Jack Bauer recalls that when he visited his aunt on Swift Street in the 1930s, he saw the police come to break up fights among the hoboes camped along the overgrown millrace between the Argo Dam and powerhouse. Hoboes also slept farther east at Dow Field—the bottom of what is today the Arboretum but was then a university dump—and, of course, at Hobo Park. Bauer cut across the "park" in the 1930s to get to St. Thomas School, and he was often chased. He was young and strong and could run fast, but if he was worried, he would go into the railroad station and ask Mr. Mynning, a friend of the family who worked in the mail office there, to escort him to the bridge.

World War II put a stop to most hoboing, since able-bodied men who weren't drafted could enlist or find factory jobs. When Betty Gillan Seward began working at the train station in 1941, there were only a few hoboes left, she recalls, and "they slept, whenever they could, in boxcars, but never in the station. Usually they slept on the banks of the river behind the station."

The hoboes never left altogether. In 1976, when photographer Fred Crudder took his future wife, Sally, on their first date, he suggested going to Hobo Park, by then officially called Broadway Park. She thought he was kidding, but when they arrived, sure enough, there were some people sleeping under newspapers there. For years after that, early morning walkers sometimes found homeless people camped in Broadway Park, and one latter-day hobo maintained a wood-and-canvas shack in the woods above the Argo millrace in the 1990s.

THE NEW RIVERSIDE PARK north of the river was started for the same reasons as the original one: to clean up a blighted area that by then was being used as an unofficial dump. The new park, too, was pieced together parcel by parcel, although in this case city officials were more successful in persuading people to sell or donate their property. In a nine-year period from 1925 to 1934, the parks commission, under the leadership of Eli Gallup, acquired sixteen parcels of land totaling eight acres located between the river and Canal Street.

During the Depression, Gallup enlisted workers from the federal WPA jobs program to clean the site, remove piles of rubbish, and tear down old buildings. To fill in the low, marshy floodplain, Gallup used waste material from construction projects, like ashes and rubbish. He had the WPA workers remove the topsoil—which was of good quality though quite stony in places—throw it into ridges, and fill in the resulting trenches with any available material. After the land was raised, the topsoil was replaced and the park developed. Gallup put in a regularly supervised playground—much appreciated by residents on the north side of the river—two tennis courts, and a baseball field. For drinking water, he ran a pipe out from the Donovan School.

The third park abutting the Broadway Bridge, Argo Park, was the last to be completed. In 1907 Detroit Edison donated the land just north of the present Argo Pond canoe livery for a municipal beach. The rest of the tract, including the dam and the millrace, was not acquired until

The original Riverside Park all cleaned up. *(Courtesy of Stan Shackman.)*

1963. Detroit Edison first invited the city to buy its holdings along the Huron River, including the Argo, Barton, and Geddes Dams, in 1959, but the purchase had to wait until 1962, when voters approved a bond issue to finance it.

TODAY DTE (MichCon and Detroit Edison) is the last industrial user remaining near the Broadway Bridge, although they no longer produce power there. What will replace their building when, or if, they choose to sell is a topic of lively speculation. Housing is one perennial favorite suggestion. Though the idea would have seemed ridiculous a century ago, the gradual transformation of the surrounding area into attractive parks makes housing a very real possibility.

Riverside Park, once slaughterhouses and factories, is now the "green sward" that Copeland envisioned. During the school year, St. Thomas and Gabriel Richard schools use the park as a practice field, while in the summer numerous teams enjoy the baseball diamond. Argo Park, linked with Riverside by a pedestrian bridge, provides an attractive hiking area right in the city with the river on one side and the millrace on the other.

As part of the recent Broadway Bridge project, the city cleaned up the original Riverside Park on the south side of the river and put in benches, plantings, walks, and lights. Finally, a hundred years later, Mayor Copeland's vision is coming true.

# Cinema's First Century

*The rise, fall, and revival of Ann Arbor's downtown theaters*

The first movie shown in Ann Arbor was *The Great Train Robbery.* Filmed a century ago, in 1903, the twelve-minute adventure didn't make it to town until the following year. On September 26, 1904, it appeared as the last item on a sold-out seven-part program at the Light Armory at Ashley and West Huron. Handcuff king Fred Gay led a bill that included minstrels, jugglers, and a boy tenor.

Films may have started as an afterthought, but they soon became a draw in their own right. One of the first movies to tell a story, *The Great Train Robbery* featured a long list of technical firsts, among them the first intercut scenes and the first close-up—an outlaw firing a shot right at the audience. The *Ann Arbor Times-News* reviewer reported that it required "no great stretch of imagination for the spectator to persuade himself that he was looking at a bit from real life."

"*The Great Train Robbery* has been called the picture that launched a thousand nickelodeons," laughs Art Stephan, president of the Ann Arbor Silent Film Society. Within three years of its showing, three nickelodeons (named for their 5¢ admission charge) popped up in Ann Arbor, along with three new vaudeville theaters whose entertainment included movies.

Ann Arbor's wide audience, encompassing both townspeople and university students and faculty, has supported an abundance of theaters ever since. "Ann Arbor is one of the great movie towns in the country," says Russ Collins, executive director of the Michigan Theater. These days, popular films appear almost exclusively in huge multiplexes on the edge of town. But for most of a century, Ann Arbor supported a wide array of downtown theaters, from the first nickelodeons and vaudeville houses to glorious movie palaces like the Michigan.

THE THEATORIUM, "Ann Arbor's Pioneer Picture Theater," opened in November 1906 at 119 East Liberty (now, aptly, the home of Liberty Street Video). It showed three short movies for 5¢, changing the offerings three times a week.

The Theatorium wasn't alone for long. In December the Casino opened at 339 South Main (now part of the Real Seafood Company restaurant). It advertised that it would cater to women and children and "give good clean shows which all can patronize." The Theatorium and the Casino were joined in 1907 by the first campus-area theater, the People's Popular Family Theater. Soon renamed the Vaudette, it was at 220 South State, where Starbucks is now.

Opening a nickelodeon was cheap—all that was needed was an empty storefront, a projector, and some folding chairs. The entrepreneur would put up a sheet at one end, install a box in the door for selling tickets (giving new meaning to the term *box office*), and get a player piano or phonograph for background music—and he or she was in business. Called the "poor man's show" or "democracy's theater," nickelodeons were a craze all over the country, appealing mainly to poorer audiences. The *News* didn't make much of the nickelodeons' openings, although it ran their ads.

Also showing films were two new vaudeville theaters. The Bijou, at 209 East Washington, opened the same month as the Casino, followed by the Star, at 118 East Washington, in August 1907. Although they also charged 5¢ admission and were scarcely bigger than the nickelodeons, both had stages at one end that enabled them to present live shows as well as movies. Both received more notice in the local papers than the nickelodeons had.

Maybe protesting a little too much, the Bijou ad invited audiences to "come and see the cozy theater and enjoy strictly high class moral entertainment." The Star has gone down in history as the site of a student riot on March 16, 1908.

According to Ann Arbor police lieutenant Mike Logghe's *True Crimes and the History of the Ann Arbor Police Department*, the riot started as a student protest against manager Albert Reynolds, who allegedly had tried to win a large bet by getting a U-M football player to throw a game. When protesters failed to get Reynolds to come out (reports differ on whether he exited through the back door or was hiding in the basement), they began throwing bricks stolen from a construction site across the street. The riot lasted all night, in spite of appeals by both law dean Henry Hutchins and U-M president James Angell. Eighteen students were arrested, but charges were later dropped when they agreed to raise money for repairs.

A much larger and more impressive early theater was the Majestic, at 316 Maynard (now a city parking structure). Unlike the nickelodeons, the Majestic enjoyed detailed local press coverage of its planning and

Whitney Theatre.

The Whitney, 117–119 North Main, originally a venue for traveling stage shows, in 1917 showed *Birth of a Nation* as if it were just that. The early movie was touring the United States with a twenty-piece orchestra. *(Courtesy of Bentley Historical Library.)*

The Majestic Theater, 316 Maynard, was built for live stage shows. *(Courtesy of Bentley Historical Library.)*

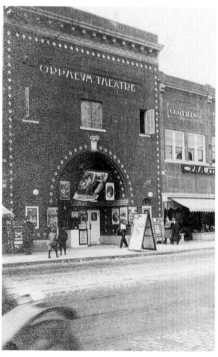

Orpheum, 326 South Main, was the first theater in town built specifically as a movie house. *(Courtesy of Susan Wineberg.)*

arrival. The Athens, 117 North Main, the town's major location for live stage shows, had closed in 1904, leaving a keenly felt gap.

The Majestic was built by lumberyard owner Charles Sauer, who converted an indoor roller skating rink into a huge theater—eleven hundred seats—complete with stage, dressing rooms, balcony, box seats, ladies' waiting room, confectionery, and manager's office. It opened September 19, 1907, with *The Girl of the Golden West*, a live musical about the 1849 gold rush. The Majestic showed movies from the beginning, but vaudeville acts were its main draw—especially after 1908, when the former Athens Theater, remodeled and reopened as the Whitney, reclaimed its position as the preferred place for prime stage shows.

Of the six early theaters, the Majestic was the only one to last. By 1912 all three nickelodeons were gone—the Theatorium became a photography studio, the Casino a grocery store, and the Vaudette a shoemaker's shop. All around the country nickelodeons were closing, Art Stephan says, mainly because the early movies weren't very good: "They were not very exciting—just a novelty." The small vaudeville theaters lasted a little longer, but by 1915 the Bijou was gone. The Star was renamed the Columbia and then closed for good in 1919.

DESPITE THE NICKELODEONS' FAILURE, a few far-thinking producers kept developing and improving movies, making them longer and more sophisticated. In 1913 the Majestic announced that it was switching to movies as its lead attraction. Manager Arthur Lane promised audiences "high class feature motion pictures" such as *Ben Hur* and *Tess of the D'Urbervilles*. In 1914 the Whitney also started occasionally showing movies. Seeking to lure middle-class audiences, it promised "good clean pictures that anyone would be glad to see."

Then, in a five-year period, four new theaters specifically designed to show movies opened. The Orpheum at 326 South Main was the first, built in 1913 by clothier J. Fred Wuerth. The architect, "Mr. F. Ehley of Detroit," designed an arched facade reminiscent of Adler and Sullivan's 1889 Auditorium Building in Chicago (the arch now frames the entrance to the Gratzi restaurant). Inside, the decor included fancy paneling and box seats. The opening performance featured *The Hills of Strife*, about feuding mountaineers, plus two other movies and a live show by the Musical DeWitts. It drew such a crowd that people had to be turned away.

The next year, 1914, Selby Moran built the Arcade at 715 North University, at the end of an arcade that ran along the north side of a tailor shop. Just three years later, Moran expanded the theater from twenty-six rows of seats to forty-three and added a balcony and boxes. The projector (or "motion picture machine," as they called it then) was on the second floor—actually in the tailor shop, outside the theater proper. "We used to go to doubleheaders at the Arcade on Saturdays," recalls John Eibler. "My mother would drop us off and take a chance when to come back. The time was doubtful when we'd come out—we had to see the whole thing." He remembers seeing "cowboy and Indian" pictures, particularly Tom Mix features.

The Rae, at 113 West Huron, opened on September 11, 1915. At 385 seats, it was the smallest of the new theaters. Its name was an amalgam of the first initials of its three owners—Russell Dobson, Alan Stanchfield, and Emil Calman. Stanchfield, the on-site manager who eventually bought out the others, visited theaters all over Michigan and Illinois to learn the tricks of the trade. He did almost everything himself—took tickets (he knew the ages of all the kids and could charge accordingly), climbed a ladder to run the projector, and hawked refreshments up and down the aisle between reels. Bob Hall, a regular customer, recalls watching cowboy movies and serials. "Sometimes the policeman on the beat would come in and stand at the back to watch," Hall says.

In 1918 Fred Wuerth added a second theater, naming it after himself. (He also built one with the same name in Ypsilanti.) Set perpendicular to the Orpheum, the Wuerth was reached from Main Street through a skylighted arcade to the north of the owner's clothing store. A Hope-Jones organ was placed so it could be heard in both theaters.

ONE OF THE MOST important films ever, *Birth of a Nation*, bypassed all four of the new theaters in favor of the Whitney. D. W. Griffith's Civil War epic was presented as if it were a live road show, traveling around the country with a twenty-piece orchestra. Admission to the four showings on May 18 and 19, 1917, was $1.50—at a time when most ticket prices were 5¢ or 10¢.

Although seriously flawed by Griffith's racist portrayal of newly freed slaves, the film was a turning point in movie history, showing audiences how engrossing this new medium could be. "It's hard to overstate the importance of *Birth of a Nation*," says Collins. "Griffith coalesced a film language recognizable today, the technique of telling a story with film." The following week the Whitney showed *Intolerance*, which Griffith produced as an answer to criticism of *Birth of a Nation*.

The days of releasing many prints simultaneously across the nation were still in the future: *Birth of a Nation* had been shown in bigger cities in 1915 and *Intolerance* in 1916. But movie exhibition was already becoming more organized. At first, all the early movie theaters were run by their owners. With the exception of the Rae, however, all were eventually leased to the Battle Creek–based Butterfield theater chain.

Gerald Hoag, Butterfield's manager of the Majestic in the 1920s, faced the challenge of handling the rushes college students made on the theater, usually after a victorious football game. "They'd holler and yell and demand a free movie. They always got in," recalls Bob Hall, who as a small boy took part in one of these rushes. "I was scared stiff—I was afraid I'd get squashed—but I wanted to see a free movie. My mother didn't like it. She castigated me when I got home."

Hoag, a big Wolverine fan, hired football players as ushers. In the days before regular radio sportscasts, Hoag obtained scores from the ticker-tape machine at Huston Brothers' pool hall on State Street and announced them to his audience. Then he got a better idea: he leased a direct telegraph wire from the press box wherever the U-M was playing and had Fred Belser, a telegraph operator at Western Union, sit on stage and transcribe the messages. Hoag would read the play-by-play to the audience while an assistant moved a toy football across a mocked-up field. At halftime Hoag presented a vaudeville show.

One of Hoag's claims to fame was discovering Fred Waring and His Pennsylvanians. In 1922 Waring's band played at the annual J-Hop at Waterman Gym. Although two more famous bands were also playing, Hoag noticed that most of the dancers drifted over to Waring. Hoag booked him at the Majestic, where he stayed six weeks, playing one-hour sets interspersed with movies. That engagement led to work in Detroit and other big cities, and for the rest of his career Waring credited Hoag with giving him his big break.

The acme and the last hurrah of the silent movie era in Ann Arbor were the opening of the Michigan Theater on January 5, 1928. The grandiose "shrine to art" reflected a national trend toward extravagant movie palaces. Starting in the second decade of the twentieth century with scrumptious theaters modeled loosely on the Paris Opera, designers segued into increasingly fanciful Egyptian, Spanish, Chinese, Mayan, and Babylonian themes. "Movies were considered low-class entertainment. The movie palaces were designed to legitimize movies as middle-class entertainment," explains the Michigan's Russ Collins.

The Michigan was built by Angelo Poulos, a Greek immigrant who was co-owner of the Allenel Hotel and an organizer of St. Nicholas Greek Orthodox Church. Although the Michigan's style is usually referred to as Romanesque Revival, architect Maurice Finkel explained in a

Wuerth Theatre, 320 South Main, showed the first talkie in 1929. *(Courtesy of Bentley Historical Library.)*

The Michigan Theater opened in 1928 as a silent movie palace. The next year they switched to talkies. *(Courtesy of Bentley Historical Library.)*

People lined up to see *It Happens Every Spring*, written by Ann Arbor's Shirley Smith. *(Courtesy of Bentley Historical Library.)*

*News* interview that he worked in a mixture of styles—classical, medieval, Romanesque—that he thought would fit with U-M academic buildings and fraternities. (Many Ann Arborites will remember Finkel's widow, Anya, who managed Jacobson's hat department for years and was known for her frank advice.)

The Butterfield chain transferred Hoag to the Michigan along with most of the rest of the Majestic staff, from ticket takers to ushers. From then on the Majestic was devoted completely to movies, since the Michigan was a better place for stage shows, and the Arcade was demoted to a second-run theater.

The Michigan opened to a sellout crowd. Entertainment included an overture written for the event and a live show, *The Dizzy Blondes Dance Revue*. The featured movie, *A Hero for a Night*, was supplemented by shorts, a comedy, and a newsreel. But the Michigan was out-of-date the day it opened: the first successful talkie, *The Jazz Singer*, had premiered the year before.

TALKING PICTURES CAME to Ann Arbor on March 21, 1929, when the Wuerth showed *The Ghost Talks*. While other local owners hesitated to spend money on sound systems, Fred Wuerth had figured out that after the initial investment, he could save money replacing live vaudeville acts with short one-reel films. Talkies had been around in bigger cities since *The Jazz Singer*, and Ann Arborites were ready: the waiting crowd lined up down Main Street and around the corner onto Liberty.

Other theaters had to add sound quickly to remain competitive. On June 16, 1929, the Michigan showed its first talkie, *Weary River*. The Majestic also switched to talkies that year. The Arcade, too, was scheduled for conversion, but it burned down before the work could begin. (The Rae also burned the following year; at both theaters, the fire started when highly flammable nitrate film ignited, but the only injuries were minor burns to the projectionists.)

Both the Orpheum and the Whitney closed in 1929 but reopened in the mid-1930s. With no one building new theaters during the Great Depression, the rest of the lineup stayed the same. First-run movies played at either the Michigan or the Majestic, because they were the largest theaters and the ones best located to take advantage of both town and gown patrons. Second-run and B movies played the theaters downtown.

The Michigan and Majestic were the theaters to take dates to on Friday and Saturday nights. Jack Dobson remembered going to movies for 35¢ and then to Drake Sandwich Shop for a malted or a milk shake.

Al Gallup started dating a little later; by that time, he recalls, "both the Majestic and the Michigan were forty cents." But even with the price increase, "for a dollar you could have a date. You'd go to Drake's after the show for a Coke." Ted Palmer preferred the Betsy Ross restaurant in Nickels Arcade: "There were no college kids in the Betsy Ross. We'd get a lemon Coke or a cherry Coke—one Coke and two straws."

Although not as fancy as the Michigan, the Majestic still got important films—including 1939's *Gone with the Wind*. "Everyone wanted to see *Gone with the Wind*," recalls Bob Steeb. "I went with my wife. We worked at Wahr's [bookstore] on State Street and took the day off to see it."

For many people who grew up in Ann Arbor, though, the fondest cinematic memories are of kids' movies. On Saturday mornings, if they could spare the money and time, they could see full-length movies made for children at the Michigan. Or they could head for the Whitney or the Wuerth, where the movie might not be as good but there'd also be a serial.

Serials typically consisted of six or seven weekly installments, each twenty or thirty minutes long. Episodes always stopped at a perilous moment—most famously, with the heroine about to be run over by a train. "We could hardly wait for the next Saturday," recalls Palmer. "We'd replay the movie all the way home, shooting the bad guys."

During World War II the bad guys were Axis soldiers. Coleman Jewett remembers watching serials such as *Don Winslow of the Navy* and *Spy Smasher*. Even the Phantom, Jewett says, added Nazi-hunting plots.

On Saturdays in the late 1940s and early 1950s, "kids would get in for ten cents," recalls Bob Mayne, a projectionist at the Wuerth. "We'd show ten cartoons, then a serial—Hopalong Cassidy, Roy Rogers, Buck Rogers—then a feature film like Gene Autry." Once Mayne projected a Donald Duck cartoon backward. "The kids loved it," he remembers, "although my boss was mad."

The Orpheum's fare was originally very similar to the Wuerth's, but it later established a niche playing to the more intellectual crowd with documentaries, revivals of prestigious American films, and foreign films—*The Red Shoes* is the movie people most often mention having seen at the Orpheum. Coleman Jewett also saw *Camille* and *The Hunchback of Notre Dame* there, while Mark Hodesh recalls going with his parents to see travelogues.

A rite of passage among kids was to sneak into the theater. At the Orpheum or Wuerth, those in the know would sometimes sneak into the other theater through a connecting tunnel. Of course any place that backed onto an alley was fair game—the kids exiting would hold the door for those who wanted to come in. Ted Heusel, who ushered at the Michigan when he was a teenager, told his friends to just pretend they were giving him a ticket. At the Majestic, some kids learned how to get in by going up the fire escape.

Once the economy recovered in the early 1940s, Butterfield considered remodeling the Majestic but instead decided to build a new theater. The Majestic closed on March 11, 1942, and the State Theater opened a week later. Not wanting to appear unpatriotic, Butterfield management emphasized that the necessary permits were issued and materials purchased before the attack on Pearl Harbor the previous December.

Six buildings along State were razed to make room for the new Art Deco theater. (The architect was C. Howard Crane, who also designed Orchestra Hall and the Fox Theater in Detroit.) The Majestic's manager and staff all moved over to the new theater. "It was a big deal when it opened," recalls Gallup. The premiere movie, appropriate for the times, was the Dorothy Lamour–William Holden musical *The Fleet's In*, about a sailor with an inflated reputation as a lady-killer.

A highlight of Ann Arbor movie history was the 1949 premiere at the Michigan Theater of *It Happens Every Spring*, a baseball movie starring Ray Milland and Jean Peters. The film was based on a story written by U-M vice president emeritus Shirley Smith, and the Ann Arbor showing actually preceded the "world premiere" that took place in the movie's location, St. Louis, two weeks later. A searchlight spanned the skies, the U-M concert band played in front of the theater, and the street was blocked off while U-M president Alexander Ruthven and Ann Arbor mayor William Brown presented Smith with their version of an Oscar.

THE RISE OF TELEVISION in the 1950s hit the oldest theaters first. At the Whitney, once host to such glamorous stars as Maude Adams, Katharine Cornell, and Anna Pavlova, the top balcony was closed off for safety reasons. "Four four-by-fours were holding up the whole projector. It was pretty heavy—the whole thing would shake," recalls Bob Mayne, who once managed to sneak a look. The two lower balconies, Mayne adds, became "a necker's paradise." Walter Metzger recalls that the kids thought (possibly correctly) that there were bats in the top balcony, and their fears made scary movies at the Whitney even scarier.

"It was rat infested, or at least rumored to be. We told the girls that rats were running around so they'd stay close," laughs Gallup. In 1952 the Whitney was closed by court order. The building was torn down in 1955.

The Wuerth, also, had clearly seen better days when its run ended. Carol Birch recalls the theater in the 1950s as "creepy. It was run down— people didn't go there much. It was dark to get to your seat." In 1957 the Wuerth and the Orpheum both closed.

To cater to the art-movie audience that had patronized the Orpheum, Butterfield built the Campus on South University. "It was a real nice one-show theater," recalls Mayne. Lois Granberg, ticket taker at the Michigan, became manager, and most of the rest of the staff, including projectionist Mark Mayne (Bob Mayne's father), transferred from the Orpheum. Doug Edwards, who was a projectionist at the Campus, recalls that although it was less opulent than the Michigan and the State (where he also worked), "it was the newest, most modern, with chrome and pastels and a concession stand. It was the place they'd have gimmick films, like surround sound." During the height of the 1960s foreign-film craze, crowds lined up along South University to see the latest Fellini or Bergman work.

When a group headed by Ken Robinson and attorney Bill Conlin built the Fifth Forum in 1966, Conlin was also thinking of providing a successor to the Orpheum. "We had a contest in the *Ann Arbor News* to name the theater," he recalls. The Fifth Forum's first big success was *Georgy Girl*, with Lynn Redgrave. The Fifth Forum kept showing the romantic comedy for more than six months, Conlin says—in contrast to the Butterfield theaters, which were able to book movies only for short periods.

The Fifth Forum was the last commercial movie theater built downtown. The cinematic migration to Ann Arbor's edges started the following year, when the Fox Village Theater opened on Maple Road. In 1975 the city got its first multiplex, a four-screen United Artists theater at Briarwood mall. Films at "the one-screen movie theaters changed every week and then were gone," explains Patrick Murphy, a projectionist who worked in several Ann Arbor theaters at the time. "Showing four for a month was better, economically speaking." Expanded choices and easier parking soon lured most casual moviegoers to the mall. "We would show movies at the Campus to ten or fifteen people," recalls Edwards.

Butterfield fought back, dividing the State into a quad in 1977 with two screens downstairs and two more upstairs in what had been a balcony, but the firm was just buying time. In 1979 Butterfield quit programming at the Michigan. The theater-loving community, worried that the beautiful building would be torn down or altered for an incompatible use, mobilized to save it. The mayor at the time, Lou Belcher, personally promised that the city would buy the theater, going to council and the voters for authorization only after the fact. The daring deal paved the way for a 1982 millage that led to its restoration and operation by the nonprofit Michigan Theater Foundation.

The Briarwood multiplex expanded from four theaters to seven in 1983. The following year, Butterfield gave up the ghost, selling its remaining theaters to Kerasotes Corporation. Kerasotes kept the State but sold the Campus. "It was more valuable as real estate," explains John Briggs, who was local president of the International Alliance of State and Theatrical Employees at the time. The Campus was torn down and replaced with a minimall.

Kerasotes tried to make the State profitable by replacing union projectionists with lower paid workers. New technology could fit a whole movie on a single huge spool of film, rather than on small reels that had to be changed every twenty minutes—so one person could run four or even eight movies at a time. Union members and U-M students picketed, and in 1988 Kerasotes sold out to Hogarth Management, a real estate company owned by bookstore founders Tom and Louis Borders. Kerasotes "suffered some financial loss, but that didn't run them out of town. The changing times with the cineplex at Briarwood is probably what did it," says Edwards, who was one of the picketers. "The 'GKC' rugs are Kerasotes's only contribution to the State," laughs Murphy.

Hogarth leased the main floor of the State to Urban Outfitters but kept the two upstairs screens. "I was involved in the restoration of the Michigan Theater and had a soft spot for movie theaters," says Roger Hewitt, who ran Hogarth Management. "I wanted to keep the movie space, and Tom and Louis were supportive." Under Hewitt's direction, the State's original marquee was also restored. Hogarth initially leased the upstairs to the Spurlin family of Aloha Theaters; after the Spurlins left in 1997, the Michigan Theater was hired to do the programming and publicity. Movies that formerly would come to the Michigan for just a few days can now be transferred to the State for a longer run.

The Fifth Forum was not only the last commercial theater built downtown but also the last to close. Conlin's group sold it to Goodrich Theaters, which renamed it the Ann Arbor Theater and divided it awkwardly between two smaller screens. It showed its last film in 1999 before being remodeled into an office building with an interesting metal facade.

Ironically, the Briarwood multiplex that devastated in-town movies was itself destroyed by the next new development. The whole United Artists chain went bankrupt in 2000 under pressure for newer, even bigger, movie houses—represented locally by Showcase Cinemas and Quality 16. After standing empty for several years, the Briarwood theaters reopened under the management of Madstone, a small chain that mixed first-run films with art movies and classics. The Madstone closed in the summer of 2004. It was replaced by the Village 7 theater, which has since been replaced by Briarwood Dollar Movies.

The venues have changed, but Ann Arbor is still a good movie town. Between them, Showcase and Quality 16 offer forty screens of first-run fare. For more exotic productions, we have the Michigan and the State. "Very few towns with a population of a hundred thousand have the choices of movies we have," says Collins.

# Social Fabric and Communities

# The Underground Railroad
# in Ann Arbor

*In the years before the Civil War, a handful of local abolitionists helped*
*fugitive slaves make their way to freedom in Canada.*

———————

*A few days since we had the rare pleasure, in connection with many of our*
*friends in this place, of bestowing our hospitalities upon six of our brethren,*
*who tarried with us some sixteen hours to refresh themselves, on their jour-*
*ney to a land of freedom.* —Signal of Liberty, *May 12, 1841*

The *Signal of Liberty* was the weekly newspaper of the Anti-Slavery Party of Michigan. "This place" was Ann Arbor, where editor Guy Beckley produced the paper from an office on Broadway. The *Signal of Liberty* was one of a series of Michigan papers that in the years before the Civil War called for the abolition of slavery in the United States. On May 12, 1841, it also provided a rare glimpse into Ann Arborites' practical efforts on behalf of escaped slaves: an article by Beckley and Theodore Foster recording an escape on the Underground Railroad.

"Believing as we do that it is morally wrong to continue our fellow beings in involuntary servitude, it is with the utmost pleasure that we aid and assist them in their flight from southern kidnappers," Beckley and Foster wrote. They described the fugitives as "from twenty-one to thirty years of age—in good health and spirits and apparently much delighted with the prospect of a new home, where the sound of the whip and clanking of chains will no longer grate upon their ears and mangle and gall their limbs."

According to a follow-up story on May 19, the escaped slaves successfully completed the final leg of their journey to freedom in Canada. "We take great pleasure in announcing to our readers that they have all landed, as we intended they should, safe on British soil," Beckley and Foster wrote. Today's Canada was still a group of British possessions then, and slavery had been abolished in all British territories eight years earlier, in 1833. In Michigan, slavery was illegal, but slaveholders still had the right to apprehend escapees; in what is now Ontario, however, the attorney general had ruled that any person on Canadian soil was automatically free.

That promise made Canada the destination of choice for blacks who escaped slavery in the South. The Underground Railroad was a network of sympathetic northerners who helped the fugitives on their way once they reached the free states. There are several stories about the origin of the Underground Railroad's name, but all point to situations in which slave hunters had been hot on the trail of fugitives, only to have the prey disappear as completely as if they had gone underground. Extending the metaphor, the escapees were referred to as "passengers" or sometimes "baggage," while the helpers along the way were "conductors" and the stopping points "stations."

Susan Hussey, the daughter of Battle Creek conductor Erastus Hussey, explained in a 1912 interview, "Passengers over the Underground Railroad were of one class—fugitive slaves. They traveled in one direction—toward Canada. There was no demand for return trip tickets."

Two of the railroad's "lines" crossed in Ann Arbor, and from the *Signal of Liberty* article and other sources we know that fugitives passed through here on their way to Canada. But beyond that, there is much we do not know and probably never will.

Of the millions of slaves held in the southern states, only a tiny fraction escaped to freedom. There is no record of how many reached Canada; the generally accepted figure is about forty thousand. Yet this comparative handful of people played a critical role in bringing the tensions between North and South to a head. It was one thing for northerners to know in an abstract way that southerners kept slaves. It was quite another to be compelled by federal law to send fellow human beings back into servitude.

## "Worse than Horse Thieves"

A very early act of the U.S. Congress, in 1793, set down procedures for identifying escaped slaves and returning them to their "owners." As the abolitionist movement gained strength in the North, a number of states passed laws intended to hinder enforcement of the federal "fugitive slave" law. Nonetheless, helping a slave escape remained a federal crime until 1864.

Presumably for that reason, Beckley and Foster were vague about where the "six brethren" stayed and exactly who assisted them. Had the helpers been caught, they would have faced fines or jail sentences. The fugitives would have been returned to slavery in the South, where they would probably have been severely beaten in a warning to other slaves.

Beckley and Foster also knew that their neighbors in Ann Arbor were divided over abolition. The Anti-Slavery Society was formed in 1836, and some religious groups, particularly Quakers and Wesleyan Methodists, were devoted to the cause. Ann Arbor's First Congregational Church was founded in 1847 by former members of the First Presbyterian Church, who broke away in part because they wanted to take a stronger stand against slavery. But there were also a significant number who were not supporters of the cause.

"Our neighbors accuse us of being 'worse than horse thieves,' because we have given to the colored man a helping hand in his perilous journey," Beckley and Foster wrote. "We are also held up as transgressors of the law and having no regard for the civil authority."

As late as 1861, a speech by Parker Pillsbury, a noted abolitionist, was broken up by a mob. Speaking at a church at 410 North State Street (still standing, the building is now a private residence), Pillsbury had to escape out a back window, followed by his audience. The attack so unnerved other area churches that most of them closed their doors to another antislavery speaker, Wendell Phillips, when he came to town later that year. (The Congregationalists agreed to let him speak, but only after a special vote of the trustees.)

Despite those mixed feelings, no record has been found that Ann Arbor residents ever returned a fugitive slave. Slaves were in more danger from their former "owners," and from bounty hunters, who sought to collect large rewards for their capture. The situation worsened after 1850, when the new Fugitive Slave Act was passed. It swept away all due process for blacks accused of being runaway slaves, increased penalties for helping escapees, and made it a crime for local law enforcers not to return slaves.

Even free blacks, of whom there were 231 in Washtenaw County in 1850, were not safe from the slave hunters. Laura Haviland, an abolitionist from Adrian, wrote about one such case in her 1881 memoir, *A Woman's Life-work*. In the 1840s, Haviland writes, she helped a fugitive couple named Elsie and William Hamilton. The Hamiltons left Adrian after their former "owner" appeared and tried to recapture them, moving to several other places, including "a farm near Ypsilanti for a few years." According to Haviland, the Hamiltons had left Ypsilanti by 1850, but their former "owner," believing they were still there, sent his

Guy Beckley published the *Signal of Liberty* above his brother Josiah's general store in the Huron block on Broadway, a few blocks from his home at 1425 Pontiac Trail. *(Photograph of Signal of Liberty courtesy of Bentley Historical Library; photograph of the Huron block courtesy of Bentley Historical Library; photograph of 1425 Pontiac Trail courtesy of Stan Shackman.)*

son north to capture them. The son didn't find the Hamiltons, but he did find a family of free blacks, the David Gordons, who came close to the description he had of the Hamilton family. Claiming the Gordons were the Hamiltons, the slaveholder's son demanded their arrest. Antislavery activists helped the Gordons confirm their freedom.

PATHS TO FREEDOM

Most of the fugitives who passed through Michigan came from states directly to the south. (Slaves escaping from the more easterly southern states could go through Pennsylvania and New York or on a ship along the coast.) "The fugitives came from various localities in the slave states, but most of those who passed on this line were from Kentucky, some were from Missouri and occasionally from the far south," reminisced Nathan Thomas, the conductor from Schoolcraft, south of Kalamazoo, in a letter he wrote in 1882. In another 1841 article, Foster and Beckley mention a fugitive "from the lead mines of Missouri."

The line Thomas was referring to went east and west across the state, roughly along the route of today's I-94. Fugitives usually came north from Quaker settlements in Indiana to Cassopolis, near Niles, where there was another Quaker settlement. They then traveled east through Battle Creek, Jackson, and Ann Arbor. A north-south route came from Toledo (where James Ashley, founder of the Ann Arbor Railroad, was an active member) to Adrian, an important hub where Haviland and a group of fellow Quakers ran a school, the Raisin Institute, for students of all colors. Refugees traveled from Adrian to Clinton and thence through Saline to Ann Arbor or Ypsilanti. From Washtenaw County, fugitives went on to Detroit, where they would cross the Detroit River at night in rowboats. Later, when the Detroit River was too closely watched, the route shifted northward to cross the St. Clair River.

By the time the fugitives hooked up with the Underground Railroad, they would have done the hardest part by themselves: getting out of the South. "Their travel with some rare exceptions was entirely by night and generally on foot until they passed from the slave to the free state," wrote Thomas. "[They] generally received friendly aid to only a limited extent from persons residing in the slave states. But success depended mainly upon their own efforts. They obtained food at night from the Negro quarters during their passage through the south."

Once fugitives arrived in free states, help was easier to get, although they still had to avoid bounty hunters. "They did not bring much property with them; and their clothing was generally barely sufficient to cover

Among the places slaves might have hid is Samuel Dexter's mansion just outside the village of that name. *(Courtesy of Bentley Historical Library.)*

them. The most destitute cases were relieved by their friends after their arrival in the free states," Thomas recalled. Stations were at intervals that could be covered on foot in one night, usually every fifteen or sixteen miles. There conductors could hide the refugees or arrange for others to do so, feed them, and see to their passage to the next station.

Slaves had been escaping during all of their captivity, but the number rose after the War of 1812, when returning soldiers spread the word about how close Canada was. According to Thomas, the line he worked on did not help its first fugitive until 1836. "The second [fugitive] in the fall of 1838 came from the far south through the Quaker settlements in Indiana," Thomas wrote. "He spent the winter with old father Gillet [Amasa Gillet of Sharon Township] in Washtenaw Co. and went to Canada the following spring. Others followed and the underground railroad was gradually established through the state." According to Thomas the line had no overall president, but the management was entrusted to one person in each area. He went on to list them, including Guy Beckley in Ann Arbor.

Erastus Hussey of Battle Creek, interviewed in 1885, explained that he was recruited as a conductor in 1840. He named the other major conductors on his line, including those in Washtenaw: "At Dexter we had Samuel W. Dexter and his sons. At Scio was a prominent man, Theodore Foster, father of Seymour Foster of Lansing. At Ann Arbor was Guy Beckley, editor of the *Signal of Liberty,* the organ of the Liberty party [an antislavery party that ran candidates in 1840 and 1844], who published the paper in connection with Theodore Foster. At Geddes, was John Geddes, after whom the town was named and who built a large flouring mill there."

Turning to secondary sources, we can add more names to the list of participants. Starting in 1892, Wilbur Siebert, a professor of history at Ohio State, interviewed as many survivors of the Underground Railroad as he could find. His 1898 book, *The Underground Railroad from Slavery to Freedom*, includes a list of stationmasters by county. For Washtenaw he lists, besides those already mentioned, Moses Bartlett, Ira Camp, Joseph Fowler, Jotham Goodell, Harwood, John Lowy (probably the aforementioned John Lowry), and "Ray." Chapman's 1881 *History of Washtenaw County* adds more: Asher Aray, Richard Glasier, James Morwick, Sylvester Noble, Russell Preston, and Eber White. Research by Carol Mull, Underground Railroad historian, has revealed that "Ray" and "Asher Aray" were the same person.

Twentieth-century sources in newspapers, articles, and oral traditions include still more names and places, but many of these are not verified— and people's very fascination with the railroad is largely to blame. Its history combines the drama of life-and-death pursuit with reassuring images of interracial cooperation and white resistance to slavery. Because the idea of the Underground Railroad is so compelling, many stories have been told about it that appear to rest on little more than imaginative speculation.

HISTORY AND MYTH

In Ann Arbor's onetime black neighborhood north of Kerrytown, it's common to hear that the Brewery Apartments at the corner of North Fifth Avenue and Summit Street were a stop on the Underground Railroad. Twenty-five years ago, there was even an unsuccessful campaign to locate a museum there. Yet, no nineteenth-century evidence links the building to the railroad. The story appears to have arisen when neighbors noted the cellars extending from the building in the direction of the Michigan Central tracks and speculated that they might have been dug to smuggle fleeing slaves to and from passing trains. Though escaped slaves occasionally traveled by train, the extensive cellars were built for a much more mundane purpose: storing beer.

There are many similar stories, in which a family tradition or a physical quirk in a building is cited as evidence of participation in the Underground Railroad. Most are probably groundless. When it comes to the

Sources disagree on whether John Geddes, hat in hand, was a conductor. *(Courtesy of Jeanette Monaghan Schuck.)*

Underground Railroad, "unfortunately it seems very clear that there's a lot more mythical belief than reality," Eastern Michigan University historian Mark Higbee told the *Ann Arbor News* in 1996.

"The Underground Railroad is the sort of thing that in the 1880s and 1890s people liked to say they were involved in, or their parents were involved," adds another historian, John Quist. "It's just hard to find contemporary verification and there's a lot of embellishment going on."

The Underground Railroad did exist. Clearly, escaped slaves passed through Washtenaw County, and some were helped by people here. However, it is impossible to go much farther with definite details of when they came, who they were, where they went, how many there were, or where they ended up. Reconstructing the local Underground Railroad is like putting together a jigsaw puzzle when some pieces are missing and the remaining pieces can be put together in several different ways.

In evaluating the historical evidence, first-person accounts written at the time are assumed to be the most accurate source of information. Unfortunately, because of the railroad's clandestine nature, few records were kept. In rare cases, conductors kept notes and hid them, but none have been found in Washtenaw County except for some references in the *Signal of Liberty*, which are intentionally obscure.

Next in value are accounts written by participants after the fact, including those of Hussey, Thomas, and Haviland. Written many years after the events described, these tales may have been embellished in retelling, but there's nothing to suggest that they were made up out of whole cloth. It adds credibility that the three memoirs do not contradict one another.

Last in the order of reliability are stories passed on by word of mouth and deductions based on physical evidence. But while such stories in themselves prove nothing, they should not automatically be assumed false, either. Like Bible stories used to prompt archaeological digs, they can help direct research in useful ways, even if the original tale is not confirmed.

With specifics so cloudy, trying to assess the size of the Underground Railroad locally is largely guesswork. No nineteenth-century source tried to estimate how many fugitives were helped in Washtenaw County. The nearest number comes from Erastus Hussey, who claims in his memoir to have helped about a thousand fugitives who reached Battle Creek.

Some of the people Hussey assisted presumably stayed in the free black communities of mid-Michigan. Most, however, would have continued east through Washtenaw County on their way to Canada. Since an unknown additional number arrived by the southern route, it seems reasonable to take a thousand as a working figure for Washtenaw County as well.

The movement was at its peak from the mid-1830s to the mid-1850s. Dividing the one thousand figure evenly over that twenty-year period suggests that an average of fifty escaped slaves a year may have passed through Ann Arbor with the aid of the Underground Railroad. But who helped them, and where did they stay?

## CONDUCTORS ON THE RAILWAY

*He was considered by many to be at least a very eccentric character, but as history has shown since, it was the entire American nation that was more eccentric than good, old John Lowry.*
> —*Judge Noah Cheever, describing a Saline farmer*
> *active in the Underground Railroad*

After the Civil War, many people wanted to claim connections with the Underground Railroad. When the railroad was active, however, only individuals with strong convictions and considerable courage were prepared to aid escaped slaves in defiance of both social convention and federal law. So it's wise to view the lists of local participants compiled after the fact by Siebert and the county history with some caution. Whether from boasting, forgetfulness, or confusion, some names on the lists may be inaccurate. At a minimum, though, they provide a picture of the people who were believed in the late nineteenth century to have been part of the Underground Railroad.

Dr. Charles Lindquist, curator of the Lenawee County Museum, has done a lot of research on his county's role in the Underground Railroad. He suggests that the best strategy to identify participants is to "find corroborating evidence—if they lived in places supposedly involved, if they were Quakers, if they subscribed to the *Signal of Liberty*, if they were active in the Anti-Slavery Society."

"It was definitely illegal, so they were very secretive," Lindquist adds. "It was impossible for there to be just one place [for fugitives to stay in each town]. They'd have to have different places, not a pattern, or they'd get caught." Lindquist also notes that it would have been easier to hide in the country than in town.

The list that follows is an educated guess about the local participants in the two Underground Railroad lines that passed through Washtenaw County, compiled through use of the Siebert and county history lists and Lindquist's rules of thumb.

### The East-West Route

AMASA GILLET: When fugitives entered Washtenaw County from the west, Gillet's farm in southern Sharon Township may have been their first stopping point. Nathan says that Gillet sheltered the second person to pass down this line of the railroad. The 1881 county history calls him "an anti-slavery man" and concurs that "his house was known as a station on the 'Underground rail way.'" Gillet was active in the Anti-Slavery Society and was an important member of the local Methodist church.

SAMUEL DEXTER: The founder and namesake of Dexter Village is identified as a conductor by Erastus Hussey. Local Quakers enjoyed the irony that the Dexters could entertain visitors on the porch of their southern-style mansion while hiding fugitives inside. The Dexter house, known as Gordon Hall, still stands on Dexter-Pinckney Road just outside the village. It has a separate area in the basement, reached only from the outside, where the slaves may have hid.

THEODORE FOSTER: Foster's antislavery work is well documented. A schoolmaster and store owner in the hamlet of Scio, where Zeeb Road crosses the Huron River, Foster was an active member of the Anti-Slavery Society, was editor with Guy Beckley of the *Signal of Liberty*, and was named as a conductor by Hussey. In the 1950s, Foster's grandson, also named Theodore, set down a story he had heard from his father, Seymour, about a game of hide-and-seek when Seymour was a boy. "Some youngsters ran into the basement and attempted to tip over an oversize barrel or hogshead," Foster recounted. "Upon doing so, they were much surprised and frightened to discover a colored man squatting there. The frightened children ran to their mother with tales of their discovery and Mr. Foster's children became aware of the meaning of their father's night rides and calls by strangers at the back door. They often heard someone knock at the door after dark and their father would hitch up the horse and be gone most of the night." The Foster home is no longer there.

EBER WHITE: A farmer and one of the founders of Ann Arbor's First Methodist Church, White lived on what was then the western edge of the city. According to the county history, "in slavery days [he] was a prime mover in the underground railroad, and many a slave after reaching Canada has thanked God for the help given him by Eber White and his trustworthy friends." White's house at 405 Eberwhite (on the corner of Liberty) has been replaced by a modern house; the land he farmed is now the neighborhood around Eberwhite School.

SYLVESTER NOBLE: The county history says that Noble was a member of the Underground Railroad, as does his obituary, which states that "during the days of slavery his sympathies were strongly engaged on the side of the oppressed and his house was frequently made a station on the underground railroad." His home at 220 West Huron is no longer standing.

JAMES MORWICK: "During slavery days he was a prime mover in the famous Underground Railroad," according to the county history. An architect, Morwick lived at 604 East Washington, in a house that is now a student rental.

ROBERT GLAZIER: Glazier (sometimes spelled *Glasier*) "was considered one of the best 'conductors' on the route," according to the county history. "He has assisted in passing many a slave into Canada where they would be safe from their cruel master. His 'route' lay from Ann Arbor [east] to Farmington and on one occasion he made a trip to Adrian with William Lloyd Garrison." Supporting evidence is that Glazier was a member of the Michigan Anti-Slavery Society and a devout Quaker. Glazier's house, which began as a log cabin, still stands at 3175 Glazier Way.

JOHN GEDDES: Hussey names Geddes as a conductor. His role was challenged almost as soon as Hussey's 1885 interview appeared, however, when an Ypsilanti newspaper article asserted that Geddes "never had anything to do with it [the Underground Railroad]." Historian Quist, whose U-M doctoral dissertation looked at antislavery efforts in Washtenaw County, found no record that Geddes was an active abolitionist.

Besides Hussey's mention, the main other evidence is that Francis Monaghan, who worked for Geddes as a farmhand and bought the property in 1885, passed on to his descendants stories he heard from Geddes about his involvement in the Underground Railroad. But in recent years, both Geddes's letters and his diary have come to light, and people who have read them say they contain no references to the Underground Railroad or abolitionism or slavery or even radical politics.

GUY BECKLEY: Beckley published the *Signal of Liberty* from an office above the store of his brother, Josiah Beckley, on Broadway, across the street from the Anson Brown Building on Broadway (which today houses the St. Vincent de Paul store). His home, just a few blocks away at 1425 Pontiac Trail, is the Ann Arbor structure most identified with the antislavery cause; it's where school buses stop on historical field trips. A specific spot for hiding fugitives has never been found in his house, although a back part has been torn down. It's possible that because Beckley was so publicly identified with the Underground Railroad, fugitives were hidden elsewhere if danger was perceived. An ordained minister, Beckley moved to Ann Arbor in 1839, remaining active in the abolitionist cause until his death in 1847.

JOSIAH BECKLEY: A farmer and brickmaker, he was supposed to have played a less active role in the antislavery movement than his brother, helping mostly with funding. His two Ann Arbor houses are strong possibilities for Underground Railroad sites.

> *1317 Pontiac:* Former owner Fran Wright says her deed research established that Josiah Beckley bought the land in 1835 and probably built the house the next year. Present owner Jack Kenny says that there is a hiding place at the back of a downstairs closet big enough for three or four people. Jerry Cantor, who grew up on the north side, said that when he was a boy he was told that fugitive slaves hid in the barn on this property.

> *1709 Pontiac:* Former owner Deborah Oakley says that her deed research established that Josiah Beckley bought the land in 1827, the year he came to Ann Arbor, and built the house sometime

between 1831 and 1843. Josiah probably built the house in the late 1830s, moving there from 1317 Pontiac. We know he resided there when he died in 1843. Present owner Martha Wallace says there is a false wall in the basement "made with brick the same generation as the house—old and crumbly" that may have concealed a hiding place for fugitive slaves.

### The Southern Route

PRINCE BENNETT of Augusta Township is not mentioned in any of the nineteenth-century accounts of the Underground Railroad, but a strong oral tradition suggests that he was a conductor. Barbara McKenzie, Bennett's great-granddaughter, says that she was told that "Underneath his front porch there was a trapdoor that led to a room where you could put runaway slaves." Bennett, whose home on Tuttle Road no longer stands, certainly was an abolitionist: a founder of Augusta's Evangelical Friends Church, he was active in the Anti-Slavery Association, and his obituary describes him as "a prominent anti-slavery man of olden times."

JOHN LOWRY: In 1899, Judge Noah Cheever, who had been in Ann Arbor since 1859, published a booklet called *Pleasant Walks and Drives about Ann Arbor.* Cheever recommended stopping at the farm of John Lowry [probably the John Lowy listed in Siebert], explaining that "Mr. Lowry's house was one of the stations to the underground railroad and he assisted a great many slaves on their way to Canada. . . . Mr. Sellick Wood, lately deceased of our city, told me that when he was a young man he drove a number of loads of fleeing negro slaves from Mr. Lowry's home to the Detroit River and saw that they were safely carried across to Canada." Lowry's house, now gone, stood on the west side of Ann Arbor-Saline Road, near Brassow.

### THE ROUTE TO CANADA

From Ann Arbor, the next stop to the east was Ypsilanti. A. P. Marshall's *Unconquered Souls: The History of the African American in Ypsilanti* includes a discussion of the city's involvement in the Underground Railroad. Marshall says that George McCoy transported fugitives in wagons with false bottoms and gave them shelter in his barn, while Helen McAndrew hid them in either her octagon house or her barn. Both of these homes have been torn down. "The only house we can absolutely verify is the Norris house," Marshall says. Mark Norris lived at 213 North River Street and was a prominent early settler whose role in the Underground

Railroad is documented in letters retained by his family. Others have suggested that fugitives were hidden in Ypsilanti's black church, but Marshall is doubtful. "The church was in an old livery stable and didn't have a basement. It's the first place [slave hunters] would look."

Going north out of Ann Arbor, up Pontiac Trail from the Beckley houses, or straight north from the Geddes and Glazier houses, fugitives would pass the hamlet of Salem. While no contemporary evidence has been found that Salem residents aided the fugitives, *The History of Salem Township, Washtenaw County, Michigan,* published in 1976, lists seven possible Underground Railroad sites, based on older documents and stories told by local residents. The hamlet's support for abolition is indisputable: in the 1840 election it led the county in voting for the antislavery Liberty party, giving the abolitionists sixty-three votes, compared with fifty in Ann Arbor and twenty in Ypsilanti.

From Ypsilanti, the former slaves originally traveled east through Plymouth, River Rouge, and Swartzburg to Detroit. When that route became too closely watched, the line shifted northward, passing through a string of towns—Northville, Farmington, Birmingham, Pontiac, Rochester, Utica, Romeo, Richmond, and New Haven—on the way to the St. Clair River. Finally, the fugitives were smuggled across to Canada by boat.

## Living Legacies

It is estimated that forty thousand former slaves and their families were living in Canada at the time of the Civil War. About half of them eventually moved back to the United States. They came over a period of decades to rejoin family, to return to a warmer climate, or to pursue jobs or education. In her memoir, Laura Haviland mentions a former slave named John White who after emancipation "removed to Ann Arbor, Michigan to educate his children."

Many Ann Arbor families trace their descent to these black Canadians. The local black Elks Lodge, according to member William Hampton, "was formed by a group mostly from Canada." Several well-known historic figures, including Charles Baker, co-owner of the Ann Arbor Foundry, and Claude Brown, who ran a secondhand store in the Main Street building that now houses Laky's Salon, came to Ann Arbor from Canada.

At least three Ann Arbor families have connections with North Buxton, a remarkable settlement in the middle of southwestern Ontario, near Chatham. North Buxton was founded in 1849 by William King, a minister who married the daughter of a southern plantation owner. When King's wife inherited her family's fifteen slaves, King freed them, buying land in Canada for them to resettle. They became the nucleus of a black community whose residents grew a wide range of crops, owned and operated businesses, ran hotels, organized churches, and published a newspaper. Their schools were so good that white people from neighboring communities sent their children there. And they claimed a number of firsts, including the first black Canadian elected to public office.

Ann Arborite Ruth Spann's great-aunt came from North Buxton, and Lydia Morton's great-grandfather lived in nearby Fletcher. Viola Henderson's great-aunt, Mary Ann Shadd Gary, ran a school in Windsor for black refugees. After the passage of the 1850 Fugitive Slave Act made life more dangerous near the border, she moved inland to North Buxton, where in 1853 she became the first black woman in North America to edit a weekly newspaper. After the war, she returned to the United States, where she was the first black woman to graduate from Howard University Law School.

Dwight Walls, pastor of the Greater Shiloh Church of God in Christ in Ypsilanti, is descended from John Freeman Walls, a former slave from North Carolina, and Jane Walls, the white widow of his original "master." The Wallses escaped the South; reached Canada by boat from Toledo; and settled in Puce, Ontario. Dwight Walls's grandfather moved to Detroit to work after World War II, but his family still has many Canadian connections. He reports that a number of black Ypsilantians have Canadian roots, including the Bass, Perry, and Kersey families, as well as the Grayer family of his mother.

Descendants of the original settlers still live in North Buxton, although only two families still farm and the children go into Chatham for school. Artifacts from the original settlement, including King's bed and many photographs, can be viewed in the Raleigh Township Centennial Museum. In Puce, Walls's cousins run the John Freeman Historic Site and Underground Railroad Museum, which includes the log cabin his ancestors lived in and the graveyard where they are buried.

Amherstburg, where many fugitives arrived by rowboat, honors their place in black history with the North American Black Historical Museum and Cultural Centre. These and several other sites—including the homestead of Josiah Henson, the man believed to be the model for Uncle Tom in Harriet Beecher Stowe's novel *Uncle Tom's Cabin*—form the African-Canadian Heritage Tour.

Sites in Michigan are harder to find. In Battle Creek, the store where Erastus Hussey once hid runaway slaves is gone, its place noted by a historical marker. Another marker tells the story of the Merritts, a Quaker family who hid slaves. In nearby Schoolcraft, Nathan Thomas's house still stands. Privately owned, it is periodically opened to the public. In Cassopolis, there's a historical marker on the former site of the Quaker meetinghouse, once a key center for fugitives entering from Indiana.

Researchers A. P. Marshall and Charles Lindquist, and Mary Butler, Battle Creek archivist, all speak of the frustration of working with such ephemeral evidence. But more information may come to light through a U.S. Parks Service project to identify and mark Underground Railroad sites, on which the Guy Beckley home has been listed. The larger than expected attendance at the National Underground Freedom Center, which opened in Cincinnati in 2004, also shows that there is increasing interest.

The period of slavery is an enormous blot on American history. The Underground Railroad was a heartening exception, in which people of all races worked together to help slaves to freedom. Retelling the story, we celebrate the courage and ingenuity of those who escaped, the kindness of both blacks and whites who helped them on their journey, and the ability of the fugitives to start life over in Canada—and, for many, yet again in the United States.

# Dixboro

*The quiet village on Plymouth Road rose and fell with the roads.*

Dixboro, a small village on Plymouth Road just a few miles northeast of Ann Arbor, probably owes its survival to its location. Serving travelers between Ann Arbor and Detroit gave the crossroads settlement an economic basis that sustained it while other nearby towns, such as Brookville and Geddesburg, dwindled to mere names on old maps.

Dixboro's founder, Captain John Dix, was only twenty-eight years old when he came to the Michigan Territory, but he had already led a remarkable life. Born in Massachusetts in 1796, Dix had gone to sea at age sixteen, fought in the War of 1812, and been shipwrecked in New Zealand. He bought the site that would become Dixboro in 1824, the same year that John Allen and Elisha Rumsey founded Ann Arbor.

Dix laid out his new town on both sides of a Potawatomi trail that was being used by settlers moving west from Detroit. He set aside a village square with sixty-four lots around it and built himself a house on one of the lots on the east side. His house doubled as Dixboro's post office and general store. As soon as he was settled, Dix dammed Fleming Creek to power a sawmill and a gristmill.

After nine years, Dix left, resettling in Texas. Dixboro continued to function but never rivaled Ann Arbor. Some believe this was because Dix's departure deprived the town of strong leadership; others point to the fact that the railroad followed the Huron River instead of coming through Dixboro. Dix sold most of his holdings to brothers John and William Clements. They continued to run the store, the post office, and a tavern. Rival stores and taverns started up as well, along with a few other small businesses—two blacksmiths, a cider mill, a cooper shop, and a steam-powered sawmill.

Dixboro never incorporated as a city. It has always been governed as part of Superior Township. But for more than a century the village had its own one-room schoolhouse on the public square. The first school, built sometime between 1828 and 1832, was replaced in 1888 with the red brick building that still stands. In 1858, a church, now Dixboro United Methodist Church, was built behind the school. The two institutions

The Dixboro Methodist Church, circa 1916, was built in 1858 and has been the center of village life ever since. *(Courtesy of Tom Freeman.)*

served as the center of village life. "Everyone took part in the [church] functions, even if they didn't go to church every Sunday," recalls Richard Leslie, who grew up in Dixboro between the two world wars. "The church really ran the town."

Dixboro was surrounded by farmland, and many of the town's residents were farmers. Lifetime resident Tom Freeman compares Dixboro to a European town where people live in the center and go out to their farms during the day. His mother, Carol Willits Freeman, who wrote the village history, *Of Dixboro: Lest We Forget*, grew up in a house in the center of town, on Plymouth Road between Dixboro and Cherry Hill Roads. Yet her family had three cows, a horse, a few pigs, and some chickens and grew crops to the south of their house.

The Leslie family, who lived on the same street as the church, farmed in many of the fields to the north and kept eight or ten cows. One of Richard Leslie's jobs when he was a boy was to take his family's cows across Plymouth Road to their grazing land behind Oak Grove Cemetery. In the days before automobiles were ubiquitous, only occasionally would a passing car slow their progress.

IN 1924, Plymouth Road was paved. The project took two years: one summer to widen and grade the narrow dirt road and one to pour the cement. Gravel for the project was taken from the Cadillac Sand and Gravel Pit, near today's Humane Society headquarters, and was transported by a little train, called a "dinky," that moved on a temporary track.

Plymouth Road looking east, circa 1916, eight years before it was paved. *(Courtesy of Tom Freeman.)*

Dixboro men got jobs helping with the road, while their wives earned extra money serving meals to the workers.

Much of the paving was done by convict labor. Carol Freeman, interviewed for a video made by Dale Leslie, the son of Richard Leslie, laughingly recalled, "They all told us they were in for bootlegging." Dale Leslie himself recalls a story told by his great-aunt: when she asked one of the convicts why he didn't work faster she was told, "Lady, I've got twenty years to build this road."

The paved road gave Dixboro an economic boost. The Dixboro General Store, which was built sometime before 1840, was sold in 1924 to Emmett Gibb. Counting on increased business from the improved road, Gibb modernized the store and put on an addition to the east. The extension created a big room on the second level, which was an excellent place for community dances. "We'd shake Mr. Gibb's groceries off his shelves," recalls Harvey Sanderson, who played banjo in the Parker Orchestra. It played for the dances from 1924 to 1930; the Parker family supplied most of the orchestra's members (Sanderson's wife was a Parker). The Parkers owned the old Parker mill on Geddes Road, today a county park.

Several other businesses opened in response to the increased traffic on Plymouth Road. The gas station (now an antique store) sold Dixie gas and became an evening hangout for men in the neighborhood. As late as the 1950s, recalls Gavin Smith, now Superior Township fire chief, "it was a fun place to go and get the gossip." The Farm Cupboard restaurant opened in 1928 in what had been the Frank Bush home. After a fire destroyed the house in 1935, the Bushes' barn was moved onto the site

An economic boom created by paving Plymouth caused several area businesses to expand, including the Dixboro General Store. *(Courtesy of Tom Freeman.)*

and converted into a restaurant; it survives today as the Lord Fox. Other road-oriented businesses followed in later years—the Prop Restaurant (now a chiropractor's office), a second gas station on the corner of Ford and Plymouth (now an empty lot), and the Red Arrow Motel, which is still there, but not used for that purpose. On football Saturdays, traffic was so heavy that residents couldn't cross the road, and even the church got in on the action. From 1926 to 1961, churchwomen raised money by selling chicken dinners to the passing throngs of U-M sports fans.

For more than a century after the village was founded, most of the houses built were for children or grandchildren of long-term residents. Carol Freeman and her husband, Glen, had a house on Church Street that included five acres of land. Later they rented out the house and built a newer one next door. Their children built houses on the remaining land and have recently been joined by a married grandchild. The Leslies did the same thing, with three of their children building homes next to the cemetery on family land.

Dixboro's first major expansion came in 1951, when the Dixboro Heights subdivision was built in what had been a cornfield farmed by the Leslies. Dixboro Heights was filled with veterans starting families, and the community soon outgrew its one-room school. A two-room school was built in 1953, and then in 1958 Dixboro joined the Ann Arbor school system. In 1974, after a large addition was completed, the school was renamed the Glen A. Freeman School, after Carol Freeman's husband. Today Dixboro children are bused into Ann Arbor, and the former Freeman School is used by Go Like the Wind Montessori school.

Traffic on Plymouth Road decreased in 1964 when the first phase of M-14 was finished. While this hurt some of the businesses (the first casualty was the gas station at Ford and Plymouth), it did no harm to Dixboro's residential attractiveness. Since Dixboro Heights, three other subdivisions—Ford Estates, Autumn Hills, and Tanglewood—have been built, and houses have filled in a few empty lots in the older part of the village. The Fleming Creek subdivision adjoins the village to the southwest.

The church is still the center of Dixboro life—residents meet there, for instance, to discuss the effect of new developments on the area. And although the population is large enough that people no longer know everyone else, there is still great community spirit. Every winter, townspeople set up an ice rink in the former village green. "There's no committee," Tom Freeman says. "Each fall it just happens." For years, the merry-go-round on the school playground—like the upkeep of the cemetery—was a Boy Scout project. One year Ron Smith, now a township firefighter, repaired it as part of an Eagle Scout project. He has continued taking care of it ever since.

# Delhi Village

*Once a thriving industrial town, it never recovered from the tornado of 1917.*

On summer weekends, many Ann Arborites escape to Delhi Metro-park, five miles west of town on the Huron River. Picnicking on the riverbank or jumping from rock to rock in the river, few realize that the rapids that make the park so impressive contain the foundation stones of five nineteenth-century mills or that the small settlement nestled southwest of the park was once a thriving village.

When Michigan was settled, water was the main source of energy, and so most early towns were founded on rivers. Delhi, where the Huron River drops steeply as it rounds a bend, was a particularly good place for mills. At its peak in the 1860s and 1870s, Delhi was a small industrial village, with two gristmills, a woolen mill, a sawmill, and a plaster mill; its own post office (called Delhi Mills); and a railroad station with four scheduled train stops per day.

The first to see the possibilities of the location was Jacob Doremus, a shoemaker who emigrated from New York State in 1831. He bought a tract of land along the river, built a small sawmill, and started clearing the land and selling rough-cut lumber to local farmers. In 1836, he platted a town, which he called Michigan Village, and began selling lots. He built a primitive dam with timber, stone, and earth. Local resident Isaac Place built a millrace on the north side of the river to channel the water.

Taking advantage of the increased water power, Doremus replaced his original sawmill with a better one at the end of the Place race and then built two additional mills, also on the north side of the river—the Ithaca Flour Mill and a four-story brick woolen mill that he named the Doremus Carding and Clothing Works.

Doremus was one of the founders in 1833 of the Webster Church (still extant, it is the oldest continuously used church in Michigan) and an organizer of the local school. In 1846, he tried to change the name of the town to Doremusville, a move that Delhi historian Nick Marsh theorizes may have been to honor his wife, Esther, who died that year.

Delhi, looking north, in 1874 when it was still a thriving mill town, with homes and mills lining both sides of the Huron River. It was all downhill from there: the first mill closed the same year. *(Courtesy of Bentley Historical Library.)*

But the other residents objected and decided to rename it Delhi after the dells and hills in the area.

Doremus died the next year, and the mantle of town leader was passed to his younger partner, Norman Goodale. Goodale built a new flour mill on the south side of the river, which he called simply the Delhi Mill. (A millrace, called the Church race, had already been built on that side of the river for a short-lived scythe factory.) The new mill, four stories high, with an unusual indoor water wheel, could be seen for miles around.

With Goodale's death in 1869, ownership passed to his nineteen-year-old son, Frank, and his partner, John Henley. Frank was the senior partner since he owned more of the stock, but Henley, who knew more about the business, continued to run the mills.

By then, however, the rise of steam power was freeing industry from its dependence on flowing water. Small mills like Delhi's were already facing competition from large urban factories that bought and sold on a national scale. The woolen mill was the first to go: it closed in 1874, done in by competition from larger clothing mills in the East that were being supplied by larger sheep herds in the West. After Henley died in 1881, the other mills' profits also began to go down drastically, due to a combination of hard economic times and Frank Goodale's inexperience. In 1889, Goodale and his mother lost ownership of the remaining mills.

Delhi after the 1917 tornado, looking south. *(Courtesy of Al Gallup.)*

The tornado demolished the house that Eli Gallup was renting and threw his Model T across the road. *(Courtesy of Al Gallup.)*

In 1900 the Delhi mills merged with the Michigan Milling Company, which razed and sold for scrap the Ithaca Flour Mill, the sawmill, and the plaster mill. In 1903, the company closed the last operating mill, the Delhi Mill, and it was dismantled in 1906.

Delhi had lived on water power, and it withered as water power became unnecessary. In 1903 the post office closed, replaced by Rural Free Delivery out of Ann Arbor, and the railroad station was torn down and replaced by a shed, where the occasional passenger flagged down passing trains.

MUCH OF WHAT REMAINED of industrial Delhi was devastated by a tornado on June 7, 1917. The storm, the worst in half a century, destroyed the school, the metal truss bridge, what was left of the Delhi Mill and the woolen mill, and many houses. Future Ann Arbor parks superintendent Eli Gallup, then a young graduate of U-M's forestry school, was living in a rented house in Delhi when the tornado hit. The house was demolished, and his Ford was thrown to the other side of the road.

Luckily, no one was fatally hurt in the storm, but with little reason to rebuild, many of the remaining residents moved away. The town continued to be home for a handful of families who lived in the remaining houses on two streets, one parallel to the river and the other perpendicular, running straight from the bridge. Many of the residents were tradespeople who worked elsewhere—carpenters, railroad workers, American Broach employees. "We enjoyed living there," says Richard Darr, who grew up in Delhi in the 1930s. "Nobody was wealthy, but we knew everyone and took care of each other." His brother Bob remembers, "In the spring we would take off our shoes and leave them off all summer."

IN THE SUBURBAN MIGRATION after World War II, Delhi began to grow again, with small ranch houses built mainly along Railroad Street and a few spurs. The longtimers called the new homes "the subdivision." Today a second building boom is occurring, this time with much larger and more expensive houses, filling in the area to the west up to the river.

In 1957, the fifty-acre Delhi Metropark opened, east of the bridge in what had been a cornfield. The park is part of the Huron-Clinton Metropolitan Authority, which was organized after World War II to save some southeast Michigan land for parks before it was all filled by development. A third Darr brother, Arnold, remembers that when the park opened it consisted of just a few roads and some benches by the river. There are now picnic tables, playground equipment, a shelter, fishing sites, and canoe launching and rental.

Today Delhi has forty-nine houses and an estimated population of 123. The Goodale house burned down, but the Henley house is still there, albeit with a different roof. The schoolhouse still stands, although it hasn't been used as such since Delhi consolidated its schools with Dexter's in the 1960s. Crossing the metal truss bridge (built about 1889 and replaced after the tornado, using some of the old parts) one can easily make out the two millraces. Also still discernible are faint traces of a mill on either side of the river, plus some stones from the dam—the last testaments of the mills that ceased operating almost a hundred years ago.

# The Story of the Schwaben Halle

*On the eve of World War I, German Americans built a virtual palace of ethnic solidarity.*

The Schwaben Halle at 215 South Ashley was sold several years ago, but the Schwaebischer Unterstuetzungs Verein (Swabian Support Association), the group that built it, is still alive and kicking. Better known simply as the "Schwaben Verein," the club was founded in 1888 by recent German immigrants. Although the local German community is by now pretty well assimilated, the Verein survives, in large part because of the fun the members and their families have sharing their common ancestry. "Eat, drink, and dance. What else do Germans do?" laughs member Walter Metzger. At the spring Bockbierfest, says president Art French, "the food is different, but we still eat and drink and dance. Any excuse for a party."

Swabians, who take their name from a medieval kingdom in southern Germany, began immigrating to Ann Arbor as early as 1825, usually when there were economic or political problems in Germany. The 1880 immigrants were escaping the effects of Bismarck's rule, as well as an economic depression, choosing Ann Arbor because Germans from earlier migrations were already here. But although other Germans in town helped them get established, the new arrivals felt a need for mutual support in the new country.

Tailor Gottlieb Wild, who was born near Stuttgart and served a four-year apprenticeship before coming to America, brought the idea of a Swabian club to Ann Arbor. His story, as related in Samuel Beakes's 1906 *Past and Present of Washtenaw County*, is like that of many other Ann Arbor German immigrants: "He came to America when but seventeen years of age, and made his way to Ann Arbor, having relatives in this city, who had come to the New World in 1835."

In 1887 Wild moved to Toledo to work as a journeyman tailor. He became involved with a Swabian social group there, and when he returned to Ann Arbor the following year to open his own shop, he encouraged his fellow Swabians to form their own association. (Wild's tailor shop, like the Schwaben Verein, proved impressively durable—

it evolved into a popular campus-area men's store that survived until 1988.)

The Schwaben Verein's official purpose was to provide a primitive kind of mutual health and life insurance: members paid a $1 initiation fee and 30¢ a month in dues, and in times of need the group would help out with hospital or burial expenses. But from the beginning, the real attraction was the camaraderie. "It was a way to be with people who spoke their language, followed their customs, who had the same outlook on life," explains president French.

THE GROUP'S FIRST MEETING was held on June 22, 1888, on the second floor of Wild's tailor shop. Business was conducted entirely in German, a tradition that would continue for nearly a century. Many of Ann Arbor's retail establishments were owned and run by Germans, so as the group grew they easily found other places to meet. They moved from Wild's shop to rooms in Michael Staebler's hotel, the American House (now the Earle, at Washington and Ashley), and when that in turn proved inadequate, to rented rooms above Arnold's Jewelry Store on Main Street.

In 1894, just six years after its founding, the group was financially secure enough to purchase a building, the former Wagner's blacksmith shop on Ashley between Washington and Liberty. All seven members of the executive committee signed the mortgage. They reserved the second floor for their meetings and rented the downstairs to blacksmith Henry Otto (who was better known locally as the leader of Otto's Band).

In 1908 the Schwaben Verein bought a second property: the Relief Fire Company Park, south of Madison and west of what is now Fifth Street, then on the outskirts of the city. (Since 1888 the fire department had been changing over to professional firefighters, and volunteer companies were phased out.) The park was used for open-air events. "Parades and picnics were memorable occasions," the *Ann Arbor News* reported. "Entire families turned out, the children to enjoy games and sports while their elders talked on and on about the 'old country' and the occurrences in their lives in their adopted land."

Hardware store owner Christian Schlenker, who was president of the Verein at the time, is credited with spearheading the construction of a permanent headquarters. "Entirely due to his persistence and influence, they decided to build the new Swabian Hall," W. W. Florer states in *Early Michigan Settlements* (1941).

The key was a deal between the group and Mack & Company, then Ann Arbor's largest department store, at 220–224 South Main. Walter

Construction of the Schwaben Verein. *(Courtesy of Bill Mundus.)*

Mack agreed to rent most of the planned structure, including the two upper floors and part of the basement. Mack, though the son of a German immigrant, was not a member of the Verein ("Mr. Mack was never affiliated with any fraternal organizations but has concentrated his energies and attention upon his business interests and family life," writes Beakes), and he did not help with construction costs. However, he agreed to build a steam heating plant, pay fire insurance for the whole building, and provide water for the sprinkler system.

IN MAY 1914 the blacksmith shop was torn down, and construction began on the new building. Local historian Carol Mull, who has done extensive research on the building, finds it probable that some of the brick from the blacksmith shop was reused in the new building. Architect George Scott designed the Schwaben Halle, and Julius Koernke, a German immigrant who had settled in Ann Arbor in 1890, served as contractor.

Enclosed walkways connected the third and fourth floors with Mack's Main Street store, and the buildings' basements were joined by a tunnel. Mack used the basement for storage and the upstairs for a dining room, a beauty shop (the holes from the plumbing were still there when the Verein sold the building), and a big toy display at Christmas. The Ashley Street storefront was rented to Hagen and Jedele Men's Clothing.

The Verein reserved the second floor for its own activities. A large front room was used for dancing and banquets; it had a stage at one end for plays and performances. There was a dressing room behind the stage, and beyond that were the bar and kitchen. Beautiful woodwork, tin ceilings, a fireplace, and a stained-glass front window with the Schwaben name on it all added to the hall's beauty. In 1988, to celebrate the Verein's hundredth anniversary, some of the members donated stained glass for the side windows and transoms.

During World War I, when other German groups were fading out or switching to English, the Schwaben Verein kept meeting and didn't experience any overt harassment. "The society subscribed to war loans throughout the war and helped in every deserving war charity brought to its notice," wrote the *Ann Arbor News* in 1922. While admitting a little defensively that the group was "still carrying its German name," the paper insisted that "the organization is essentially American and stands for everything which is American."

The war and subsequent anti-immigrant fervor, as well as Prohibition, cut into the activities of many German groups, but the Schwaben Verein emerged stronger than ever. Helping German war victims from the Württemberg area gave it an additional reason for existing. And although Prohibition lowered attendance at the park, the club met the challenge by selling the land and using the proceeds to help pay off its Ashley Street building.

Member John Hanselmann bought the park and divided it into house lots. The club continued having picnics at Hanselmann's Grove on Waters Road off Ann Arbor-Saline Road or at members' farms, such as Walter Aupperle's property on Frains Lake Road. (The German Park organization on Pontiac Trail is a different group, although there is some overlap in membership.)

In 1922, just eight years after finishing the Halle, the group was able to celebrate paying off the mortgage. "On the eve of Thanksgiving day a gathering of 100 men stood in a darkened room of the Schwaben hall and in hushed stillness watched the mortgage on the building disappear in flames," reported the *Ann Arbor News*. "The flickering light of the flames showed up solemn faces and glimpses of the Star Spangled banners which decorate the room. As the last shred of paper fell and the flame died out lights flooded the room and 100 voices rose in acclamation."

At Christmas the hall hosted Swabian-dialect plays. *Left to right:* Gottlob Schumacher, Gertrude Flautz, Martin Rempp, William Metzger, Emmy Heinzlemann,
and Anton Vetter ham it up. *(Courtesy of Walter Metzger.)*

THE VEREIN PAID OFF its mortgage just in time to be ready for the next
wave of immigrants. "They came from the very same villages as the men
of the eighties and of former decades," writes Florer. "A revival of interest in plays, concerts, and other social activities began and has continued ever since."

One of the 1920s immigrants was Gottlob Schumacher, who until
his death in 2001 was the group's oldest living member. Schumacher first
visited the Schwaben Halle three days after his arrival in Ann Arbor in
October 1923. Staying at the American House, Schumacher was introduced to a fellow Swabian named Gottlob Gross, who brought him over
to the club. In a 1988 interview Schumacher recalled that since it was
Sunday the hall was supposed to be closed, so the men went up the back
stairs from the alley. They rang a bell, and the barman looked through
a sliding window before letting them in. Although it sounds like a scene
from a Prohibition-era movie, Schumacher insisted that the bar offered
nothing stronger than hard cider—although even that was illegal during
Prohibition.

Schumacher officially joined the Schwaben Verein three months later.
One of his favorite activities was acting in plays the group wrote and
performed in Swabian dialect. Walter Metzger, whose parents emigrated
from Swabia, recalls that a huge crowd always attended these plays, put

on near Christmas. "They filled up the Schwaben Halle, sitting in folding chairs and the benches around the side," he says. The programs would consist of two or three short, sitcomlike sketches: "There would be a married couple. They would bicker and make fun of each other," Metzger explains. "Then others would come in—neighbors, relatives. They were humorous. You had to laugh the entire time." In between the plays, the audience could buy sandwiches and beer at the bar.

The cast was all amateurs, just members who enjoyed that sort of thing—Schumacher, Anton Vetter, Hans Meier, Martin Rempp. Bill and Fred Wente, who worked at Herz Paint Store, did the sets. Bill Staebler, who owned a beauty shop, did the makeup, and members' wives sewed the costumes. Metzger was just a boy then, but he was put to work with his older brother Hans, who could drive, delivering advertising placards to outlying towns such as Manchester and Bridgewater that had large German populations. Metzger also served as a curtain puller and once even had a nonspeaking role.

In 1938 the Schwaben Verein had been in existence for fifty years. One hundred and fifty members and guests celebrated the anniversary at a banquet at the city's biggest hotel, the Allenel (where the Courthouse Square apartments are now). After dinner they reconvened at the hall for a program that included music by the Lyra Männerchor (men's chorus), followed by dancing and a radio program of Swabian folk tunes and songs—broadcast live via shortwave from Stuttgart especially for the occasion.

The plays stopped during World War II, but the group weathered the war, just as it had survived World War I. It no doubt helped that many of the young men leaving to fight the war were themselves of German ancestry. Although local German Americans were firmly on the Allied side, they didn't forget their relatives in Germany. "We had our own CARE program, helping individually in areas we knew about," explains French.

The war triggered one last influx of German immigrants. The Schwaben Verein continued a full schedule of activities, including *Kirchweihe* (literally a church dedication festival, observed as a harvest festival, with strings of radishes, beets, turnips, and cabbage serving as decorations); a children's Christmas party; an anniversary dinner; and the Bockbierfest, featuring a special beer traditionally made for Lent. For years a group of women, headed by Karoline Schumacher, who was chef at the Old German when she and her husband owned the restaurant from 1936 to 1946, would make and serve such German specialties as liver sausage, roulades, goulash, spaetzle, sauerkraut, and German potato salad. And of course beer was the drink of choice for most events.

German bands from Toledo or Detroit with names like Langecker's Wanderers, Tyrolers, Dorimusikanten, or Eric Nybower provided the music for dancing. Sometimes the Schuhplattler, a group affiliated with German Park, would perform traditional German dances. For its centennial in 1988, the Verein imported a band from Germany named Contrast.

People who regularly attended these functions became very close. Art French met his wife, then Kathy Rempp, at a Schwaben event. And Kathy's parents, Mina and Martin Rempp (who, like his son-in-law, was a long-term president), met at a Schwaben event in Toledo.

"We still call each other our extended family," says Marianne Rauer. "We are our own psychiatrists." Fritz Kienzle, the group's flag bearer, once dropped out for three and a half years but missed it so much he went back. "You've got to have that gravy on your potatoes," he explains.

The Schwaben Verein has changed as the local German community has become more assimilated. Originally members had to be from Swabia, but later the group accepted anyone who spoke German. Today, members just have to have some German connection.

Most in the group now are American born, although there are still fourteen German-born members. "The meetings were mostly in German until about twenty years ago," says French. "There are less and less who can converse in German, so we have to keep translating in order not to keep them out. But we still open and close the meetings in German."

Though the Verein is still officially an all-male group, in the 1970s, with no change in the rules, women started coming to the hall during meetings. Wives of members who drove their husbands to the meetings, or who just didn't want to be left alone at home, came up and waited in the bar area, visiting and playing cards until their husbands finished the meeting and joined them.

After Mack & Company closed during the Great Depression, the first floor was rented to other tenants, including a bar called Mackinaw Jack's, which left the facade covered with fake logs. Later, Hi-Fi Studio, an electronics repair business, packed the space with old TVs and stereos. Even the second-floor meeting room was rented out when the Verein wasn't using it. Over the years it's hosted everything from the local Jewish congregation (in the early 1920s) to sports clubs, sister city events, and weddings and other private parties.

French says the group currently has seventy members, of whom twenty or twenty-five regularly attend bimonthly meetings. The average age is about fifty. "Lots join with their dads," explains Harriet Holzapfel, whose husband, son, and father-in-law were all members. "There's an age gap," says Rauer, "but once they are married and have kids they come back. They want their kids to have the Christmas party and family events."

But the group's desire to keep the large hall waned, especially since the rest of the building wasn't producing the rental income it once had. Art French says he'd been looking for a long time, but "I couldn't get tenants. Everyone wanted to buy—no one wanted to rent." So in March 2001 the Schwaben Halle was sold to Bill Kinley of Phoenix Contractors and Ann Arbor architects Dick Mitchell and John Mouat.

The new owners removed the fake log siding from the front of the building and restored the facade as closely as possible to its original look. Inside they made changes to meet current standards, such as wider, fire-code-compliant stairs and an elevator for handicap access.

Meanwhile, the Schwaben Verein members meet just down the street at Hathaway's Hideaway, the former second ward polling place now owned by the Hathaway family. "We're still active, still accepting new members, we still have the activities. We just don't have a building," says French. For big events they rent space at either the Links at Whitmore Lake or Fox Hills golf course on North Territorial Road.

Many in Ann Arbor's German community were sad to see a building that encompassed so much of their past sold. "It was like the soul of the German community, such a beautiful place," says Marianne Rauer. But Fritz Kienzle points out that the Schwaben Verein was always more than just a building. "People said when you sell you lose all your heritage," he says. "But the heritage is in you, in your memories."

# A Tale of Two Lakes

*Side by side, separate resorts catered to blacks and whites.*

P eople once came from all over southeastern Michigan to play golf, dance, swim, and fish at two resorts on neighboring lakes north of Chelsea. But the guests rarely mingled, because one group was white and the other was black.

Both resorts were established in the 1920s—Inverness, on North Lake, by a white former Detroit business owner and Wild Goose Lake, a short hop away, by three black families from Ann Arbor. The latter was born in controversy. When word first got out that some farmers were considering selling their land to blacks, neighbors circulated a petition urging them not to do so. When grocer Perry Noah refused to sign— he reportedly told the petitioners, "My father died in the Civil War to free these people"—his store was briefly boycotted.

The sellers, descendants of the area's original settlers, refused to be intimidated. And that is how dual resorts, each with its own country club and a beach, grew up almost side by side.

THE LAND AROUND the two small lakes, about five miles north of Chelsea, was first permanently settled in 1833. Charles and John Glenn and their sister Jane Burkhart came from upstate New York with their spouses and children. Charles Glenn reportedly had decided to move west after his first wife and their two young children were killed when flax she was spinning caught fire.

The siblings bought adjoining tracts of government land and built houses. Charles Glenn's original house at 13175 North Territorial Road still stands. John Glenn had a fancier Italianate house down the road. The Burkharts settled just south of Wild Goose Lake.

Other settlers quickly followed, enough to justify a post office at North Lake in 1836. That year the Glenn family organized a Methodist church. Nineteen people gathered at John Glenn's house for the first service, with Charles Glenn presiding as lay preacher. Ten years later the two brothers built a small church that also served as a school. In

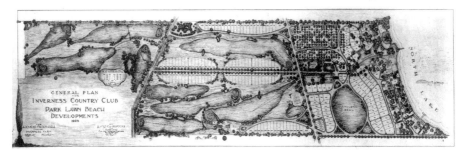

Original plat for Inverness. *(Courtesy of Sylvia Gilbert.)*

1866 John Glenn deeded land for what is now the North Lake United Methodist Church. He also gave land for a cemetery on Riker Road.

The land around the lakes, hilly and full of glacial gravel, was best suited to fruit farming. Charles's son Benjamin Glenn went into the nursery business with his cousins William and Robert, starting apple trees from seeds they procured at a cider mill. (At Wild Goose Lake today, aged apple, pear, and cherry trees are the remnants of a much larger orchard.)

The local grange built a hall that served as the community's social center. The North Lake Band, which played in neighboring towns, was based at the Grange Hall from about 1897 to 1906. In 1925 the North Lake church bought the building for $1 and moved it to church property to use as a Sunday school, dining room, and kitchen.

In 1920, Doug Fraser, president of American Brass and Iron Company in Detroit, retired and moved to North Lake. Fraser had ulcers, and his daughter Lauretta had contracted whooping cough, tonsillitis, and diphtheria; he hoped farming would be a healthier way of life for them both.

Fraser and his wife, Laura, bought John Glenn's seven-bedroom Italianate farmhouse from John's grandson Fred Glenn. The dining room was so large, Lauretta Fraser Sockow remembers, that the family preferred to eat meals in the sunroom next to the kitchen.

Sockow, now in her nineties, remembers how she loved the rural area as a child. She attended the one-room North Lake School at 1300 Hankerd, now a private home. Her family joined the North Lake church and sometimes hosted barn dances, playing music on their Victrola. Fraser grew apples, strawberries, raspberries, and currants and also raised pigs, but his pride and joy, according to Sockow, was his registered cattle. Unfortunately, her father eventually developed an allergy to them. "His arms swelled up to the size of a football," Sockow recalls, and he had to sell his animals and machinery and find another way of making a living.

Doug Fraser boating on North Lake with daughter Lauretta. *(Courtesy of Sylvia Gilbert.)*

Glenn house, later the country club. *(Courtesy of Sylvia Gilbert.)*

Inverness clubhouse today. *(Courtesy of Adrian Wylie.)*

His property reached all the way to North Lake, so in 1927 Fraser decided to start a resort. Invoking his Scottish heritage, he called it Inverness and gave its streets such names as Glencoe, Aberdeen, and Bramble Brae. He divided the land between his house and the lake into lots for cottages and set up the deeds so that all owners would have lake privileges. He put in tennis courts behind his house, and he built a nine-hole golf course, expanding into additional land he'd bought along North Territorial Road. He moved his family to Ann Arbor and turned the former Glenn home into the golf course's clubhouse.

Fraser's gamble paid off. In the 1920s, greater prosperity and rising car ownership created a new demand for resort communities, even in once-remote areas like North Lake. Ads for Inverness noted that it was "only sixty miles from Detroit," and Fraser encouraged potential buyers to drive out for the day to sample activities such as pony rides for children and dances for adults (the clubhouse living room was big enough to accommodate two sets of square dances simultaneously). Sockow remembers that one neighbor might play the piano and another the violin.

Sylvia Gilbert, who today lives in the house built for the farm's hired man, says the original clubhouse "was gorgeous. There was a beautiful powder room upstairs, wicker furniture. You could eat in the dining room or the sun porch." Gilbert recalls dances where people would dress in kilts and Halloween parties with elaborate decorations. Her house has since been moved from its original spot to 7095 Glencoe, around the corner.

Inverness attracted people of means from Detroit and Ann Arbor. Doctors, dentists, and businesspeople built large cottages. Laurence Noah, Perry Noah's son, earned money by doing chores for the summer people, such as delivering wood and taking away garbage. In the winter, Laurence and his father cut ice from North Lake and stored it to sell in the summer.

A MILE AWAY, at Wild Goose Country Club, the members enjoyed the same amenities as at Inverness—swimming, dancing, fishing, and golf. But for the people who frequented it, Wild Goose represented a much rarer opportunity.

"Blacks had no place to go," explains Mercedes Baker Snyder. Her father, Charles Baker, along with Donald Grayer and Iva Pope, bought the land and organized the resort. Baker, co-owner of the Ann Arbor Foundry, was interested in the venture because "he loved golf, and blacks couldn't play at public courses," explains Mercedes's husband, Charles Snyder.

Wild Goose sign. *(Courtesy of Adrian Wylie.)*

The first cottages at Wild Goose Country Club were log cabins built from Sears Roebuck kits. *(Courtesy of Mercedes Snyder.)*

Shirley, Sherman, Carl, and Mercedes Baker at Wild Goose Lake with their father, Charles, and grandfather Pawley Sherman. *(Courtesy of Mercedes Snyder.)*

The partners developed the club on the 250-acre farm of Sam and Fred Schultz, who were descendants of the original settlers, the Glenns. The petition drive that residents of North Lake started to keep out the black resort community didn't deter the Schultzes. After the sale was completed on June 1, 1927, the Wild Goose Country Club was formed, with ninety-three lots for cottages and a stretch of communal lakeshore with a fishing dock. As at Inverness, the original farmhouse eventually was converted to a clubhouse. A nine-hole golf course began behind the clubhouse and went across Wild Goose Lake Road toward the lake. A dance hall was built on a hill.

Pawley and Carrie Grayer Sherman, Charles Baker's father- and mother-in-law, became the first residents when they moved from Ann Arbor to the farmhouse. Mercedes Snyder, who came out for weekends to visit her grandparents, remembers that it had three bedrooms downstairs, two big living rooms, and a big kitchen but no plumbing. Her dad would play golf while the children romped around, walked in the woods, or swam in the lake.

The first two cottages, one built by the Shermans, the other by Donald Grayer, were log cabins made from Sears Roebuck kits. A couple more cabins were built before the Depression. The rest of the eighteen or so members merely owned unbuilt lots, which sold for $100. "At that time most Ann Arbor blacks worked in fraternities or cafeterias," explains Charles Snyder. "Fifty cents an hour was considered a good wage, so they couldn't afford to build."

Mercedes Baker Snyder and her husband, Charles, still enjoy the lake. *(Courtesy of Adrian Wylie.)*

Most of the members were relatives or friends of the organizers. A much larger group, consisting of other friends and extended family members, came to visit and swim, dance, or golf. Visitors often traveled for hours to get there; in those days there weren't many recreational facilities open to blacks.

Coleman Castro used to come in the 1930s to fish with Don Grayer Jr., his future brother-in-law. Ann Arbor resident Donald Calvert recalls coming out in the late 1940s or early 1950s to swim with friends at Wild Goose Lake. Back then, he says, the resorts favored by his white classmates, such as Zukey Lake or Groomes Beach at Whitmore Lake, did not allow blacks.

In its heyday, Wild Goose hosted big dances organized by Jim and Harriet Moore (a Sherman daughter), who moved into the clubhouse after the senior Shermans moved out. The public dances attracted blacks from all over southeastern Michigan. U-M dentistry graduate D. J. Grimes, who was one of the first black dentists in Detroit and a cousin of Jim Moore, told his Detroit friends about the dances and also put Moore in touch with good bands. Ann Arbor residents would go home after the dances, but the Detroit visitors often stayed, sleeping in rooms the Moores rented to them, either in the clubhouse or in another house they built across the road.

THE LAKESIDE RESORTS' golden age was brief. Once the Depression hit, "people didn't need cottages. People didn't need to play golf," says Sockow. Sales at Inverness dropped so precipitously that her father had to incorporate and bring in other investors to keep going. Although he ceded control of the development to a board of directors, he kept managing the country club until his death in 1952.

Cottage building completely stopped at Wild Goose Lake during the Depression. The dance hall was knocked over during a big storm in the 1930s and was never rebuilt. Russell Calvert, Donald's brother, remembers that the golf course was still there in the late 1940s and 1950s but had become less popular because by then blacks could play on municipal courses. It eventually fell into disuse and is now overgrown.

North Lake residents and Wild Goose Country Club members apparently reached a state of grudging coexistence after the failure of the initial petition drive. Wild Goose people patronized North Lake businesses and report that they were treated well. But the two groups did not socialize much.

After World War II, building at both lakes resumed. The prewar cottages were winterized and often enlarged, and the old prejudices began to ease. In the 1960s a Wild Goose resident, Bessie Russell, joined the North Lake church. "They were glad to have her," recalls Mercedes Snyder. "They needed someone to play the organ."

Today, both former resorts have turned into bedroom communities where working people and retirees live year round. At North Lake, the Inverness Country Club is going strong, with a waiting list to join. Buying a house in the original subdivision bestows automatic membership. The clubhouse has been replaced with a more modern building that looks like a ranch house.

The Wild Goose clubhouse was sold and is again a home. Much of the communal land, including the golf course, has also been sold and is divided into residential lots awaiting development.

The biggest change at Wild Goose Lake is that the population is now about 50 percent white. "As older blacks die, young blacks don't want to live in the country," explains Charles Snyder. But residents still often have family connections—including some that cross the old color line. Members of one of the new white families are the in-laws of Coleman Castro's son, Tommie.

# Architecture

# Cobblestone Houses in
# Washtenaw County

*They're a spinoff of the Erie Canal.*

C obblestone Farm on Packard Road is one of at least seven cobblestone houses in Washtenaw County. Highly distinctive but incredibly laborious to build, they're examples of a folk art that flourished
between the completion of the Erie Canal in 1825 and the Civil War.

Cobblestone houses first appeared in western New York State immediately after the canal was completed. Their creation was due to a
fortunate combination of circumstances: a labor force of skilled masons
looking for work after the canal's completion, an abundance of glacial
stones, and a population eager to build new homes with profits from the
canal. Most of the known examples (nine hundred in all) are in New
York, but as New Yorkers moved west, they took the craft with them
and built scattered cobblestone houses in southern Ontario, southern
Michigan, Illinois, and Wisconsin—wherever they found the style's namesake building materials, glacial stones, formed during the Ice Age, small
enough to hold in one hand.

Even the most informative book on cobblestone architecture, *Cobblestone Landmarks of New York State*, by Olaf William Shelgren Jr., Cary
Lattin, and Robert W. Frasch, is unable to trace an inventor of the style.
The authors assume that most masons did only three or four cobblestone
houses and that "they learned the cobblestone technique from each other
or by examining finished buildings."

Cobblestone houses' exterior walls were constructed with the stones
arranged in neat rows, usually either vertically or horizontally but
sometimes in fancier designs, and held together with cement that formed
ridges between the layers. The simple lines of the prevalent architectural
styles of the period, such as Federal, Classic Revival, and Greek Revival,
lent themselves perfectly to this type of construction.

The masons experimented, and the homes became more involved and

The city-owned property known as Cobblestone Farm, built in 1844 for naval surgeon Benajah Ticknor, is today the site of many community activities. *(Courtesy of
Stan Shackman.)*

elaborate as the years went by. But even the simplest style was very labor
intensive, requiring hand placement of each stone. In the earliest homes,
the stones were embedded right in the cement, forming an integral part
of the outside wall. Later, the stones were more of a veneer, with just an
occasional longer stone poked all the way into the cement. Toward the
end of the era, the houses became very fancy, with tinier stones used
merely for a veneer and arranged in elaborate patterns.

The cobblestone houses in Washtenaw County fit in with what is
known about the homes in general: all were built in the 1830s and 1840s;
all are in places where western New Yorkers settled; and all are of simple
design, either Classic Revival or Greek Revival. Where the building time
is documented, it runs from two to seven years, showing how laborious
the work was. While two of the homes may have been done by the same
mason, the other five seem to have been done by different individuals.
All are located either on the Huron River or near streams, where stones
were easier to find.

Cobblestone Farm, built in 1844 at 2781 Packard, is now a city-owned
museum. Both the owner and the builder had New York origins. He-
man Ticknor, who bought the farm for his brother, Dr. Benajah Ticknor,
had farmed in Pittstown, New York, near Troy; the probable builder,
Steven Mills, learned to be a mason in Phelps, in western New York.

Ann Arbor's other cobblestone house, at 2940 Fuller Road, across

Cobblestone houses, built from stones small enough to hold in one hand, are very labor intensive because the construction process entails putting in the stones one by one. *(Courtesy of Stan Shackman.)*

from Huron High, was built in 1836 for Orrin White, the first settler in Ann Arbor Township. White migrated to Ann Arbor from Palmyra, in Wayne County, New York, the county with the largest number of recorded cobblestone houses. Former owners Nan and Robert Hodges believe that the house was also built by Steven Mills because it is very similar to the Ticknor-Campbell house: both are Classic Revival, and they have identical herringbone patterns of angled stones and similar interior layouts.

Lima Township's cobblestone house, at 10725 Jerusalem Road, is similar to the Ann Arbor cobblestone houses in size and design. Original owner Lester Jewett, who hailed from Seneca, New York, was, like Benajah Ticknor, a medical doctor. According to stories that have been passed down, the house took seven years to build. Dr. Jewett had two brothers who also settled on Jerusalem Road. They, too, built stone houses, but they used larger fieldstones. Family legend is that the stone houses brought them luck.

The Rufus Knight home on Scio Church Road also has a similar look except for smaller upstairs windows. Knight, a miller who arrived in this area in 1826 from Wheatville, New York, was a pathfinder who, according to the *Portrait and Biographical Album of Washtenaw County, Michigan, 1891*, "ground the first grist which ever went between the stones in this county." He set another record—the first marriage to be entered in the county archives—when he married Sallie Scott in 1827. The 1891 book's description of Knight ends, "The old cobble stone house is still in use and as good as ever although it was erected as long ago as 1849."

A hens and chicks Greek Revival–style cobblestone is found at 3555 West Delhi Road, just a little to the west of the Delhi settlement. It is

The Orrin White house across the street from Huron High School is believed to be built by Steven Mills, the same mason who constructed Cobblestone Farm. *(Courtesy of Bentley Historical Library.)*

believed to have been built by William Burnett, who owned the property for thirty years and is buried there. In the twentieth century the house was part of the Detroit Edison holdings and home to the manager of the peach orchard. In 1937 Henry Ford bought it as part of his effort to recreate mill industries in southeast Michigan.

A second Greek Revival house in Scio Township (the owner prefers not to reveal its exact location) was the home of farmer Morris Richmond, who hailed from New York and built his house in 1847, taking more than two years to do it. The house was obviously built by someone who knew about architecture, since it features classic Greek Revival attributes: gable entrance, symmetrical windows, and even a raised area under the beams forming a frieze.

The most rustic of the seven Washtenaw County cobblestone homes is probably the only owner-built house in the group. Located on the corner of Baker and Shields just south of Dexter, it was built by Obed Taylor, who, according to information researched by his great-great-grandson, Welton Chamberlain, had been a surveyor and a road builder in Northbridge, Massachusetts, before coming west. After his arrival in Dexter, he was hired by Vrelan Bates to dig out a millrace for a saw mill on Mill Creek. Taylor worked for three years, digging with pick and shovel, for which he was rewarded with forty acres of nearby land.

He used the stones that he dug out to construct his house, burning the larger pieces of limestone for cement and using the smaller stones for the walls. Records indicate that he must have finished his home by 1844 because in that year he was hired by Judge Samuel Dexter to build a fence just like the one around his own home.

People curious about cobblestone houses and willing to travel farther afield can see all the cobblestone houses they could ever desire by going to western New York State and driving along Route 104, built on an old sandbar that parallels the Erie Canal. In Childs, New York, is the Cobblestone Society, located in a cobblestone church; a cobblestone home and a cobblestone one-room school are also on display. A little closer to home, in Paris, Ontario, near Brantford, are Canada's finest examples of cobblestone homes, all built by Levi Broughton, a mason from Normandale, New York.

Right here in Washtenaw County, we are lucky to have the seven we have: all slightly different, all well kept up, and all beautiful. The best time to view cobblestone houses is when the sun shines on them, giving the stones a beautiful three-dimensional look.

# The Remarkable History of the Kempf House

*Following brass bands around Basel turned Reuben Kempf's career from the ministry to music.*

The Kempf House, at 312 South Division, a nationally recognized gem of Greek Revival architecture, is now a city-owned center for local history. It is named for Pauline and Reuben Kempf, the husband-and-wife music teachers who lived in it from 1890 until 1953. The Kempfs were guiding lights in the local music community who often loaned the Steinway in their front parlor—Ann Arbor's first grand piano—to the university. It was played in the May Festival (a University Musical Society concert series) 1894–1995 by such luminaries as Victor Herbert and Ignacy Paderewski.

The Kempf House was actually built in 1853 by Mary and Henry DeWitt Bennett. The Bennetts came from Stephentown, New York (southeast of Albany), where they had doubtless seen numerous examples of Greek Revival architecture. Henry Bennett, described by contemporaries as a genial and warmhearted man, served as postmaster and, later, as steward and secretary of the U-M. After Bennett retired, they moved to California.

The house was sold in 1886 to a neighbor, who rented it out for a few years. Then in 1890, Pauline and Reuben Kempf, married seven years and the parents of a daughter, Elsa (a son Paul was born six years later), moved into the house. They lived there for the next sixty-three years.

Both Pauline and Reuben were raised in Ann Arbor's large German community, and both showed early musical promise. Pauline was the daughter of Karl Widenmann, the German consul for Michigan and owner of a hardware store on the northeast corner of Main and Washington. The family lived in a big house on Fourth Avenue until Pauline was fourteen, when her father was diagnosed as having a brain tumor. He sold his business and moved his family to Whitmore Lake, where he died eight years later. The family could not afford to send Pauline to music school to study singing, but two professors at the university, im-

Pauline and Reuben Kempf enjoy sitting on their porch with daughter Elsa (*left*) and a woman thought to be a neighbor. *(Courtesy of Bentley Historical Library.)*

pressed with her talent, arranged for her to give a recital in the Athens Theater (later the Whitney) at Main and Ann. The proceeds were enough for one year at the Cincinnati Conservatory of Music.

Reuben Kempf, born in 1859, a year before Pauline, grew up on a farm in the area now occupied by Briarwood mall. According to his daughter-in-law, Edith Staebler Kempf, "he learned to play the organ at the Bethlehem Church school, and by the time he was a teenager played the pipe organ quite well. But this didn't impress his parents. They said, 'You *will* study for the ministry.' In those days they didn't ask you."

Reuben was sent to Basel, Switzerland, in 1877, to the same theological seminary that had graduated Friedrich Schmid, the first German pastor in Michigan and a hero to the local German community. But Reuben had been there only a few months when his parents received a letter from the principal, recommending that they not force him to be a minister but let him follow his own wish to be a musician. Evidently he had been following brass bands around Basel. Edith Kempf says it broke his parents' hearts, but they allowed him to transfer to the Royal Conservatory of Music in Stuttgart, where he studied organ and piano and was a classmate of Victor Herbert.

When Reuben returned to Ann Arbor, he opened a studio on the corner of Main and Liberty, on the third floor. He supplemented his income by playing the organ at St. Thomas Church. In 1883 he married Pauline Widenmann, their common music interests forming an obvious bond.

Reuben Kempf organized the Lyra Mannerchor (men's chorus) to bring town and gown together through the universal language of music. Elsa Kempf served as the group's mascot. *(Courtesy of Bentley Historical Library.)*

When they moved to Division Street from their first home on the corner of Main and William, they set up a studio in the front parlor where they could both give lessons.

THE KEMPFS' HOUSE was conveniently located: children could walk to their lessons from all over town. The front door was left unlocked so that students could walk in without knocking. If a lesson was still in progress, they would wait their turn on the red sofa. Geraldine Seeback, who was a student of both Kempfs, remembers them as warm and caring but also very strict. Once, when she did not have her piano lesson prepared, Reuben hit her on the knuckles.

SEEBACK WAS A musical prodigy who first sang publicly at age five, standing on three Bibles in church. Her mother paid for her voice lessons by doing the Kempfs' laundry. Seeback still has the metal-wheeled child's wagon, which originally belonged to Paul Kempf, that she used to carry the laundry back and forth. When Seeback finished high school, Pauline Kempf helped arrange for her to go to the Cincinnati Conservatory.

Besides giving lessons in their studio, the Kempfs were very active musically in the community. Pauline was the first choir director of the

Congregational Church, and Reuben was the first organist and choir director at St. Andrew's. He was also music director of the University Glee Club and the Michigan Union Opera and organist of the Ann Arbor Masonic groups. Because Reuben had connections in both the town and university communities, U-M president James Angell asked him to form a singing society in an attempt to bridge the gap between town and gown. Under Reuben's direction, the group, first called the Beethoven Society and then Lyra Gesangverien (singing society), gave regular concerts for the next thirty-five years.

The Kempfs often entertained, hosting diverse groups from students to dignitaries. A former maid remembers being extra busy during the May Festival buying food needed for the many guests. There was always a live-in maid (the present office at Kempf House was the maid's room), and Pauline's mother, the widowed Mrs. Widenmann, also helped with the cooking. She particularly excelled at baking and noodle making. Edith Kempf remembers that "there was lots of good food, all made from scratch."

REUBEN KEMPF DIED in 1945 at age eighty-six. Pauline stayed on until her death in 1953, when the house was sold to Mr. and Mrs. Earl V. Parker. When Earl Parker died in 1969, the newly created Historic District Commission spearheaded a movement to convince the city to buy the house.

Today, thanks mainly to the efforts of Edith Kempf, the music studio has been almost entirely re-created, complete with the famous grand piano (which has only eighty-five keys, three less than the modern ones), the red couch, the two mirrors that Pauline's voice students used to check their posture and their mouth formations, Reuben's desk, a music stand, and the Lyra flag. Even the prints of Germany on the walls were there during the Kempfs' occupancy.

The sitting room, decorated to be contemporary with the studio, holds a horsehair couch from Reuben Kempf's parents' farm (in perfect condition because only the minister was allowed to sit on it) and an Ann Arbor Allmendinger organ.

# Ann Arbor's Oldest Apartments

*Eighty years later, they're back in the spotlight.*

Ann Arbor's oldest surviving apartment houses, built between 1923 and 1930, were glamorous affairs designed by the area's leading architects. Many included such amenities as doormen, on-site maids, cafes, and beauty parlors. Even so, they drew mixed reactions: some Ann Arborites welcomed them as elegant and cosmopolitan additions to the city, while others deplored their size and their effect on existing neighborhoods.

Now they're back in the political spotlight. Since 1994 the city has been fighting to protect the buildings, one of which was demolished by the U-M in 2003. Meanwhile, as city planners look for ways to expand downtown housing, they're confronting many of the same issues raised by the original apartment-building boom eighty years ago.

IN THE NINETEENTH CENTURY the U-M campus was surrounded by student rooming houses. Apartment buildings as we know them today, where each unit has its own kitchen and bath, didn't arrive in significant numbers until after World War I.

As the U-M's enrollment and employment swelled in the 1920s, multistory apartment buildings were a good solution to the housing crunch. But the idea took some getting used to.

The city hired the Olmsted Brothers, son and stepson/nephew of the famous landscape architect and city planner Frederick Law Olmsted, to make recommendations for Ann Arbor's future development. Besides encouraging street improvements, more parks and playgrounds, and scenic drives, the Olmsteds' 1922 report urged the city to enact a zoning ordinance. Council responded by dividing the city into four zoning categories: single residential, residential, local business, and industrial. Apartment buildings were permitted only in the "residential" district near campus.

That zone included one existing apartment building: the twenty-unit Cutting, built in 1906 on the southeast corner of State and Monroe. "For its time the Cutting was a remarkable structure, one of very few apartment buildings in the city, where rich people lived and where elegant old ladies sat looking out on the world through lace-curtained plate-glass windows," recalled Milo Ryan in his 1985 memoir *View of a Universe*. "A carriage was usually to be seen waiting at one of the three entrances."

Florence Mack, widow of department store owner Walter Mack, lived in the Cutting with her son Christian. Broadcaster Ted Heusel, who as a boy lived nearby, recalls that Christian "was so spoiled he used to take a cab home from the Blue Front, two blocks away." The Cutting was torn down in 1962 for a parking lot. "People lived there forever," recalls veteran Ann Arbor real estate agent Maynard Newton. "When it was to be torn down, they tried to sue, saying they had a proprietary right because they'd been there so long."

The 1920s apartment houses followed the example of the Cutting: they were elegant buildings designed in the latest styles, mainly Tudor and Spanish Revival. And, as in the Cutting, their tenants made up a who's who of Ann Arbor.

THE ANBERAY, built in 1923 at 619 East University, was the first of the postwar apartment buildings. U-M architecture professor J. J. Albert Rousseau designed it in a U shape around a court. The light brick, zigzag roof, and balconies on each of the three levels, often filled with flowers, give it a Spanish flavor.

Early Anberay tenants included grocery heiress Elizabeth Dean, whose bequest to the city continues to bankroll the tree-planting Dean Fund; Palmer Christian, U-M organist; and Francis Kelsey, the archaeology professor whose finds from the Near East make up a large part of the Kelsey Museum's fabulous holdings. This illustrious tenant mix continued into the 1960s. Ray Detter, a tenant at that time, recalls that his neighbors included Herbert Youtie, an expert on the Dead Sea scrolls; Renaissance scholar Palmer Throop; and Jacob Price, a U-M history professor who ran for city council.

Washtenaw Apartments, at 332 East William, dates from 1925. Although a simple red-brick building, it has elegant touches, such as a decorated stone entrance and stone wreaths on top. Carl Wurster, who grew up on Division Street around the corner, remembers his dad saying that the place was being constructed from very shoddy materials and would never last—but more than eighty years later, it still stands. When finished, the building didn't impinge very much on the lives of Carl and his sister, Elizabeth. Carl delivered papers there, and tenants occasionally rented spaces in the Wursters' garage. The only person Elizabeth and Carl knew in the building was their math teacher, a Miss Shipman.

The 1926 Hildene Manor, at 2220 Washtenaw, looks from the outside like an English manor house with classic Tudor details—dormers, half-timbering, nine-over-nine windowpanes, and heavy wooden doors. Inside are eight six-room apartments, plus common areas and a three-room caretaker's flat. Set back on a wide expanse of lawn, "it was *the* apartment in Ann Arbor—the most expensive and the best," recalls Ted Heusel.

The Wil-Dean, 200 North State, and Duncan Manor, 322 North State, are perfect mirror images of each other, except the first is faced with light brick and the second with red brick. Harold Zahn and Dugald Duncanson hired recent U-M architecture grad Gardiner Vose to design the buildings, and construction on both started in 1928. Zahn took ownership of the Wil-Dean, which he named after his son Dean William; Duncanson claimed the other, naming it Duncan Manor. Asymmetrical, with balconies, tile work, and casement windows, the buildings fit in with the best of the Tudor apartment houses.

The 1929 Kingsley Post, at 809 East Kingsley, a Spanish/Moorish Revival design by R. S. Gerganoff, is nothing like the architect's most famous Ann Arbor building, the Washtenaw County Courthouse. With its elaborate ornamentation—tiles, rounded windows, wrought-iron decorative balconies, arched entrance—the Kingsley Post stands in striking contrast to the comparatively drab post–World War II apartment buildings flanking it.

In the early 1950s, when they were first married, Ted and Nancy Heusel lived in a third-floor efficiency in the Kingsley Post. Jimmy Murnan, manager of the Lydia Mendelssohn Theater, lived on the same floor but in a more luxurious apartment overlooking the river valley and the railroad tracks. Murnan, a big circus fan, would invite the Heusels over to watch circus trains unload.

The Planada, at 1127 East Ann, opened in 1929. It catered to employees at the then new University Hospital a block east—the 1931 city directory lists nurses, therapists, interns, and research assistants among the residents. Like the Kingsley Post, it was a Spanish/Moorish Revival design but less symmetrical. The *Observer*'s Eve Silberman, who lived in the Planada in the 1980s, recalls that "the apartment definitely had more character than any I've rented before and after." Silberman particularly liked the gargoyles in the lobby. She moved, however, because she did not like sharing her apartment with a mouse.

Forest Plaza, 715 South Forest, was built in the same year as the Planada. Although there had already been a number of successful apartment projects and its site was in the "residential" zone, the original plan for the building set off a storm of controversy. The older apartment

The 1906 Cutting, corner of State and Monroe, was the first apartment building in Ann Arbor. *(Courtesy of Bentley Historic Library.)*

The Planada, because of its location on Ann Street, was an attractive place for people employed at University Hospital to live. But its location worked against it when it was torn down to provide parking for the Life Sciences complexes. *(Courtesy of Stan Shackman.)*

At the Wil-Dean, 200 North State Street, and its near twin, Duncan Manor, corner of State and Lawrence, tenants still enjoy the elegant Tudor styling. *(Courtesy of Stan Shackman.)*

buildings were three and four stories high; Forest Plaza's developers wanted to go up nine stories—a sketch that appeared in the *Ann Arbor Daily News* shows an elegant tower that would have looked at home on New York's Park Avenue. The "Spanish Renaissance" design was expected to cost $400,000, including the land.

Presaging future controversies, neighbors led the fight against the new building while real estate agents and businesspeople defended it. U-M professors Frederick G. Novy and Charles Cooley, who lived in houses on either side of the site, argued that the new structure would block their light and air and would increase congestion in the neighborhood.

After much discussion, a compromise was reached: Forest Plaza was scaled down to five stories and set far back on the lot. The resulting building, while not as ornate as originally proposed, still has many attractive details, including Spanish tiles, terra-cotta decorations, and rounded windows. The increased setback actually adds to its elegance, making it reminiscent of glamorous apartments on Connecticut Avenue in Washington, D.C.

Like other apartment houses of the era, Forest Plaza provided homes for many upper level university people. A 1930 *Michigan Alumnus* photo essay mentions that Forest Plaza was the home of Harry Kipke, football coach and later regent. Mark Hildebrandt recalls being taken there as a child to visit his parents' friends Jan Vandenbroek, a U-M engineering professor, and his wife. Hildebrandt remembers Vandenbroek's apartment as "classy but comfortable, with soft dark-red carpeted floors, Spanish irregular plaster, wrought-iron sconces."

Forest Plaza's current manager, Chris Heaton, says that long-term residents have told him that the building used to have a doorman who would park cars for the few residents who owned them and a maid living on the first floor, who was available to do housework.

The debate over Forest Plaza led to new ground rules for apartment construction. Part of the compromise allowing Forest Plaza to be built was an agreement that city council would revisit the zoning law, which it did. At a public hearing, a speaker called for more limits on apartment buildings, citing several instances in which "the homes next door to apartment houses have stood vacant since the construction of the larger building, being of value neither for a single home nor for another apartment house, as the one apartment is usually enough to care for the district."

On May 5, 1929, city council voted that future apartment buildings could be no more than three stories or forty-five feet high. Clothier and theater owner J. Fred Wuerth dissented, protesting that "the growth of

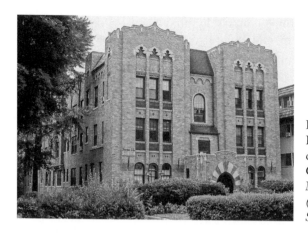

Kingsley Post, 809 East Kingsley, was designed by R. S. Gerganoff in Spanish/Moorish Revival style. *(Courtesy of Stan Shackman.)*

the city would be held up by discouraging outside capital." Supporters answered that the law would encourage developers to construct a larger number of smaller buildings and so would help preserve the city's residential character.

Neither side realized that the apartment boom was already essentially over. Only one more apartment house, Observatory Lodge, was built before the Great Depression, followed by World War II, virtually halted construction in the city.

If Observatory Lodge was the last apartment house of its generation, it at least was a spectacular expression of the best of the age. Built in 1930 at 1402 Washington Heights, Observatory Lodge, like the Planada, was just a few steps from the 1925 University Hospital. One admirer calls its design "a feast of Tudor Revival details," including oriel windows, heavy Tudor-style doors, half-timbering, and a quirky squirrel weathervane. Inside are stained-glass windows, beautiful tile work, and a lobby fireplace. Residents in its thirty-four units also enjoyed the services of a beauty parlor and barbershop. And it must have been approved before the 1929 height limit went into effect: it's four stories high.

APARTMENT CONSTRUCTION RESUMED in the 1950s and 1960s, when U-M enrollment more than doubled. This time around, apartment developers created buildings catering to U-M students as well as staff.

Maynard Newton recalls that when he came back from the Korean War in the mid-1950s, students still rented rooms in boardinghouses— "big, comfortable houses, run by a landlady usually called 'Ma' something, such as Ma Guenther on Oakland or Ma Jeffries on Monroe. These ladies thought the value was in the house," Newton recalls. "But savvy Realtors realized the land was what was valuable."

Developers began buying up old houses around campus and downtown, demolishing them, and building modern-style apartments on the lots. A few, like the Nob Hill complex off South Main, were thoughtfully designed and integrated into their neighborhoods. Most, however, were bare-bones cubes derisively dubbed "cash boxes"—both because of their flat roofs (unlike the peaked roofs of the surrounding older houses) and because they were built to squeeze as many rental units as possible onto their lots.

In 1963 city council amended the zoning ordinance to limit apartments to bigger lots and to require that they be set farther back from their lot lines. These two provisions, followed by the formation of historic districts in and around downtown, virtually eliminated teardowns of existing structures to build apartments.

The 1963 zoning change also abolished the height restriction for apartment buildings, instead setting limits on the "floor-to-area ratio" (FAR). Two high-rise apartment projects, the eighteen-story University Towers on South University, finished in 1965, and the twenty-six-story Tower Plaza, at William and Maynard, approved in 1965 and finished in 1969, were built under the new regulations. Tower Plaza was particularly controversial.

The Tower Plaza debate echoed the one nearly forty years earlier over Forest Plaza. Proponents saw the high-rise as an asset to the city, opponents as an affront to downtown's existing scale. Eunice Burns, who was on council when Tower Plaza was approved, recalls that she and the other three Democrats were called antidevelopment because they voted against it. (With the backing of council's Republican majority, it passed anyway.)

In classic Ann Arbor fashion, council then appointed a study committee and hired a consultant. The resulting report, *Central City High-Rises and Parking*, suggested a system of premiums, allowing developers more height in their buildings if they added amenities such as public space in front, parking, or landscaping. These changes, plus further increases in minimum apartment lot size and setbacks, were enacted in 1967.

It would be impossible to build a high-rise like Tower Plaza under the current FAR limits. Still, residents who have arrived since the 1960s take Tower Plaza for granted. Some even admire its clean lines and appreciate that the landlord included a cutaway first story and shopping arcade, even before the system of premiums was enacted.

The 1923–30 apartments, also scoffed at by some when they were new, today look very elegant next to the cash boxes abutting the Kingsley Post, or the monolithic Mary Markley dorm near Observatory Lodge.

The 1930 Observatory Lodge, 1402 Washington Heights, was the last apartment built before the Depression put a stop to most construction. (*Courtesy of Stan Shackman.*)

"They are a good example of apartments of that era," says Heather Edwards, Ann Arbor's historic preservation coordinator. "They gave people the chance of living in the downtown vicinity in buildings pleasing to look at that also met all their needs."

Four are already in historic districts: the Wil-Dean, Duncan, and Kingsley Post are in the Old Fourth Ward, and the Washtenaw is in the East William Street district. The Historic District Commission has worked to preserve the other five, but the process has been slow. In 1994 city council voted to designate 120 buildings as "individual historic properties" (IHPs), a classification intended to protect historic buildings that are outside of historic districts. Included in the list were the Anberay and the Planada, both then owned by the Draprop Corporation.

Draprop sued, claiming that the city had no legal right to designate buildings as IHPs without the owners' permission. The circuit court upheld the city's right to do so, but in 2001 the Michigan Court of Appeals declared Ann Arbor's IHP district invalid. "They said it didn't meet the definition of a historic district—that it didn't hold together geographically or thematically," explains Louisa Pieper, historic preservation coordinator at the time.

At the recommendation of the state Historic Preservation Office, the Historic District Commission divided the original IHP list into thematic sublists—apartments, of course, but also churches, early homesteads, industrial and commercial structures, landmark homes, schools, and transportation—and appointed study committees to research each area and decide which properties were the most significant.

The apartment committee recommended protecting all five surviving early apartment buildings that weren't already in historic districts—the Anberay, Forest Plaza, Hildene Manor, Observatory Lodge, and the

Planada. Any city restrictions would not apply to the last two, however, since the university owned them. Observatory Lodge, in need of repairs, was closed several years ago but is now being converted into offices. A sadder fate awaited the Planada: when the university bought it, the report to the regents warned that "the building will be demolished and the site integrated into the adjacent campus." It was torn down in fall 2003, and is now replaced with a parking structure.

While the legality of the IHP is being investigated, the issue of height of buildings is also part of an ongoing discussion. The eight-story Corner House Lofts on the corner of State and Washington is the tallest new residential building in the city in more than thirty years. And like its predecessors in the 1920s, it has been controversial. The city planning commission voted against approving the project, only to be overruled by city council.

The passage of the greenbelt measure in November 2003 gave even more impetus to the height debate. A number of people—even some who had been no- or slow-growth advocates—began asking whether preserving more green space around the city obliged Ann Arbor to accept greater population density within its boundaries. Mayor John Hieftje enthusiastically supports the idea of more downtown density, although he says he began thinking about it independently of the greenbelt.

Noting that only about two hundred new residents moved into downtown Ann Arbor in the 1990s, Hieftje says he'd like to see a thousand more arrive in the next decade. He argues that an increased downtown population would provide the economic base for the return of practical stores, such as food markets, and would ease parking and congestion problems, especially if the new residents also worked downtown. While this increased density would obviously require more multifamily dwellings, Hieftje says they would probably be condominiums rather than apartments.

Does Hieftje mean that Ann Arbor will see a new generation of high-rises? "Taller buildings would upset the delicate pedestrian balance downtown," Hieftje replies. "I'm protective of Main Street and a block or so off it, as well as State Street. But I can see them maybe on Thompson, Maynard, or Huron." Eighty some years after Ann Arbor's first apartment-building boom, the town is still debating how and where future generations of downtown residents will live.

# Alden Dow's Ann Arbor

*Inspired by a trip to Japan when he was a teenager, the Dow Chemical heir spurned the family business to devote his life to architecture. From city hall to the U-M's administration building, he put a quirky modernist stamp on the city.*

Judy Dow Rumelhart was walking down Fifth Avenue one day recently when it started to rain. Looking around for shelter, she spotted the Ann Arbor District Library, a building originally designed by her uncle, Alden Dow. "And I thought how lovely it is," Rumelhart says. "The library is one of my favorites."

"The library and city hall are two of the ugliest buildings in Ann Arbor, and ISR [the U-M Institute for Social Research] is right up there," says library board member Ed Surovell, expressing a dissenting opinion on the library and two other Dow designs. "They do not have the kind of imposing presence of a public building that creates civic pride."

Alden Dow (1904–83) is an unlikely figure to provoke such controversy. Though Frank Lloyd Wright once called him his "spiritual son," Dow had none of the older architect's egotism or self-promotion. Shy and studious, Dow had to be encouraged to take on major public commissions by his devoted wife, Vada. He got much of his work through family connections; his father, Herbert, was the founder of Dow Chemical.

Alden Dow's entrée to Ann Arbor was through his sister Margaret and her husband, U-M physician Harry Towsley. His first residential commission, in 1932, was the Towsley home in Ann Arbor Hills. Over the next thirty-six years, Dow designed seventeen more Ann Arbor buildings; in the 1960s, his work was so highly regarded that both the city of Ann Arbor and the U-M hired him to design their administrative centers: the Larcom Municipal Building (1961) and the Fleming Administration Building (1964).

Like Frank Lloyd Wright, with whom he studied, Dow sought to integrate his buildings into their environment. His motto was "Gardens never begin, and houses never end." Especially in his residential projects, he was capable of blending building and landscape brilliantly.

The going was tougher when the commission was a civic building downtown. He sometimes attempted to domesticate these urban settings by specifying massive upper-story planters, but in Ann Arbor, most of these have long since been abandoned as impractical.

Despite the common elements he sometimes used, Dow was no assembly-line architect. His Ann Arbor buildings have evoked comparisons as diverse as "a Mondrian painting" (the Fleming Building) and "a chest of drawers" (city hall). But especially in recent years, those characterizations have not always been flattering.

Shortly after taking office, former U-M president Lee Bollinger announced that he wanted to move his office out of the Fleming Building, which he called "fortresslike." (Its slit windows, arched entryway, and looming overhangs do give the Fleming Building a defensive look, but the popular belief that Dow designed it to shut out student protesters is unfounded—the plans were completed well before the campus demonstrations of the 1960s turned violent.)

Others have since risen to the building's defense, including Robert Venturi and Denise Scott Brown, the celebrated "postmodern" architects whom Bollinger retained to develop a new master plan for the university. But Bollinger's comments are a sure sign of Dow's declining stature in the city he did so much to shape.

ALDEN DOW WAS BORN in Midland in 1904, the fifth of Grace and Herbert Dow's seven children. His parents had assumed that he would go into the family business, but they also encouraged his creativity by exposing him to art, historic buildings, and gardens. When he was a teenager, the whole family took a trip to Japan. "They went in a big ship and stayed for three or four months," relates his niece Judy Dow Rumelhart. The trip exposed Dow to two of his greatest influences as an architect: the exacting simplicity of Japanese design and the striking modernism of Frank Lloyd Wright, whose newly completed Imperial Hotel the family admired.

Dow spent three years at the U-M studying mechanical engineering but then begged his parents to let him switch careers. He transferred to Columbia's School of Architecture, and in 1930, while he was still a student, his father got him his first commission: a clubhouse for the Midland Country Club. Upon graduation, Dow joined a Saginaw firm, and he married Vada Bennet, his childhood sweetheart, in 1931. His sister and brother-in-law Margaret and Harry Towsley promptly hired him to design their home.

As originally designed, the Towsley house was basically a three-

Vada and Alden Dow. *(Courtesy of Alden Dow Home and Studio.)*

bedroom ranch, although much more elegant than those that would become ubiquitous after World War II. Its features included clerestory windows, a copper roof, and raised planter boxes designed to blend house and landscape.

Dow designed the interior of his houses in minute detail and even dictated the color schemes. "He loved strong colors, primary colors, and jewel tones," recalls Rumelhart—"cherry red, cerise, emerald green, purple amethyst, ruby topaz."

Considering Dow's great interest in gardens, it's ironic that his most influential innovation at the Towsley house was the way he designed the driveway: he specified an attached garage facing the street, believed to be the first in the country. "We thought the house looked like a gas station," recalls family friend Jack Dobson.

Asked whether it was strange to grow up in such an unusual house, Rumelhart replies, "I loved the house. . . . and had a sense of pride of being in it. I thought all architecture should look like that."

During construction, Dow fought repeatedly with city building in-spectors, who he saw as trampling on his artistic license. For instance, he wanted to give the house unusually low ceilings, 7'6" instead of the required 8'. Denied, he recorded his losing battles in a series of four bas-reliefs in the front hall; one shows an architect being stomped by an authoritarian foot while another depicts him strangled in red tape.

Although the house had been planned as a starter home, the Towsleys

lived there all of their lives. They just kept asking Dow to design additions, which he did in 1934, in 1938, and again in 1960. Dow put his
latest ideas into each revision, such as a landscaped backyard viewed
through a big dining room window and so many built-ins that there was
little need for furniture: he provided a built-in safe, walk-in refrigera-
tor, clothes drawers that opened on both the bedroom and dressing room
sides, and even metal drawers especially designed to store Margaret
Towsley's extensive collection of linen tablecloths. The original color
scheme was vividly patriotic in the main living areas: cherry-red rug and
turquoise walls.

In 1933, Alden and Vada Dow spent six months at Taliesin, Frank Lloyd
Wright's studio-home complex in western Wisconsin. While Alden
studied architecture, Vada completed her own fellowship in painting,
weaving, and pottery.

Dow and Wright maintained a friendship for years after the Dows'
time at Taliesin. The two architects visited each other in their homes,
and Dow even named one of his daughters Lloyd. They had a serious
falling out, however, in 1949, when Wright lost a commission to design
the Phoenix Civic Center because his fee was too high—and Dow agreed
to take the job in his place. According to Craig McDonald, director of
the Alden Dow Home and Studio in Midland, it was Vada Dow and
Olgivanna Wright who finally persuaded their husbands to make peace.

After Taliesin, Dow set up his own firm in Midland. Despite the
Depression, Dow Chemical was booming, and he designed homes for
an ever-increasing circle of clients. As his reputation grew, he received
commissions from as far away as North Carolina (a residence for the
president of Duke University) and Texas (an entire company town, Lake
Jackson, for Dow Chemical during World War II). But Midland always
remained his base: of the 138 buildings he designed in his career, 104
are in his hometown.

Ann Arbor is second only to Midland, with eighteen Dow buildings.
Surprisingly, very few are private homes; he built only two more resi-
dences here, both for doctors who knew Harry Towsley: the Sibley and
Katherine Hoobler house (228 Belmont Road) in 1949 and the Joe and
Julia Morris house (7 Regent Drive) in 1962.

In the early 1960s, Joe Morris asked Harry Towsley whether he
thought Dow would design him a house. Towsley suggested that he
write and ask, and Dow responded by inviting Morris to Midland for
lunch. During lunch, Morris recalls, the architect "talked about sailboats,
about housing—he had an idea about housing for Third World countries

Alden and Vada Dow (*front row, left*) at the U-M in 1924. Alden's sister Margaret (*third row, right*) would soon become his most important Ann Arbor patron. (*Courtesy of Alden Dow Home and Studio.*)

by making plastic modular units and dropping them in by helicopter. When we returned, I told his secretary we hadn't talked about my house. She said, 'Wonderful. He needs to get his mind off his work.'"

The Morrises waited two years before Dow had time to work on their house. When they finally sat down to review the plans, they found that Dow had definite ideas about what he wanted. For instance, Joe recalls, Dow's original plan did not include room to eat in the kitchen—"He said we would never eat in the kitchen."

"We insisted we would," Morris continues. "So he relented and designed a [built-in] kitchen table." The furniture that Dow didn't build in, he selected, including daybeds, dining room table and chairs, and the chairs and sofa in the living room. All of the built-ins and carefully coordinated furniture result in a very clean look. Morris calls it "magnificent simplicity."

JOE MORRIS WAS ONE of many clients invited to visit Dow's combined home and studio in Midland. A beautiful and unusual building, it was a good advertisement for his artistry.

Like the Towsley house, Dow's evolved in a series of additions. It began in 1933 as a long train car–like studio. In 1935, he added its most striking feature, a room half-submerged in a pond. Officially called "the floating conference room," but known informally as "the submarine room," the room invites comparisons to Wright's more famous Falling Water because of its ingenious use of water.

In Midland, Dow was able to build the low ceilings he was denied in Ann Arbor. "I got a kick out of his studio," recalls Fred Mayer, retired as U-M's director of university planning. "He was about 5′6″, so the studio was designed for him. I'm 5′8″, so it was okay with me."

The low ceilings and small proportions in Dow's house reminded Morris of "Beatrice Potter homes in *Peter Rabbit.* There was the same childhood comfort in his home." Bill Reish, who visited Midland in the seventies to discuss an addition to Greenhills School, recalls the "sunken room at duck-eye level, with ducks floating by." Former library director Gene Wilson missed that view—"The pond was leaking the day I was there, so he had it drained."

People remember Dow's appearance as slightly eccentric. "He was wearing different-colored shoes, I think yellow," Wilson recalls. Adds Rumelhart, "He wore his hair longer than the conventional doctors I was used to."

Craig McDonald, who was Vada's assistant in the last years of her life, recalls Alden as "quiet and understated. He was somewhat shy, but expressed himself through design." The late Guy Larcom, who oversaw construction of Ann Arbor's city hall, remembered him as "a small man, undistinguished—but impressive when he talked about architecture."

"He could be very intense if he got excited about something," Rumelhart says. "He could pick a flower and be overwhelmed. He had a creative intensity.

"I loved Alden," Rumelhart continues. "He said it was okay to be a singer. The medical world was terrified of the arts, but he told my parents, 'She's talented. She should be doing what she is doing.'"

Dow's PEAK PERIOD in Ann Arbor came during the 1950s and 1960s, when he built six university and three civic buildings. The U-M's Margaret Bell Pool (1952) was his first college commission; it opened doors, and he eventually worked on nine other campuses in Michigan.

Before it was built, the U-M had two pools reserved primarily for men, while women had only the "Barbour bathtub" in the basement of Barbour gym. Margaret Bell, head of women's physical education, had long wanted to redress this injustice. According to Sheryl Szady, who

The egalitarian design of the ISR offices did not extend to the space assigned to the female support staff, which consisted of a large open area with no private space whatsoever. (*Courtesy of Alden Dow Home and Studio.*)

has researched the history of U-M women's athletics, "She said, 'Before I leave, I'm getting a pool.'" Bell organized bridge parties, sold tiles, and organized benefit parties to raise the necessary funds. Margaret Towsley, a friend of physical education professor Marie Hartwig and a generous patron of progressive causes, probably contributed to the project.

The new pool was state of the art. Designed for synchronized swimming and for Michifish shows (elaborate performances with costumes, lighting, and staging), it had an air flow system that sent cool air over the spectators in the bleachers and warm air over the pool. Underwater speakers allowed the synchronized swimmers to hear the music.

According to Szady, the day before the pool opened, Bell, Hartwig, and another woman "hopped in and played around." At first, men were allowed to swim at the pool only on Friday nights. The pool became coed in 1976 when the building was enlarged to become the Central Campus Recreational Building. In 1997 the kinesiology department put on another addition, but Dow's original building is still discernible, especially the second-story planters, the only ones in Ann Arbor that are still maintained.

In 1964, Dow designed two large buildings just half a block apart on Thompson Street: ISR, the first new building in the country dedicated solely to social research, and the administration building, later named in honor of Robben Fleming, the university's tenth president.

The two buildings have striking exteriors, but both have been criticized as being designed from the outside in, sacrificing interior utility to achieve an exterior effect. For instance, as originally designed, the massive white aggregate panels that face ISR would have left the offices behind them with no exterior windows. According to retired psychology professor Bob Kahn, one of ISR's founders, Dow had to be persuaded to move the panels out slightly so that small slit windows could be added.

Dow planned ISR's interior in detail. The space was divided into modules, each with a large open area facing a window wall, with two offices on either side of the open area and two slightly bigger offices in the corners. "The offices would be almost all one of two sizes to minimize status," recalls Kahn. Dow was proud of the egalitarian effect, noting in his 1970 book, *Reflections*, "All occupants have a similar relationship, through glassed area, with the outside."

But research projects did not always divide neatly into the modules Dow prescribed. And despite his egalitarian goals in designing the faculty offices, the ISR layout also perpetuated what, in hindsight, looks like a far greater inequity: while the researchers had private offices, the female support staff was assigned to desks that sat in the middle of the central area, without a shred of private space. Room dividers were eventually added—but these in turn blocked out light to the side offices.

Maintenance on the windows also presented a problem. They were locked with special keys and pivoted open to wash. People would open the windows to let in air and then not secure them because they didn't have the key. Once, "a person on the fifth floor was leaning against the window when it pivoted," recalls retired ISR administrator Jim Wessell. "He almost fell out. Luckily he was caught by someone nearby."

The windows on the Fleming Administration Building opened the same way but were arranged very differently: in geometric patterns reminiscent of a Mondrian painting. While intriguing from the outside, the design created some very curious interior spaces, with long, thin windows in unpredictable locations.

Dow's most unusual campus building, the Fleming Building is also the most controversial. Ed Surovell calls it "a cube in space" and says of the entrance, "you have to hunt for it like a medieval castle." People who work in the building complain of the "mazelike" layout.

The Regents' Room on the first floor is designed with an arched ceiling, which, according to Craig McDonald, was used "to give a feeling of being in a larger space." Two similar arches take up the rest of the first floor: the middle arch is a corridor connecting the east and west entrances, and the other serves as offices. The cavernous look has caused people to compare the space to a beer vault or a wine cellar, and audiences at regents' meetings often decry the absence of windows and call it "the cave."

Rumelhart defends the design, saying, "Alden took the assignment and created a painting. He was a great fan of Mondrian and he fulfilled that feeling." Also siding with Rumelhart is architect Denise Scott Brown. Asked about the Fleming Building, she calls it "honorable architecture" and says it is "nicely proportioned."

"Taste cycles," adds Brown's husband, Robert Venturi. "There was a time when Victorian architecture was thought ugly and torn down. We have to be tolerant of the immediate past."

Changing taste is one problem with the building, but of the more utilitarian problems, many are not Dow's fault but are the result of growth. "It was never intended to have as many people as it does now. When there was a big lobby on every floor, it was more aesthetically pleasing," says Dick Kennedy, retired vice president for government relations.

"You'd get off the elevator and see a bank of windows onto the plaza," recalls Kay Beattie, who worked in the building in its early days. "You had the feeling no one worked there." Beattie also remembers that, in vintage Dow fashion, each floor had its own vivid color theme—longtime employees describe them with names like "Howard Johnson orange" and "football field green."

As controversial as the Fleming Building is, it could have been even more eye popping. According to Fred Mayer, university architect Howard Hacken vetoed Dow's original plans to finish the exterior in white stucco with blue windows and gold trim. "Very rah-rah," Mayer laughs.

DOW LEFT A STRONG MARK on the U-M campus, but it was nothing compared to his impact across Division Street. In the library and city hall, he defined the two most important buildings in Ann Arbor's public life.

The library was built first, in 1956. "After the war there was no established library architecture," recalls Gene Wilson, then a library staff member, later director. "Dow had built the Midland library, and we thought it was grand."

His Ann Arbor design had all of the Dow hallmarks. Even today, after two additions, one can still recognize his hand in the elevated planter faced with turquoise enamel paneling and the lovely little garden on the south side.

As soon as the new city hall was finished, it was surrounded by picketers supporting a fair housing ordinance. *(Courtesy of Alden Dow Home and Studio.)*

"I always liked it," Wilson says of the library. "It was state of the art for its time." But, he admits, there were problems. "Dow was more concerned with visual impact—he wanted it to be noticed, he didn't let function get in the way. There was a circulation desk but no reference desk, and there was no clear delineation between public and private areas. We had to scramble around to make [the layout] work."

Like many other clients, the library also found that Dow's elevated gardens were difficult to maintain. Wilson doesn't recall exactly when the library stopped tending the second-story planters, but says, "it would have been very early. There never was a way to get to them except by a long ladder put up by the sidewalk—any maintenance was done by the janitor climbing the ladder. One day the ladder slipped and the janitor fell and broke his leg. After that we lost enthusiasm."

Dow's other great downtown project, the Ann Arbor city hall, has been a conversation piece ever since it opened in 1961; in addition to being called "a chest of drawers," it's been compared to "an inverted wedding cake" and "an upside-down carport." It's also been called "a poor man's Guggenheim," an allusion to Frank Lloyd Wright's famous upward-spiraling museum in New York City.

The building is an inverted stepped pyramid, with the floors growing wider as they go up. The second floor is a large promenade that Dow thought might be used for public meetings or for city council members to step outside to caucus. (Rumelhart has always thought it would be a good place to perform plays.)

Inside, Dow put elevators, stairs, conference rooms, and department heads' offices near the building's core. The space around the periphery of the building was kept open. "The idea was that there were to be no prestige offices, no best windows," recalled Guy Larcom. "It was all open to public view."

Kathy Frisinger, then the city's assistant director of central services, oversaw the move into the new building. She remembers that although employees were glad to be together after being scattered at seven different locations, many didn't like the open floor plan. "You could see from one end to the other," she explains. "If you talked to someone, everyone could see you talking, see which office you went into."

The promenade never got much use, and there were serious problems with roof leaks. Former switchboard operator Mary Schlecht recalls that when it rained, the police department downstairs had buckets all over the place. The planters Dow specified on the second and third floors also leaked. "The plants grew well on the north side, but it got too hot on the south and you had to water almost every day," a former employee recalls. City hall's maintenance people, like their counterparts at the library, eventually gave up on the planters; they're now filled with rocks.

Dow ordered the building's furnishings with his characteristic eye for vivid color. "I'll never forget that day when seven Steelcase trucks came. Big semi trucks drove up with turquoise and orange furniture," laughs Frisinger, who supervised the unloading. "I saw mine were to be orange and I said, 'I don't think so,' and did a quick switch." Nonetheless, she says, "I basically enjoyed the building. I liked the big offices, the open spacious feel in the building. Dow was ahead of his time."

As city hall has become more crowded, its once open spaces have given way to a warren of cubbyholes. Furniture and curtains have been placed in front of most of the big windows in the inner offices to give more privacy. The top floor, recently remodeled after the district court moved to the county courthouse, today comes the closest to the spacious feeling Dow originally intended.

Dow WORKED UP TO his death in 1983, but the debate continues on his rightful place in architectural history. The question of whether or not his buildings look good comes down to personal taste, and there can be no global or permanent answer. Setting that aside, a study of his Ann Arbor work shows that while many have serious practical problems, there were always reasons for what Dow did.

Near the top of the list of problems would have to be his flat roofs, a distinction he shared with his mentor, Frank Lloyd Wright. "Talk with any person about an Alden Dow building and they will sing its praises and then remember the trouble they had with the roof," says Greenhills' Bill Reish.

Dow's elevated planters were another recurring source of trouble. The only one still in use in Ann Arbor, at the U-M's kinesiology building, supports a few scraggly plants. Ann Arbor has apparently tended its Dow buildings less carefully than his hometown. Craig McDonald reports that numerous examples of Dow's elevated plantings are still flourishing in Midland.

Lighting could be listed among Dow's greatest failures but also among his greatest successes. It was obviously a lifelong obsession, and when it worked, it worked gloriously, as in the big windows that both let in light and created splendid views in his private homes. When his plans went astray, however, people worked in dark caverns such as those in the Fleming Building and ISR.

It could be argued that these failures were not so much design errors as a misreading of human nature, especially the need for privacy. "Human nature will confound you if you fight it too much, even with a good idea," comments Fred Mayer.

Dow seems to have been the most successful in his smaller projects, particularly the private residences, where he could think out the use of every inch of space. In the larger buildings, he was most successful in the ones built for a specific use, particularly those associated with family members such as Greenhills (Dow's niece Judy Dow Rumelhart was a member of the school's original planning committee, and his sister Margaret Towsley was on the first board) or the Towsley Center for Continuing Medical Education (as mentioned previously, Harry Towsley was Dow's brother-in-law).

Some of Dow's critics complain that he received the Ann Arbor jobs only because of his connections with the Towsley family. Certainly some of his work came directly through his sister and her husband or as a result of friendships or community contacts made through them. Fred Mayer defends Dow on this score. "Having connections will give you a chance," he says, "but if you don't do something good, it won't save you."

Most of the serious criticism of Dow is aimed at his multistory buildings. Architects don't like to speak ill of other architects, even dead ones, but off the record, several express doubts about Dow's "bulky, boring" multistory designs.

"Nothing is related to human scale in ISR. It's just a big white space," says one architect—who goes on to describe the Fleming Building as "weird." But Mayer again comes to Dow's defense. "He was a talented architect," he says. "I don't know if he will make it in the ranks of the great, but talent and creativity are evident in his best buildings."

Dan Jacobs, who's designed several additions to Greenhills, agrees. "I'm a great admirer of Dow. I admire the simplicity of his structural system."

Despite the complaints, it should be noted that all of his Ann Arbor designs, except for one razed gas station, are still being used for their original purpose. Even the Fleming Building, threatened during Bollinger's term with a changed use, is still the administration building. Asked about Bollinger's dislike of her uncle's building, Judy Dow Rumelhart lets out a good-humored laugh—but then admits that she has chided Bollinger for his criticism of the building. "He can move out, but I hope he uses it for something else, maybe English classes," she says. "Let it be used by someone to enjoy."

## AN ALDEN DOW CHRONOLOGY

Between 1932 and 1970, Dow designed eighteen Ann Arbor buildings. Details are given only for buildings not described in the main story.

1932: Towsley home, 1000 Berkshire Road

1949: Hoobler home, 228 Belmont Road

1952: Margaret Bell Pool (U-M)

1956: Ann Arbor District Library, 343 South Fifth Avenue

1958: Ann Arbor Community Center, 625 North Main. Dow designed the building at the request of his sister Margaret Towsley. Towsley not only contributed most of the cost, she also paid for many of the building's furnishings—even dishes and towels.

1959–65: Matthaei Botanical Gardens (U-M). The gardens' offices and conservatory are instantly recognizable as Dow's work thanks to the turquoise-faced second-story planters (long since abandoned). Herb Wagner, professor emeritus of botany, remembers fighting to include a lobby and meeting room in the plans; more than thirty years later, Wagner says, it remains "one of the best university botanical gardens in the nation." Dow also designed the garden superintendent's house.

1960: Leonard gas station, 2020 West Stadium Boulevard. Possibly conceived as a prototype for Michigan-based Leonard, this simple, well-landscaped gas station was Dow's first commercial work in Ann Arbor. It is the only Ann Arbor Dow building no longer standing.

1961: Guy J. Larcom Jr. Municipal Building, 100 North Fifth Avenue

1962: Morris home, 7 Regent Drive

1962: Conductron headquarters, 3475 Plymouth Road. Keeve "Kip" Seigel, founder of the high-flying Conduction conglomerate, was a friend of the Towsleys. The low-slung brick building is currently the Ave Maria School of Law.

1963: University Microfilms, 300 North Zeeb Road. Dow met University Microfilms founder Gene Power, a U-M regent, through the Towsleys. To recycle water used in processing microfilm, he included a moat on the south side of the building, creating what he called "a reflecting pool for office and cafeteria." The company is now known as ProQuest.

1964: Institute for Social Research (U-M)

1964: Fleming Administration Building (U-M)

1964: Michigan District Headquarters, Lutheran Church Missouri Synod, 3773 Geddes Road. Dow built some lovely churches in Midland, but this is his only church-related structure in Ann Arbor. Its four wings are grouped in the shape of a Greek cross; the teepeelike dome on top symbolizes the church's early missions to American Indians.

1966: Towsley Center for Continuing Medical Education (U-M). Dow's last major job for the university was arguably his most successful. One of Harry Towsley's specialties was continuing education, and the brothers-in-law collaborated closely on a simple, straightforward building distinguished by Dow trademarks such as long corridors filled with windows and plants. "It's state of the art, designed for traffic flow, with an auditorium and four break-out rooms, a huge lobby," facilities coordinator Robert Witte said. "If I was ever asked to design a medical education building, I would design it off the Towsley Center."

1967: Greenhills School, 850 Greenhills Drive. Dow laid out the building as a series of clusters, each with classrooms around the edge and a court in the middle. In the middle of each court is a common space called a "forum"; in the corners are areas for quiet activity, called "alcoves."

Starting in 1968 with grades 9–12, Greenhills gradually expanded to accommodate grades 6–12. By opening alcoves and linking them to new clusters, Dow designed additions that felt as if they were part of the original. Over the years, the brown walls and curiously colored carpets Dow specified have been toned down, and doors have been added to control noise. Still, Bill Reish says, "It works wonderfully as a school."

1970: 2929 Plymouth Road. After Gene Power stepped down from University Microfilms, he commissioned Dow to build this small office building just east of Huron Parkway. "I was glad I selected Alden, because my site presented a difficult design problem," Power recalled in his autobiography, *Edition of One*. "The zoning regulations stated that floor space could not exceed 40 percent of the land area. There had to be one automobile parking space available for every 110 square feet of floor space, and the structure could be no more than three stories high. Dow met these requirements by raising the building on columns, with only a small entrance lobby and elevator area extending down to the ground-floor level. Most of the area on that level formed a parking lot beneath the rest of the building."

Power's son, U-M regent Phil Power, recalls the office as "a lovely place to work. It had a beautiful view of North Campus. It had a fireplace, shelves with Eskimo art, orchids, a nice sitting area, and was lined with bookshelves." The building—which always reminded Rumelhart of "a giant toadstool"—is now rented to a number of small tenants.

# Frank Lloyd Wright in Ann Arbor

*Thanks to Frank Lloyd Wright, Bill and Mary Palmer raised their family in a work of art.*

On a Saturday morning in 2001, a group that included prominent local architect Larry Brink; Doug Kelbaugh, dean of the U-M's Taubman College of Architecture and Urban Planning; builder Bruce Niethammer; and George Colone, a heating specialist from Hutzel Plumbing & Heating, met to discuss a failing radiant heat system beneath the concrete floor of a fifty-year-old house. If it had been just any house, the solution would have been obvious: jackhammer the concrete and replace the pipes. But on hearing that suggestion, owner Mary Palmer recalls, "I nearly fainted. It wasn't acceptable." The reason so many people shared her concern was that the floor in question was designed by Frank Lloyd Wright.

The group worked out a solution that would preserve the part of the radiant system that still worked, about a third of the total. Hutzel would install a new boiler and radiators to heat the rest of the house—but would hide all the new components behind couches, inside cabinets, and under beds.

"'Change' is not in the vocabulary up there," says Bruce Niethammer, who's worked on the house since 1974.

"The Palmers maintained their house the best of all owners," says Brink, who trained under Wright and has consulted on hundreds of Wright homes. "They took the best care of the house from day one."

But while staying true to Wright and his principles, Mary and her husband, Bill, made the house their own, using it to express and enhance their interests in music, yoga, gardening, and art. "You take something, it becomes part of you, you become part of it," explains the Palmers' good friend Priscilla Neel, who is also an architect. "That's what makes a building individual."

IT WAS QUITE A COUP in 1950 to get the foremost architect of the century to design a house for a young couple in Ann Arbor. The Palmers had no "in" with Wright; they just asked him. But from meeting Mary Palmer fifty years later, it is clear why she would be drawn to Frank Lloyd Wright. She is a gracious woman with a hint of a southern accent (she grew up in North Carolina), and her whole demeanor—her simple but elegant style of dress, her artistic sense, and her concern with doing things right—fit into a whole, like the perfectly integrated details of a Wright design.

Mary and Bill Palmer met as students at the U-M—Mary in music and Bill in economics. After graduation Bill was asked to stay and teach. In the early years of their marriage, the Palmers lived in an old farmhouse on Geddes, now the home of attorney Clan Crawford. The older women in the neighborhood befriended Mary. "They broke the rules about not inviting instructors to dinner parties," she recalls. "These ladies knew gardens, literature—they were rich in what Ann Arbor had to offer."

Elizabeth Inglis, who lived in the family estate on Highland (today the U-M's Inglis House), was one of these remarkable women. One morning she phoned Mary to tell her that the road behind her house was being extended for building sites. Mary called Bill at work, and he came home at lunchtime. Mrs. Inglis, in gardening boots, showed them what she considered the best lot. "This is the most beautiful place in the city," she told them. The young couple took her advice and bought both that lot and the one next to it—a total of one and a half acres of varied terrain.

Mary, a woman of wide intellectual interests, spent hours reading at the U-M's architecture library while thinking about what kind of house to build on the site on Orchard Hills Drive. At the time she was very interested in antiques, so it might seem natural that she would have been drawn to a traditional style. But she was also very interested in Japan, one of Wright's sources of inspiration. She had visited Japan, audited classes on Japanese art, and taken Japanese language classes.

Mary's reading led her to Wright. The architect was then eighty-three years old but still active. Hoping to see one of his homes for herself, Mary telephoned Gregor and Elizabeth Affleck, who lived in a 1941 Wright house in Bloomfield Hills. The Afflecks responded by inviting the Palmers to dinner. Bill and Mary drove to Bloomfield Hills on a frigid February day. "We had an 'experience,'" Mary recalls. "And they had as much of an experience showing it to us as we had. How it felt to be in one of Mr. Wright's buildings opened up to me!"

On the way home Mary said to Bill, "Let's see if we can get Mr. Wright." Bill agreed that it was worth a try. He thought that the project might appeal to Wright: Ann Arbor, despite the presence of the U-M architecture school, had no example of Wright's work.

Mary wrote Wright a letter that concluded, "I hope you will design our house and we will not have to go to a lesser architect." Her mother, who lived in Raleigh, North Carolina, had told her that Wright was going to be lecturing at North Carolina State, so Mary suggested in her letter that they could meet there. Wright agreed.

The Palmers attended the lecture and then gave Wright a topographic map of their property. "He opened it and looked at it," Mary recalls. "Then he looked up, rolled it back up, and said, 'I'll design your house.' It was that simple." Not known for false modesty, Wright told them, "Wouldn't it be wonderful for your children to grow up in one of my houses?"

Thinking back, Mary Palmer suspects that Wright accepted the commission because "he saw a young couple who were really going to build—who wouldn't back out. There was a big falloff of clients, many who went to him for designs never built."

Some months later, the Palmers picked up the house plans at Taliesin, Wright's home and studio in Spring Green, Wisconsin. Wright delivered the plans and left the Palmers alone to review them. The most striking detail was that the design was made up of equilateral triangles instead of the rectangles of a traditional house.

"I must say when we looked at the triangular module it was a surprise," Mary recalls, "because we didn't ask for it. But I had some background, because I was familiar with the Anthony house in Benton Harbor." As he had with the Anthony house, Wright had produced a floor plan without a single conventional 90-degree angle—every angle is either 60 or 120 degrees.

Although familiar with architectural styles, the Palmers had never seen preliminary plans and were not quite sure how to interpret them. When Wright returned to the room after about fifteen minutes, he told them to take the plans home and think about it. They showed the plans to Mary's family in North Carolina, who also found themselves at sea. After a month or two of pondering, they got back to Wright and told him the house was too small.

Mary expected some resistance, because "the plan looked so perfect as it was," but Wright replied that he was just trying to keep costs down for their sake. "He enlarged the house with no trouble," she recalls. Wright made the bedrooms several modules larger, added a mud room and pantry to free up space in the kitchen, and put a study for Bill at the back of the house.

The plans, now kept at the U-M's Bentley Historical Library, detail not only the building materials but also the design and placement of

Exterior of Palmer house. *(Courtesy of Balthazar Korab.)*

the furniture (most of it built in) and even the color scheme—Wright's signature "Cherokee red." For the exterior, the architect specified red tidewater cypress, sand-molded brick, and a matching perforated concrete block. Part of the roof would be flat; the sloping portion would have red cedar shingles. Although Wright was not big on basements, he included a small utility basement under the kitchen. The rest of the house would be constructed on a concrete slab finished with a red glaze coat called "colorundrum." (Maintaining the slab's appearance was a major goal of the recent heating repair.)

The Palmers hired Erwin Niethammer, Bruce's uncle, to build the house. "He was one of the best builders around," recalls local architect David Osler. Niethammer was also well suited to the job because he was not easily intimidated—"He didn't take nonsense from anyone," according to Osler.

Mary Palmer recalls that Niethammer was "receptive to the unusual. He looked at the plans and said he'd never seen anything like it but thought he could build the house." He also told her they were the most "beautiful set of plans he'd ever worked with."

Gathering the materials was probably the biggest challenge. The cypress had to be specially ordered, the blocks specially fired. Working with Fingerle Lumber and Niethammer, the Palmers found the best craftspeople in the area to make the built-in furniture.

Bruce Niethammer was only four when the house was being built, but he still has a vivid memory of a Sunday drive his family took to the site. "We saw the house up on the hill and piles of dirt and lumber," Niethammer recalls.

"It was an event," recalls Priscilla Neel, who visited the site regularly during construction. So did Bob Metcalf, a U-M architecture prof and future dean. "It was a unique experience for a town to have a Frank Lloyd Wright house," Metcalf remembers. David Osler, too, was a frequent visitor. John Howe, the head draftsman at Taliesin, came by periodically to make sure things were going all right, but so far as these sidewalk superintendents could tell, Niethammer seemed to do fine on his own.

Of course the Palmers, living just a few blocks away, also viewed the progress of the house. "When it was being constructed, we all went out to see it over and over," recalls the Palmers' daughter, Mary Louise Dunn, then about ten. "We saw it was going to be marvelous."

Mary Palmer says she left most of the decisions about the house to the architect. "Mr. Wright was not autocratic—just sure of himself," she recalls. "He would say 'I don't think you'd like . . . '—and he was always right."

The Palmers moved into the house shortly before Christmas 1952. The large triangular living area at the center of the home was ideal both for family life and for entertaining. It has windows on two of its three sides and a pyramidal ceiling formed by three triangular sections.

The room is still arranged exactly as it was in Wright's plans half a century ago, with a grand piano as the focal point. People sitting on the built-in couch, a parallelogram, look toward the piano and onto the grounds beyond. Between the couch and piano on the right is a large brick fireplace. On the left side of the room are the Wright-designed dining table and chairs, and tucked behind them is the kitchen, separated from the living area by specially manufactured perforated blocks.

The ceiling in the sleeping wing is much lower, as is common in Wright houses. (The architect was a short man, and some have speculated that he would have made the rooms higher had he been taller.) A more pedestrian architect might have switched to a conventional design for this less visible area, but Wright continued his triangular pattern, even designing hexagonal built-in beds in the master bedroom and children's rooms. (Mary Palmer used to have sheets specially made but now just folds them under.) The house is situated so that the bedrooms get morning sun.

THE LIVING ROOM's unexpected angles and peaked ceiling, the sun pouring in the large windows, the view of the landscaped backyard—all

The Palmers' hexagonal living room, with the piano as focal point, is complete with furniture as arranged and designed by Wright. After more than fifty years in the house, Mary Palmer is still amazed at its beauty. *(Courtesy of Balthazar Korab.)*

combine to create a breathtaking experience. After almost fifty years, Mary Palmer says, she is still continually amazed by the beauty of the house.

When the Palmers first moved in, their two children, Mary Louise and Adrian, were still young, and they tried to lead as normal a family life as possible. "We used the house," says Mary Louise Dunn. Asked whether it was hard to live there, Dunn replies, "There was always a standard of how to treat the house—higher than most, imposed by the house. There was no basement rec room, no place that wasn't absolutely beautiful." But, she adds, "the payoff, if we couldn't do anything like everyone else, was that it was so special." The semirural location (it was outside the city limits until 1999) also allowed activities that couldn't be done in a more urban setting, such as taking Sassafras, the neighbors' donkey, down to Nichols Arboretum to ride. When Dunn was a teenager, she had parties like other kids, rolling up the rugs and dancing to rock 'n' roll.

After living in the house a few years, the Palmers put in a terrace off the living room. Wright had said that the terrace, which was part of his original plan, would be a good place to have weddings, and in time both Mary Louise and Adrian would be married there.

In 1964, after a visit to Japan, the Palmers built a Japanese garden house, which they used as a guest house and meditation area. By then Wright was dead, but Taliesin's John Howe designed it in the same style as the house, complete with a three-section pyramidal ceiling. The last major change was a garden wall that Brink executed, using Wright's design with a few necessary modifications.

Elizabeth Inglis suggested that the Palmers wait a year before start-ing to landscape, so that they could see what they had. Since the site was once an orchard, there were some beautiful trees on the lot, including apple trees that went back several decades. When they were ready to begin, Inglis sent her own gardener, Walter Stampfli, over with flats of pachysandra and euonymus. The garden turned into a lifetime passion for both Palmers. "It was a real collaboration between Mother and Father," recalls Dunn. "Mother was the artistic one. She gave unstinting consideration to the whole garden, considering it from every angle." Of her father she says, "He was a great gardener, actually planting, appre-ciating plants, doing cuttings, watering, fertilizing." The garden, which even today is being further refined, follows the site's natural contours and uses a limited palette of plant materials. Although formed with great art, it looks utterly natural.

Mr. Wright, as Mary Palmer calls him to this day, did not see the house until it was finished. She remembers his first visit: "He didn't look at the house. He went right to the piano and sat down and played." Asked what he played, she replies, "Something he composed extemporaneously." Music was a shared interest for the architect and his clients: Wright once told Mary, "If you didn't like music, you wouldn't like my architecture." Wright, whose father had been a music teacher before studying for the ministry, often compared his architecture to music.

Wright stayed overnight with the Palmers in 1958. Invited by the U-M architecture students to give a lecture, he agreed on the condition that he would talk only to them and not to their professors. Wright slept in one of the Palmers' hexagonal beds and had oatmeal for breakfast.

On an earlier visit to Michigan, in 1954, when he was to lecture at the Masonic Temple in Detroit, he stayed with the Afflecks but came to the Palmers' for dinner. Gil Ross, a U-M faculty member and the first violinist of the university-based Stanley Quartet, was a close friend of the Palmers, so they asked him if the quartet would perform for Wright. Mary recalls that they opened with a Haydn quartet. When the first movement ended, Wright stopped them, saying something was wrong. Everyone looked uncomfortable—the Stanley Quartet were first-rate musicians. Then Wright explained that their playing was fine but that their location bothered him. He walked over and helped them move their music stands and chairs between two piers leading out to the terrace, where he thought the music would sound better.

MANY OF THE Palmers' friends were people connected with music. "I first knew the music faculty as teachers, then as friends. It was the beginning of all our friendships," recalls Mary. Both Palmers were active in the University Musical Society and the Ann Arbor Symphony Orchestra and often entertained musical luminaries in their house. Dunn recalls meeting such performers as Lena Horne and Frederica von Stade.

The Palmers' yearly caroling party is also fondly remembered by those who attended. "About twenty families would sing and then eat. Mary's was a perfect place for it because of the sensational acoustics," recalls publisher Phil Power, whose parents, Eugene and Sadie Power, were good friends of the Palmers. Dunn recalls that at Christmastime her mother would bring out a special set of Welsh bells, spanning two octaves, to add to the music from the piano.

Mary's interest in music segued serendipitously into another interest: yoga. Bill Palmer got to know many foreign students in college, and Mary first heard of yoga through his Indian friends. When she went to the Y to sign up for her first yoga class, she was pleasantly surprised to run into her good friend Priscilla Neel putting her name down for the same class.

Palmer and Neel's original teacher was an American, as was her replacement. Both teachers did their best, but in retrospect, Neel says, the exercises were "by rote—more like calisthenics." When the second teacher was leaving, she told Palmer and Neel that they should take over. The second teacher had encouraged them to read some of the yoga literature, including B. K. S. Iyengar's *Light on Yoga*, which came out in 1966 with a foreword by violinist Yehudi Menuhin.

"Of all the artists who come to Ann Arbor, the one I'd really like to meet is Mr. Menuhin," Mary Palmer told Alva Sink, whose husband, Charles, then headed the University Musical Society. Later, when Menuhin came for a concert, the Sinks invited the Palmers to a small party afterward. Mary took Iyengar's book with her and told Menuhin that she wanted to go to India and study with the author. "Without batting an eye, he said, 'You must go,'" she recalls. "He was pleased someone knew about this dimension of his life." When Bill was on sabbatical, she traveled to India, carrying a letter of introduction from Menuhin, and met with Iyengar in Poona.

"She came back very enthusiastic," recalls Neel. The women and a few friends began to practice yoga at the Palmers' house. "One of us would read [Iyengar's book] on tape. Then we'd put it on and learn the positions," recalls Neel. In 1973 they convinced the Y to sponsor Iyengar's first visit to the United States. "Then he came and showed us how to really do it," Neel recalls. For the next decade, until he retired, Iyengar visited Ann Arbor regularly. After coming to Ann Arbor, he was invited to cities all around the country and attracted students to India, where Palmer and Neel helped him open a yoga institute. "Mary always entertained when Iyengar was in town," Neel recalls. "He'd stay at her house."

Iyengar was only one of many guests over the years, some drawn by fascination with Wright's architecture, others by the warmth of the Palmers and their shared interests. "Mary's an incredibly gracious hostess," says Anne Glendon, a leader in the Ann Arbor music scene. "The house and her intellectual interests are a unified whole."

Glendon recalls a spring party to honor Carl St. Clair, then conductor of the Ann Arbor Symphony, when "the grounds were beautiful with daffodils." David Osler, whose wife, Connie, started the docent program at the U-M Museum of Art, remembers a gathering at the Palmers' in honor of Marshall Wu, the curator of Asian art. "Magic," says Osler. "It was a warm fall evening. The moon was out. Everything was waxed and polished." One party that stands out in Mary's mind is a dinner she gave for Yehudi Menuhin. "He liked to sit on the floor, so we had tables sitting on the floor with white tablecloths."

Different visitors respond to different aspects of the house. Architect Ralph Youngren, impressed to find all the original furniture still in place, was intrigued by "the odd-shaped drawers and dressers" and by the Palmers' attention to detail, down to the special red gravel they ordered for the driveway. Ann Arbor Building Department head Larry Pickel was struck by how the hexagonal shape of the beds made it impossible to put pillows next to each other.

"I was fascinated by being in a Frank Lloyd Wright house," says retired U-M surgeon Herb Sloan. "I'd been in Wright houses that were museums, but not one where someone lived." Judy Dow Rumelhart, who used to live across the street, remembers how she "adored going out in the teahouse. It's a romantic house—another world." Mary Louise Dunn says that even her teenage friends responded to the architecture: "You couldn't be human and not recognize it's unique."

Although the Palmers were generous in sharing their house, Bill and Mary also guarded their privacy. They opened their home to the general public on only two occasions. In the 1980s they allowed it to be shown on the Women's City Club Tour, helping to make that year's tour the most lucrative ever. A few years ago Mary opened her house for a University Musical Society fund-raiser that sold out instantly.

Bill Palmer died in November 2000. Mary is still enjoying the house. It's Wright's only house in Ann Arbor—unless one counts a house on Holden Drive that was built in 1979, twenty years after Wright's death, from plans he drew—and living in one of his buildings is a continual balancing act. "All owners of Frank Lloyd Wright houses are plagued by curious people," says Brink. On a recent visit to the house, while looking out a window with Mary Palmer, I saw a car slow down and creep along as it passed the house. Mary told me that happened all the time. As if anticipating this kind of attention, Wright designed the house for maximum privacy. Not much can be seen from the road, and what is in view tells very little about the delights inside and out back.

"She was the perfect client for Mr. Wright," says Bruce Niethammer of Mary Palmer. Even after Wright's death in 1959, the Palmers kept the house as close as possible to his original conception. At first Mary worked closely with John Howe and Larry Brink. Howe has since died, but Mary still works with Brink. For instance, Wright designed chairs for the living room, but the Palmers used some Scandinavian chairs instead. Mary was never satisfied with them, and she turned to Brink for help. Using Wright's original design, he figured out how to make Wright's chairs and had them fabricated by Phipps of Port Huron.

And of course, it wouldn't be a Frank Lloyd Wright house without a challenging roof—but again Brink, with Niethammer executing the plans, has devised improvements that keep the look of the house intact while keeping the Palmers dry. "Mr. Wright lived on the edge in his architecture," explains Niethammer. "Low sloping roofs are not really suited for cedar shingles. It's too shady—too flat. It's pretty, but it holds moisture, because the water doesn't run off." Close attention to maintenance has saved the sloping roof, while the original tar sections of the flat roof have been replaced with lead-coated tin.

Palmer, still as enamored of Wright as ever, bristles at any criticisms, saying, "Everything you hear about Mr. Wright has two sides." On my original visit she had me move from the couch to the Wright-designed chairs to show me how comfortable they were, and later she had me make the same test with the dining room chairs. She is appalled that people will say to her, "But do you really live here?"—or, worse, "I think it's an interesting house, but I certainly wouldn't want to live here." She is unambiguously not in agreement: "I can't imagine having something so fulfilling in so many ways—visually, the tremendous serenity, the fantastic drama."

Beyond its own pleasures, the house has given the Palmers opportunities to meet fascinating people, many of whom ended up as friends. "Anyone interested in architecture comes to Mary's," says Brink. Bob Metcalf recalls a big Wright symposium in the 1970s attended by all the leading Wright scholars. In honor of the event, architecture students painted a 120-foot canvas of a building Wright designed but never built for a site in Kansas, and they hung the canvas from Burton Tower. The event ended with a big party at the Palmers' for all the participants. More recently a delegation of Japanese architects, led by Taliesin-trained Raco Indo, visited the house. E. Fay Jones, a Taliesin-trained architect best known for his Thorncrown Chapel in Arkansas, and the celebrated Indian architect Charles Correa, a U-M architecture graduate, have also visited.

"As a group, musicians seem to seek out the house as well as architects," Mary says, remembering the time she got to hear Hephzibah Menuhin, Yehudi's sister, play their grand piano. Menuhin was staying at Inglis House before a concert, and Gail Rector, then head of the University Musical Society, asked the Palmers whether Menuhin could practice on their piano. Menuhin came over and ran through her entire program. Asked if she listened, Mary replies, "Of course."

More recently, the house gave Mary Palmer the opportunity to befriend members of the Royal Shakespeare Company (RSC), who gave awe-inspiring performances of *Henry VI* and *Richard III* under University Musical Society auspices in March 2001. Current society president Ken Fischer is a great friend and admirer of Mary Palmer, and when a group from the RSC visited Ann Arbor a year before the performances to check out the facilities, Fischer took them to see the Palmers' house. They raved about the experience, and when the whole troupe came the next year, another visit was high on their wish list. Mary responded by inviting all of the actors to tea—served on the "India Tree" Spode china that Wright had personally selected for the house.

Mary gained more than fond memories from the RSC visit. She actually acquired an addition to her house: a piece of "sculpture" for her garden. Tom Piper, an RSC set designer, had been among the first group to visit. When he returned the next year, Mary took him around the garden and said, winking, "Instead of charging, I ask advice. What's missing is sculpture. I've been looking all my life, but nothing is right." After discussing the question with the rest of the RSC group, Piper suggested they give her one of the ladders from the set.

Contacted by e-mail, Piper explains, "I wished there was a way to thank her for her hospitality and jokingly suggested that she should have the whole 'hell mouth' set in the garden. That seemed a little impractical!!! So I thought she should have one of the metal ladders as a memento of the play. Frank Lloyd Wright is a great hero of mine, and it's wonderful to think of a bit of my set becoming a sculpture in the garden of one of his finest houses!"

The ladder, visible from the living room, is casually but artfully placed against a tree. As it rusts, it will fit even better into the ensemble of landscaping and house. It's just the latest development in the continuing melding of Wright's architecture with the Palmers' interests and the greater community.

In retrospect, Mary Palmer says, "What attracted me to Mr. Wright was not pictures of the houses, not visiting other houses, but his philosophy that came into the house. It widened the whole reaction—how to live in the house, incorporating the landscape, the materials, the site—the whole big picture."

Text design by Jillian Downey
Typesetting by Agnew's, Inc., Grand Rapids, Michigan
Text font: Janson
Display font: ITC Honda

Although designed by the Hungarian Nicholas Kis in about 1690, the model for Janson Text was mistakenly attributed to the Dutch printer Anton Janson. Kis' original matrices were found in Germany and acquired by the Stempel foundry in 1919. This version of Janson comes from the Stempel foundry and was designed from the original type; it was issued by Linotype in digital form in 1985.

—courtesy www.adobe.com

ITC Honda was designed in 1970 by Ronne Bonder and Tom Carnase for ITC (International Typeface Corporation).

—courtesy www.linotype.com